LUCRETIA STEWART

Lucretia Stewart was born in Singapore in 1952 and lived as a child in Turkey, Peking, the United States, Greece, and England. She now lives in London.

Educated at convents in China, England, and the United States, she studied English Literature at Edinburgh University from 1970 to 1973.

She was commissioning editor at *Granta* from 1988 to 1990 and remains a contributing editor to the magazine.

In addition to working extensively as a journalist, Lucretia Stewart is the author of *Tiger Balm: Travels in Laos, Vietnam and Cambodia* (1992), which was described in the *Times Literary Supplement* as "a worthy successor to Norman Lewis's classic"; *The Weather Prophet: A Caribbean Journey*, which was short listed for the 1996 Thomas Cook Travel Book Award; and *Making Love: A Romance* (1999). She is also the editor of The Modern Library's *Erogenous Zones: An Anthology of Sex Abroad* (2000).

THE WEATHER PROPHET

A Caribbean Journey

Lucretia Stewart

A COMMON READER EDITION
THE AKADINE PRESS
2001

The Weather Prophet

A COMMON READER EDITION published 2001
by The Akadine Press Inc.,
by arrangement with the author.

A COMMON READER EDITION and fountain colophon
are trademarks of The Akadine Press, Inc.

ISBN 1-58579-036-2

10 9 8 7 6 5 4 3 2 1

For Ben and Dorothy

Acknowledgements

The events described in this book are the result of several visits to the Caribbean. I have taken the liberty of changing both the names and occupations of various people to protect their privacy. Many people were helpful to me and I would like to thank in particular the following: Savannah Boone, Gregory Ferrari, Edwin Frank, John Fuller, Ralph Gonsalves, Tim Hector, Judy Kirton, Roger Le Breton, Raphael Martine, Makeda Mikail and Jean-Marc Thudor. The Spanish Main guest house in St John's, Antigua, is now under new management.

I am also profoundly grateful to Jonathan Burnham for his encouragement and sensitive editing, to Antonia Gaunt for reading each chapter as I wrote it, and to Holly Eley for her advice and support. That said, any mistakes are, of course, mine alone.

Atlantic Ocean

LEEWARD ISLANDS

PUERTO RICO
VIRGIN ISLANDS
Anegada Passage
ANGUILLA
BARBUDA
ST. KITTS
NEVIS
St. John's
ANTIGUA
MONTSERRAT
Passage
Guadeloupe
GUADELOUPE
BASSE-TERRE
Pointe-á-Pitre
Basse-Terre
MARIE-GALANTE
Portsmouth
DOMINICA
Roseau
Saint-Pierre
MONT PELÉE
Fort-de-France
MARTINIQUE
Le Diamant
St. Lucia Channel
Castries
ST. LUCIA
St. Vincent Passage
BARBADOS
ST. VINCENT
Soufrière
BEQUIA
Kingstown
MUSTIQUE
UNION I.
CANOUAN
CARRIACOU
St. George's
GRENADA

LESSER ANTILLES

WINDWARD ISLANDS

Caribbean Sea

TOBAGO
Port of Spain
TRINIDAD

N

VENEZUELA

0 Kilometres   150
0 miles   100

Contents

My wife's gone to the West Indies
Jamaica?
No, she went of her own accord
(old joke)

I

Trinidad – Gateway to the Caribbean

It was as if a curtain had fallen, hiding everything I had ever known.

(from *Voyage In The Dark* by Jean Rhys)

The evening before I left New York for Trinidad I fell in love – or thought I did – and this belief or emotion coloured not only the plane flight but also the first few weeks of my time in the Caribbean. I drifted from island to island like a sleepwalker dreaming of love and, by the time the sensation wore off or I fell out of love or saw it for the illusion it was, other sensations had taken over and I had become so accustomed to the heady perfume of the islands that it was as if I was permanently drunk or high. I think that I needed to fall in love, or at least believe that I had, to get up the courage to make the trip. I needed to arm myself. I sensed, without knowing precisely why, that the Caribbean would be less focused, somehow more sprawling, both literally and metaphorically, than the places I was used to.

I first went to the Caribbean in the 1970s. I went with a boy-friend who had business in the Bahamas. I didn't much like Nassau but one evening we drove across to the far side of New Providence, away from the resort developments and the off-shore banking towers. The radio was tuned to a reggae station and, as we bumped along in the amber light of dusk, 'Take Me Home, Country Roads' began to play softly. In front of us was

an old pick-up weaving all over the road. The back was cram-
med with small black children. It was a perfect moment: the
light, the music, the children laughing and waving. Ten years or
so later I went to Eleuthera, a small island near the Bahamas, a
third of which was devoted to an exclusive resort called the
Windermere Island Club, patronised by the Royal family and
members of the British aristocracy. It was, in most ways,
phenomenally dull. In the evenings, a small steel band would
play calypso staples like 'The Big Bamboo' and 'Island in the
Sun' and the elderly guests would circle sedately on the dance
floor. Windermere Island, with its wonderful pink sand beaches,
was cut off from scrubby little Eleuthera, and such entertainment as the guests were likely to want – water-skiing, tennis,
golf – was provided *in situ*. You couldn't even go to a local bar.
But I had been ill, and I was not immune to the healing properties of the Caribbean sun. I did, however, wonder where all the
black people were.

Later, as a journalist, I went to the Cayman Islands, the
Virgin Islands and St Lucia, and it was then that the differences
between the resort world and the real world, between the rich
visitors and the poor natives, between white and black, began
to be glaringly obvious. These jaunts – 'press trips' – which
were designed to reveal only what tourist boards and resort
hotel managements chose – an idyllic, extravagant, pampered
way of life where no one worried and 'No Problem' was the
name of the game – served only to remind me of all we were
not being shown.

There is a Virgin Island proverb which seemed to fill the bill:
'Belieb half what yo' see nuffin what yo' hear.' In 1988, in
Christiansted, the capital of St Croix, one of the US Virgin
Islands – a group of black youths whom I approached for
directions, told me to 'Fuck off, else we whip your ass, whitey!'
before I had a chance to open my mouth. Not long after,
Hurricane Hugo hit St Croix and, in the wake of the devas-
tation, there was widespread looting. St Croix was at least sev-
enty-five per cent black but white people had most of the good
jobs and off-island blacks and Hispanics dominated the jobs in

tourism, leaving the most menial occupations to the locals. The looting seemed to have been an attempt by the black poor to get their fair share of the island's resources.

In the St Lucian capital, Castries, I had been surprised to see my mother's maiden name, du Boulay, on hoardings in town and, down by the port, on huge oil drums: Du Boulay Bottling Co. Ltd., St Lucia (Klenzada Brite-Klenz Heavy Duty Alkaline Cleaner). I told my mother about this and she told me a bizarre story about the du Boulays and St Lucia.

The du Boulays originally came from Normandy where there is still a tiny town called Boulay-Les-Ifs. Some, including my mother's family, were French Huguenots who had fled France in the late seventeenth century during the persecution of Huguenots and had come to England. Others were Catholics who had made their way to the Caribbean and thence their fortunes as sugar planters and slave-owners. In 1869, one of these, a man called Belisle du Boulay brought a case against a black St Lucian by the name of Jules René Hermenegilde du Boulay, in an attempt to stop him using the family name.

Jules René Hermenegilde du Boulay was born in Martinique in 1835, the illegitimate son of a mulatto woman named Rose who had been a slave to the du Boulay family and as often happened, had assumed their name. In 1852, Jules, who had previously had no surname, applied for a passport and took his mother's name, du Boulay. From then onwards he used the name for private and professional purposes on the island of St Lucia. In 1864 Jules received a letter instructing him to stop calling himself du Boulay. He refused, though he admitted that he was not related to the other du Boulays.

The white du Boulays won their case but Jules took it to the Court of Appeal whence it was referred to the Privy Council. In giving judgement, the Hon. H. J. Woodcock, Chief Justice of Tobago, spoke of the 'baneful influence of slavery in the West Indies under which the possession of the Slave rendered the unfortunate bondswoman the mere creature of her Master's lust' and pronounced that '... the present suit [was] the only attempt I have ever heard of to deprive them or their progeny of a name . . .', adding 'Thank Heaven, I know of no Law which I can be called on to administer by which such an attempt can be supported.'

The whole business was further complicated by the fact that St Lucia had been French until 1803 and there was some doubt about whether French laws passed in and before 1803 before the British gained possession of the island (including the 1773 *Code de la Martinique*, which forbade even *gens de couleur libres* – free people of mixed race, like Jules, from taking the name of any white family in the islands) were valid in this instance.

On my father's side, my great-great-grandfather, Francis Stewart, was a sugar planter in Puerto Rico. Their son, Francis, married into a family of English sugar planters who had taken Spanish nationality when the abolition of slavery in 1833 forbade the owning of slaves by Britons. Slavery was not abolished in Puerto Rico until forty years later, and my great-grandmother's family were keen to hang on to their slaves.

Often I would look at a map of the Caribbean, at the Lesser Antilles, that group of small islands that stretched from Grenada to the Virgin Islands just below Puerto Rico and try to imagine each island as a country in its own right – independent, self-governing, with a parliament, a prime minister. Many of them were no bigger than the Cyclades.

When I first conceived my trip, I had also thought of going to Jamaica whence most of my neighbours in Notting Hill (where I had lived for fifteen years) had come but, looking again at the map and the vast stretch of Caribbean Sea that lay between the little islands and the Greater Antilles, it seemed better to concentrate my energies in one area. When I had travelled in Indochina, I had been accompanied by a guide and an interpreter and had been obliged to plan the entire journey at the outset. Any deviation from the agreed programme led to endless complications.

This time I wanted to wander, to go where the fancy took me. Geography alone would dictate my itinerary. I would start in Trinidad and make my way up – this was all I had in the way of a plan.

The journey from Manhattan to Port of Spain took eleven hours from door to door. All the way down the length of America's east coast from chilly New York, high over the scattered islands of the Bahamas and the wide Sargasso Sea and into the daisy chain of the Lesser Antilles, I lay back in my seat and dreamt of love. In New York, it was the first day of real winter and a cold wind was blowing down the avenues. In San Juan, Puerto Rico, where the plane stopped for forty-five minutes, it was pleasantly warm. Midnight local time at Piarco International, the air was hot and damp, like a steam bath. The airport was crawling with people and the duty free shops selling liquor, cigarettes, perfume and electrical goods were doing brisk business with late Christmas shoppers. In the customs queue I stood next to a man who was bringing his mother-in-law's body back for burial. He had something to declare. Every so often, someone, usually a young man, would be taken off into a back room and questioned, presumably about drugs.

Outside, there were even more people, a sea of dark faces searching for returning relatives. If there were any white faces, they didn't stand out. The highway into town was unlit and the Caribbean night seemed vast and dense. The journey seemed interminable, the last straw, and I dozed fitfully in my seat, head drooping forward, then jerking up for another glimpse into the black void on either side of the road.

In Port of Spain the Errol J. Lau hotel was locked and shuttered, a faint light glowing through the window. The taxi driver banged and shouted, and eventually a sleepy youth unbolted the door and showed me to my room, a fetid cubbyhole, backing on to a noisy, though apparently deserted, street. I undressed and, too tired to think, let alone wash, lay down to sleep. But all night long I tossed and turned, bathed in sweat, and kept awake by the noise. Port of Spain was – or so it seemed – one huge discotheque, and the beat went on and on and on.

I had found the Errol J. Lau – 'The city hotel for the conservative traveller . . . This is your home away from home' according to the little brochure in reception – through a guidebook. The Scarlet Ibis hotel had sounded more alluring – by name at least – but the Errol J. was recommended as 'clean and friendly'. It may have been friendly and there were certainly written testimonials from previous guests displayed in the lobby to that effect, but clean it was not. I must have dropped off for a minute or two because, around four-thirty when I had finally abandoned all thought of sleep, and the noise from the traffic outside became deafening (however laid-back the Caribbean might be, in common with everywhere else in the Third World, it rises early), I discovered, ranged neatly between my right hip and breast, no less than forty bedbug bites.

I had heard so much about Trinidad: the home of calypso and the scene of the mother of all carnivals; the birthplace of V.S. Naipaul and C.L.R. James; the cradle of modern Caribbean civilisation; an ethnic melting pot where Africans, Indians, Chinese, Syrians and whites lived harmoniously side by side. It had everything going for it. I knew I would *love* Trinidad.

But outside everything was smaller and shabbier than I had expected. In the voluminous dark of the previous evening the possibilities of Port of Spain had seemed endless. Now I trailed through narrow, dusty streets lined with buildings of little or no architectural merit. Many of the streets had fiercely British names: Kitchener Street, today the headquarters of Bue-t-ful Clothes Manufacturers ('Vogue Caribbean – We Aim To Please'), Baden-Powell Street, Sackville Street, Scott-Bushe Street, Abercromby Street. Everywhere there were signs and slogans: 'I'm Cool With A Cole Cold'; 'The Church United is the Church Ignited'; 'Total Eclipse Of The Heart'; Star Gazer 'Keep In Touch With Your Dreams'.

I walked on past the Garden of Eden *roti* shop, a building called the Rebirth House, which had an open umbrella painted on the tin roof, a shiny new Mazda with the number plate RAW 4191, and the Crystal Stream Government School with its motto, 'We'll Find Or Make A Way', emblazoned on its front. Pretty little houses with wooden fretwork 'gingerbread' trimmings, their bright colours softened by the tropical climate, that I had been led to expect from photographs were nowhere in evidence. No one paid any attention to me and eventually, after walking for some time in the wrong direction, I found the offices of LIAT (Leeward Islands Air Transport).

In London I had bought a ticket that, for an amazingly modest sum (about £290), permitted me to 'island-hop', providing I flew LIAT. There wasn't much choice: LIAT, 'the Caribbean airline' whose motto used to be 'We fly where buccaneers sailed', flew the length and breadth of the Caribbean, enabling some semblance of contact to exist between the islands. It was in regular danger of bankruptcy through mismanagement, helped, no doubt, by its immensely reasonable fares. Despite the groans and sighs that attended any discussion of LIAT's present or future, it always seemed to function efficiently enough, with tiny planes arriving and taking off, if not on time, rarely disastrously late.

But, the longer I spent in the Caribbean, the clearer it became that a myth existed, propagated in part by West Indians themselves, but given further and continual nourishment by white residents; the myth is that absolutely nothing works there. In *The Middle Passage*, V. S. Naipaul laid the blame at the white man's door: 'Again and again one comes back to the main degrading fact of the colonial society; it never required efficiency, it never required quality . . .'

Carnival wasn't due for a few months. So it seemed to make sense to leave Port of Spain soon – by daylight the view from my bedbug-ridden room was anything but appealing – and return for a decent stretch of time during carnival. I decided that I would go straight to Grenada.

After booking my flight, I went to telephone to reserve a room in Grenada. In the road which ran down the side of the vast TSTT (Telecommunications Services of Trinidad & Tobago) building, there was a handwritten notice tacked to a lamppost, as for a lost cat or dog. A faded black-and-white photograph of an elderly woman, skeletal, with a pinched sunken mouth and an expression of bewilderment, stared out below a message offering a reward of $500.00 (about US$120) to anyone knowing the whereabouts and leading to the finding of Mrs Rosie Bisnath, aged sixty-one. I imagined Mrs Bisnath alone, lost, wandering the streets of Port of Spain. It reminded me of an old calypso by the great Trinidadian singer, the Mighty Sparrow, called 'Mother's Love'. In it, he sings:

> In this place, certain men should hide their face
> The way they treat their mother is a disgrace,
> Neglect the old lady for donkey years
> When she dead, they shedding crocodile tears
> And spending money like hell
> To buy a casket made like Hilton Hotel ...

I hoped it wouldn't come to that.

I walked back in the direction of the Errol J. Lau, then wandered up Frederick Street, the city's main drag – the Bond Street or Fifth Avenue of Port of Spain. There were signs advertising 14K gold caps for teeth and bursts of noise spilt from sidewalk stalls selling cassettes. Sometimes there would be two or three of these stalls in a row, each of them playing a different tune, though the bass was so insistent that it was difficult to make out a melody. There was music everywhere – in the restaurants, shops, even in the Post Office, and in the place where I had telephoned.

There were almost no white people. I wanted to buy some postcards but the choice was limited. Those that I did find were blurred, crudely coloured and oddly old-fashioned, dating from the Fifties. Tourism and its promotion didn't appear to be a high priority. In Naipaul's Book Stores, I found a card I liked, a reproduction of a painting of a wonderful tropical scene with palm trees and brilliant sky and sea, the river mouth at Mayaro on Trinidad's Atlantic coast. Inside was a message from the Psalms.

> And he shall be like a tree planted by the
> rivers of water, that bringeth forth his fruit

in his season; his leaf also shall not wither;
and whatsoever he doeth shall prosper.

I bought it, and a pad of writing paper, then found a balcony
café on the first floor of a shopping mall where I could sit and
watch the street below. I started to write a stilted letter to the
man I thought I was in love with in New York. My head and
heart were still awash with muzzy emotion but I didn't dare
write about that. Instead I described the women in the streets
– big and brassy, exuberantly testing the limits of their day-glo,
lycra clothes.

Later, in Duke Street, hot and sweaty after the long dusty
walk in the noonday sun, I stopped at a little bar-restaurant.
There was no food left, but I had a cold, pale-gold Carib ('A
Beer Is A Carib'; 'Carib is You'). All over the bar walls there
were posters of beautiful black girls with big, bare breasts, their
hair to their waists, encouraging men to drink Carib or a stout
called Stag. I sat in a booth letting the sweat dry and, with the
second beer, got talking with Gina who owned the bar.

I told her about life in the Errol J. Lau, and she immediately
invited me to come and stay with her. I barely hesitated. She
would come to the hotel to collect me the following morning
at nine with her cousin, Justin, who had a car.

'That's real time, not Caribbean time,' she said. 'Be ready.'

That evening, hunger and curiosity (the Copper Kettle Grille
named after a two-hundred-year-old copper kettle, now apparently in the restaurant and once used by slaves on the Dorson
Barrie Estate; the aptly-named Mirage Coffee Shop and Air-
Conditioned Cocktail Lounge specialising in 'serving local
foods and choice US Steaks' appeared permanently closed)
drove me out on to the mean streets of Port of Spain, but I
didn't get far. There were few women, and too many young men
lounging on street corners for comfort – those with headfuls of
matted dreadlocks seemingly more menacing than those without
(despite the allegedly peaceful implications of the Rasta
hairstyle). As I walked by, they hissed at me, 'Psst, psst'. The
sound, so loud and obvious, yet somehow furtive – as if they

9

were trying unobtrusively to attract my attention – had an anonymity to it that was insulting. I didn't like it at all. I felt self-conscious and vulnerable and dived into a nearby Chinese café. I ordered a bowl of won ton soup and ate it very slowly, postponing the moment when I had to run the gauntlet back to the hotel.

The next morning, when I told Gina where I had been, she said 'What's the matter with you, girl? You askin' for trouble?'

We loaded up my bags and drove out to Petit Valley where she lived with her ten-year-old son, Rupert. Petit Valley, nicknamed God's Bathroom because it rained so much, was in a residential suburb of Port of Spain called Diego Martin, about half an hour from the centre of town. Gina had chosen to live in this area, where she had no friends and knew no one, so that her lover, a white married man, could visit her without being recognised.

Rupert sat in front of the television, playing a video game that bleeped every minute or so. Gina said that he spent all his time like this. She had described him as fat but he seemed a nice-looking normal-sized boy. He was shy and didn't speak to or look at me. The apartment was on the first floor of a two-storey concrete building. It had a big long main room with a kitchen at one end and a counter separating it from the living area where there was a large television set and a video. There were two bedrooms, one at the front for Gina and a windowless room at the back where Rupert slept; there was a lavatory, cold-water shower and a basin. Outside the back door, there was a narrow strip of balcony with a washing line and another tap and sink. Gina insisted that I take her room, saying that she would sleep on the couch.

Late that afternoon, when the light had softened, I stood on the balcony looking up at the hills, enjoying the view and the breeze. Away from the traffic fumes of the city, the air was sweet. Below, the backyards of Gina's neighbours were full of squawking chickens, rusting automobiles, palms, poinsettias, paw-paw and breadfruit trees swollen with fruit. Across the valley, through the tangled mass of telegraph wires and tele-vision aerials, I could see the soft green of the corrugated iron roof of St Anthony's in Petit Valley, against the darker greens of the hills around. I liked this little church with its white walls and apple-green tin roof, which became a symbol of the peace of the valley after the maelstrom of Port of Spain – though peace – and quiet – was, of course, a relative term.

Gina usually had both the television, with a dreadful fuzzy picture, and the radio – FM Music Radio: 'More Music, Less Talk' – blaring, and her neighbours did the same. I asked Gina what it would be like to be a Trinidadian who didn't like music – that is, loud music. She said: 'That would never happen. There would have to be something drastically wrong with a person like that.'

Then there were the natural sounds: babies crying, cocks crowing, dogs barking, birds singing, frogs croaking, crickets doing whatever they do; beyond them the soft thud of bat on ball, as boys played cricket on the open ground across the road and, in the distance, the church bells, the noises of traffic and car horns and the roar of an approaching maxi-discotaxi.

Maxi-discotaxis are mini-buses with blackened glass in the windows, heavily customised inside with stickers and badges – 'Men – wear a condom or beat it' is a good example – and often as many as three equalisers to ensure a powerful bass. They came past about every ten minutes and were the easiest, cheapest and noisiest way to get into town. The first time I took one Gina said as we boarded, 'Now you goin' to get some noise in your head.'

It was torture to ride in. The seats throbbed with the relentless boom-boom of dub and conversation was impossible. Some passengers would wait for a particularly loud maxi, having rejected other quieter ones. Rupert said that sometimes the vibrations caused the glass in the windows to shatter, and there were frequent articles and letters in the *Trinidad Guardian* about noise pollution and its effects on young Trinidadians. Doctors were called on to give a professional opinion. In one article entitled 'The Frustrations of Noise', the writer quoted Dr Hari Maharaj, 'psychiatrist/neurologist':

Noise in maxi-discotaxis also worries Dr Maharaj ... he was sure the excessively loud music distracts drivers. 'And why are maxi-taxis involved in so many accidents?' Dr Maharaj wondered aloud ... He would like to see studies similar to those done in the US on the effects of noise on our children. For example: To look at the academic performance of children travelling to and from school in maxi-discotaxis and compare their performance with a similar group of children in the same school who don't use maxi-taxis for travelling ... The over-stimulation of loud dub, rap, rock takes time to wear off; these children are over-excited, can't settle down to classes in mathematics after exposure to the ninety plus decibels of noise in taxis.

Dr Maharaj was evidently a *Guardian* favourite, always being called upon to give his professional opinion. Another day found him commenting on racial attacks in calypso, and drug problems among the young. Readers – presumably older people – wrote in complaining about noise:

Whenever they begin their all-night sessions, I cannot sleep because of the radio and because of their loud shouting to each other that they may be heard above the radio. When this happens, the following day I usually experience head-aches and I am irritable at work because of the lack of sleep or I find myself sleeping on the job.

The author of the letter lived next door to a *mas* ('masquerade') camp and, as Carnival approached, so the noise level increased. I was glad that I would have time to adjust to it before being exposed to the full blast of Carnival.

Gina was keen that I should 'play *mas*', which meant wearing a costume and following a particular band during Carnival. And one afternoon we went to choose a costume for me at the camp that she played with. The band, Wayne Berkeley, was one of the best and often won.

There weren't many costumes left. The more elaborate ones,

such as a Chinese mandarin or a Red Indian chief, had already all been taken – which was just as well, as they cost a fortune (about $450), and they included layers of garments, which meant that you'd probably die of heat while you were prancing round the streets. I chose the cheapest which was left, a serpent costume which consisted of something – it wasn't clear exactly what – which would cover the bottom half of my body. I had to be measured for it, and for a headdress which cost about $150, a quarter of which I had to leave now as a deposit; I would have to supply a black top.

Then we went to buy kitchen curtains. I was surprised by the number of stores which sold furnishing fabrics and the low sale prices which they offered during the holiday season. Gina told me that black people – in Trinidad at least – bought new curtains every Christmas.

Gina was a few years younger than me, in her mid-thirties. She was pretty, almost beautiful, small and slim with very dark skin that gleamed, and white teeth and pronounced cheekbones, and hair that had been 'relaxed' (another term was 'cultivated').

Almost every woman I saw had had something done to her hair, despite the health hazards involved; and there were numerous beauty parlours on the streets of Port of Spain to cater for West Indian women's desire not to have 'nappy' or 'hard' hair. I asked one woman why she bothered. 'Well, you can't do a thing with "nappy" hair – it's so boring,' she said.

Hair like mine, Western hair, was known as 'soft' hair (also 'good' hair as opposed to African hair which was 'bad'). A number of the younger men also had 'relaxed' hair and hoardings which advertised products for all the family depicted a happy, and somewhat unconvincing, nuclear family of mother, father and two smiling children, all with glossy heads showing no trace of their African origins.

One morning the *Guardian* devoted an entire page to the subject. 'One of the most widely used products is Hairlox Capital Curls,' began an article. 'To get the desired results when curling hair with this product, three steps must be observed: First, the Cold Waves Cream Reformer must be applied, then the Curl Booster, followed by the Curl Stabiliser... This is a vastly superior system for cold wave processing of excessively curly and kinky hair...'

After 'relaxing' the hair (Afro-Caribbean hair grows at an angle, hence its extreme curliness), you could then curl it, or leave it, or braid it, but all the beautiful long heads of braids were done with 'extensions'. You could also add a 'weave', a chunk of unbraided wig sewn into the existing hair. If you never brush, comb or cut it, you get dread locks. The 'relaxing', or the weaving of elaborate extensions, into the existing hair all clearly took hours. It didn't bear thinking about.

The treatments weren't always successful and, at worst, the hair would end up looking stiff and dry as if it had been starched, or as if its owner, as in a cartoon, had had an electric shock which had left it standing on end. But Gina's hair was wavy and had a soft, natural look to it.

I loved Gina's sing-song Trini accent, which sounded a bit like Welsh, and I found her expressions, her use of language, and her immediate frankness irresistible. She was extremely outspoken with a good, sometimes outrageous, sense of humour and she was passionately interested in sex, about which she talked non-stop. She attributed her own 'hot' nature to her Spanish grandmother and would give chapter and verse on sexual encounters at the drop of a hat. One incident she described involving a man whom she had met at the airport en route to Caracas; in the ensuing thirty-six hours, they had succeeded in using sixteen condoms.

According to Gina, every married man had an 'outside woman' who was known as a 'deputy'. But she dismissed most Caribbean men as 'more hot than sweet'. 'They have this big thing but they don' know how to use it,' she said disdainfully.

Gina had strong opinions on everything – for instance, capital punishment. 'I believe in Moses' law – an eye for an eye', she stated, and my appeals to reason or compassion fell on deaf ears.

Capital punishment came up because there were two men on

death row who were due to hang the following week; the papers were full of their cases.

Capital punishment was still the law in Trinidad, though no one had been put to death since 1979 (this changed in July 1994, when a man was hanged in Port of Spain just minutes before a stay of execution was faxed to Trinidad from the Privy Council in London which still acted as the ultimate court of appeal). One of the condemned men had been convicted of murdering his next-door neighbour. Local columnists wrote that he had 'only himself to blame'; the state prosecutor had offered him a plea of manslaughter. This seemed to be the general consensus on the matter. 'The simple fact is that punishment must fit the crime' was the view of the letters' page of the *Guardian*.

The *mélange* of races and colours on the streets gave Port of Spain a bewilderingly exotic air. You would see dark-skinned men and women with narrow, almond-shaped eyes and pale, kinky hair; light-skinned people with African features; skin tones ranging from pale gold to blue-black. In the rich multi-racial and multi-coloured society of the Caribbean – 'multilayered pigmentocracy' – a whole vocabulary has evolved to describe the many different shades of the people who live there: black, red, bronze, *coco-blanc* or high bronze, light-skinned, *browning* – meaning a brown-skinned woman – were just a few terms (both Naipaul and Caryl Phillips list the following as being in common usage: fusty, musty, dusty, tea, coffee, cocoa, light black, black, dark black).

I was astonished at first by this, having been brought up to believe that it was offensive to mention someone's colour – like talking about money, it wasn't 'done'; I also believed that 'black' was the correct, polite term. But, as Naipaul wrote in *The Middle Passage*, 'We were in the West Indies. Black had a precise meaning ...'

Now I, too, was 'among people who had a nice eye for shades of black'. I wasn't used to hearing the words 'nigger' or even 'negro' – to me, they smacked of racism and made me uncomfortable – but Gina used these terms freely. She said that she didn't find black men attractive – though Rupert's father was a black man from Barbados. 'I like cream in my coffee,' she said, and also told me that Trinidadian men loved 'red' women, saying, 'I don't care how bad she is, if she's red, I'll take it.'

Indians, the descendants of the indentured labourers who were brought to the Caribbean after the abolition of slavery, were dismissively called *coolies* behind their backs. Gina said that she would kill her lover if she ever caught him with a coolie woman. Chinese were known as *chinee* and anything considered a bit skimpy or cheap or mean would be described as *chinee*. 'Why you givin' me this chinee bag?' Gina would say, if the bag for the shopping was on the small side.

Racial mixes had their own special names too – just so you always knew where you were: in addition to the more familiar terms of *mulatto* – which derives from *mule* (in French *mulattre* or *métise*), *quadroon* and *octoroon*, there was *doogla* meaning half-Indian and half-negro and *chigro* meaning half-negro, half-Chinese. *Chigros* were also known as *hakwai Chinee* (*hakwai* being the Chinese word for nigger). There is a precision about these categories that could only have developed in a society where the exact colour of your skin determined your position in that society and where the whiter you are the better – and the softer your hair, the straighter and slimmer your nose... In Brazil, at one time, there had been a staggering 492 categories. Colour and race continued to be an obsession, though perhaps not to the degree that the Trinidadian writer, C. L. R. James, described in 1963 in *Beyond A Boundary*:

> Where so many crosses and colours meet and mingle the shades are naturally difficult to determine and the resulting confusion is immense. There are the nearly white hanging on tooth and nail to the fringes of white society... Then there are the browns, intermediates... Associations are formed of brown people who will not admit into their number those too much darker than themselves... Clubs have been known to accept the daughter who was fair and refuse the father who was black... in a West Indian colony the surest sign of

a man having arrived is the fact that he keeps company with people lighter in complexion than himself . . .

Just as I had always found it incredible that even a drop of non-white blood in South Africa had placed you firmly on the far side of the apartheid fence, so I was staggered by the intricacies of the social structure of Caribbean life that this vocabulary indicated. At the same time, if Gina was anything to go by – and that still remained to be seen – it all seemed pretty relaxed. Despite the much-vaunted hostility between Africans and Indians which kept Indians out of the government, away from major calypso triumphs and in control of the business community, all these variously shaded people were at least cohabiting (if infrequently inter-marrying) on a functioning day-to-day level. I could see, however, that, if you arrived in England fresh from a society where subtlety in the matter of colour was crucial, the crude distinction between white and black which lumped anyone who wasn't pure white together in a job-lot of blackness, would come as something of a shock.

I was excited to have company – and protection – and wanted to go out at night, to listen to music, to go dancing. Gina looked in the paper and found a band of which she approved playing that night at a bar called the Moon Over Bourbon Street. She called her friend, Seamus, to come with us. He had a car and we also arranged to pick up another friend, Loridel.

Seamus was an Irishman from Cork who had been training for the priesthood but had given it up in favour of dentistry and the Caribbean. He was a tall man with clammy hands and a hangdog expression. He was opposed to fornication – as he called it – and abortion. Gina said that she had wondered whether he might be an 'anti-man' – as gay men were called in Trinidad – but that sometimes he got drunk and then would sleep with a woman but afterwards he felt very bad about it. Given the general abandonment to pleasure and sexual licence that prevailed in the Caribbean, it seemed rather a waste for him to be there but perhaps he enjoyed torturing himself. A definite air of flagellation and martyrdom hung about him.

We went out into the starless night, got into the car and set off to collect Loridel. As we drove off, there was an ominous rattling sound from the rear of the vehicle and, after a few miles, Seamus stopped and got out to look and see what the problem was. The back left-hand wheel was halfway off its axle. Seamus found a spanner in the boot and screwed it back. Fortunately we hadn't yet reached the Diego Martin freeway.

Loridel was a 'watless' woman – or so Gina said. The nearest that I could get to a translation was a combination of 'wanton' – or perhaps 'unabashed' – and 'witless'. The main justification for this judgement seemed to be her refusal to wear dentures; her two front teeth were missing but, as she rarely smiled, this was not immediately apparent. Gina said that she had 'no shame – and no teeth in her mouth when she got married'. She had a Chinese husband and two small children. She was very beautiful with a fierce disdainful beauty like the high priestess of some ancient cult, and the missing teeth served, in a curious way, only to enhance her beauty. Her skin was lighter than Gina's, mahogany to Gina's ebony, matt and flawless. She had long, long legs and wore a mini dress that just scraped her bottom, mules on slender feet and a straw panama hat covering hair that had been too ruthlessly 'relaxed'. I found her speech difficult to understand, whether because of the unfamiliar Trini accent or the missing teeth I couldn't tell. Seamus, his professional instincts aroused, started to tell her about the latest improvements in the dentures market.

The Moon Over Bourbon Street was a disappointment – though perhaps the name itself should have warned me. It was smart, up-market and distinctly unfunky. It was decorated – possibly unintentionally – to look like the deck of a cruise liner. The band played 'quattro', a soft romantic Latin American music from Venezuela (named after a little guitar called a 'quattro' which, along with three other guitars, a set of maracas and an instrument made of a box and a pole comprised the ensemble). It was a cool evening and I was glad to have a jacket.

I asked when it was hottest in Trinidad. 'Carnival-time,' said Loridel. The weather wasn't the only thing that heated up around carnival. There were lots of unwanted pregnancies 'when everything gets a bit wild' and new AIDS cases to add to the existing twenty thousand known cases. The conversation languished and we drank in silence listening to the music. We drank beer or rum punches and the band played on. Finally, a group of noisy young rich kids came in and we left.

The next day was Sunday, hot and slow. Across the road some boys played a desultory game of football in the sweltering heat. Gina, who said that she hated to cook, made a lunch of baked chicken legs and macaroni. Rupert watched television or played with his video game. Everything seemed suspended in time and heat. The day dragged on until finally, in the late afternoon, we took a maxi into Port of Spain and went for a walk, just *liming* (hanging out), until it was time to go to the cinema.

I had seen posters all over town advertising a sexy thriller called *Whispers in the Dark*: 'This movie will get you hot!' and Gina was keen to see it. She claimed to have been so aroused by *Basic Instinct*, a violent sexual thriller starring Michael Douglas and Sharon Stone, that she had seen it four times. *Whispers in the Dark* was about a female psychoanalyst with a beautiful blonde patient who recounted her sexual encounters and fantasies. The audience appeared to find these amusing rather than arousing and burst into loud laughter when she described experiencing spontaneous orgasm at the thought of being tied up. Throughout, the word 'fuck' was bleeped out but everybody knew what had been said. As soon as the film finished and before the credits started to roll, the audience stood up and poured out into the street. We went to meet Rupert who had been to see *The Last of the Mohicans* and then for a snack called a *buss-up shut* which was a sort of *roti* filled with curried meat and vegetables. When we got home, some scavenging dogs had upset the dustbin and there was stinking garbage all over the road.

That night I had a nightmare about visiting an old, but unresolved, lover and discovering that he was living with another woman and had 'given' her two babies. The feelings of outrage and hurt and betrayal were terrible and I had to pretend that everything was normal. I woke up, freezing, in the middle of the night. Outside my window Petit Valley was quiet and dark. There were no blankets so I put on a sweater and lay down again, clammy and cold. I drifted back into sleep and dreamt that I had been caught in an explosion that had turned into a fire. I thought, 'This dream is about my love.'

2

Life Is Sweet

The wind is in from Africa
Last night I couldn't sleep
(from *Carey* by Joni Mitchell)

I celebrated my fortieth birthday in Grenada.

I had arrived a few days before, leaving Gina's early one morning to drive through the dawn to the airport. The cab driver took a back route on tiny dusty lanes through fields of sugar cane, scattered with egrets and the large black birds known as *corbeaux* – or the Savanna Blackbird – bathing in muddy pools. Every fifty yards or so there would be a little altar set up for a *puja* (the traditional Hindu prayer ritual) with marigolds, zinnias, oleanders and sticks of incense.

It was a hiccuppy flight. The tiny plane lurched around the sky, jumping and dipping at the mercy of clouds and air currents. We flew north-west towards Tobago over a green and cultivated landscape which rose to the island's central highlands, dense, wooded and with no sign of habitation. Trinidad's north coast was also apparently untouched by human hand. Tobago, seen from the air, looked as I had expected the Caribbean to look. The deep waters were a dark glassy blue, broken by small white explosions of surf; over the reefs, the sea became crystalline and turquoise.

The plane skimmed a pale gold beach fringed with palm trees and landed at Tobago. A group of middle-aged white tourists climbed aboard, the little craft settling under their weight. One of them, a blonde Dutch woman in her mid-fifties, had had her sparse hair braided in tight little cornrows with gold and silver beads threaded at the end of each spindly braid. Her exposed scalp gleamed shiny pink.

Airborne once more, the stewardess distributed copies of the (Barbados) *Daily Nation*. 'Barbados – "land of violence and hatred" ' was the headline of a front-page story about rising crime on the island: 'Superintendent of James Street Methodist Church, Reverend Patterson Dean, has charged that today's Barbados was one of increasing violence, aggression, hostility and hatred . . .'

This story was in marked contrast with the Barbados portrayed in *Harpers & Queen* which I had read shortly before leaving England. Under the headline 'Parties in Barbados', the social editor had gushed:

Escaping the tyranny of the British winter, I flew to Barbados and fell into a warm aquamarine sea and a social whirlpool. Ever since the thirties, when Sir Edward Cunard made it exotically fashionable, Barbados has been a much loved retreat for the British . . . The Pembertons are a marvellous couple and when I asked Mike how he had built up his empire he laughingly suggested it was his unerring judgement . . .

Photographs of 'beautiful' people illustrated pages of this sort of stuff –

Margaret Leacock knows everything there is to know about the country and everyone in it. She and her husband Jack . . . have friends in the government and friends in chattel houses (painted wooden houses that can be dismantled and moved on). They know the migrant winter visitors and the few remaining plantation owners.

Barbados was one of Britain's earliest West Indian colonies. It lay out on a limb, off to the right, outside the main arc of the Lesser Antilles, marooned in the Atlantic, some 180 miles from Trinidad. Unlike many of the other islands, it was never occupied by any other power and remained the most Anglicised of the islands so much so that it was still known as 'Little England'. Settled in 1627, it soon replaced Hispaniola as the richest of the sugar-producing islands and, thanks to the 'white gold' of sugar, became the single most important colony in the British Empire, worth almost as much, in its total trade, as the two tobacco colonies of Virginia and Maryland combined, and nearly three times as valuable as Jamaica. In 1661, Charles II marked its importance by creating thirteen baronetcies on the island in one day.

But it was also a watchword for greed and cruelty of which Eric Williams, Trinidad's first Prime Minister after independence, said: 'Barbados, a word of terror to the white servant, became to the Negro, as a slave trader wrote in 1693, "a more dreadful apprehension . . . than we can have of hell".' Now one of the most densely populated countries in the world, Barbados is a popular holiday destination ('Reach out for blue skies, Reach out for paradise, Reach out for Barbados' ran the jingle on London's Capital Radio), where, if it lives up to its reputation, female tourists in search of sexual adventure can take their pick of muscular beach boys gleaming with coconut oil (in the days of slave trading, palm oil was used to create a healthier-looking sheen on African skin) and where there are more crimes committed against foreigners than in any other Caribbean island.

Grenada, the 'Original Caribbean' (each island in the Lesser Antilles came complete with a marketing slogan, courtesy of the local tourist board), seemed small from the air and flat compared to Trinidad. Through the puffs of cloud, the island's ragged coastline came and went. Then, suddenly, came the sickening moment when the plane appears to stop all movement and hang, suspended, in the air so it seems that it must drop like a stone from the sky. We landed twenty yards from the sea.

It was a short trip from Point Salines airport to Lagoon Road and Mamma's Lodge. The island appeared green and tame, as I imagined Jersey or one of the other Channel Islands to be, and there were nice soft brown cows grazing peacefully on the green slopes. The road was good, the taxi modern, the taxi driver exuberantly cheerful ('This your first time in Grenada? You gonna love it here, the Spice Island. Everybody very friendly here'). My spirits lifted. There had been something unwieldy about Trinidad.

Rosemary, the manageress of Mamma's Lodge, was a massive woman with a head of tightly cropped hair, shiny with oil. When the cab drew up, she was sprawled outside, thighs akimbo, dozing on a chair that could barely contain her. The late Inslay Wardally, the original Mamma, whose portrait (another massive black woman) hung in reception, had had a number of children. Rosemary, her sister Cleopatra who ran Mamma's Restaurant up the road and her brother who oversaw the running of the hotel were just three of them. Rosemary herself had five children by five different men (there had been six by six fathers, but one had died). She was just forty and unbent perceptibly when she learnt that we were virtually the same age. Slow of speech and movement, Rosemary wasn't sassy or funny like Gina but was happy enough to talk about herself. She had lived with the same Grenadian man for fourteen years but one carnival, in 1990, he had 'three girlfriends'. This was too much even for the easy-going Rosemary.

'So I took a knife to his throat,' her huge shoulders shook with the memory, 'but I was only making grandcharge.' Serious or not, this episode marked the end of that relationship and she was now involved with Errol, who lived away from St George's, the capital, in the provincial town of Gouyave where nutmeg was grown and processed.

That evening I went to eat at Mamma's Restaurant, the establishment presided over by Rosemary's elder sister, Cleopatra. The night orchestra maintained a steady clamour. There were the sounds of a dozen different birds, one of which squeaked incessantly – like chalk on a blackboard; there were dogs barking, crickets and frogs. Earlier, on my balcony, I had seen one of the frogs, a tiny translucent creature with black eyes like those eerily realistic toys where the rubber glows and feels clammy. Petty crime was on the increase in Grenada and I felt exposed and vulnerable as I walked briskly up the unlit slope clutching a EC$100 note in my hand – Rosemary had advised me not to take a bag – but the main danger seemed to be from the cars that whizzed by with scant regard for anyone walking by the side of the road.

The restaurant was quite full and all the diners were white. 'I'm Dreaming of a White Christmas' poured from the loud-speakers. Cleopatra turned out to be almost as massive as her sister but without the sleepy good humour. She seemed sour and tired as she placed course after course in front of me. First came a very small bowl of callaloo soup. This, which is one of the staples of West Indian cuisine, is made from the young leaves of the dasheen plant, native to West Africa where it is called 'eddoe', but also grown throughout the Caribbean. It tastes a little like spinach or watercress soup but leaves a peppery aftertaste.

The soup – which was delicious – was followed by barracuda, then lambi (conch), then goat, then a dish of possum and on it went. There were nine courses in all and Cleopatra's stony expression did not encourage refusals. I found myself trying to eat whatever was put in front of me like a polite guest, forgetting that I was in a restaurant and paying for all this food which I had not, strictly speaking, ordered. On the wall there was a large mural depicting all the different kinds of fish, seafood and meat that we might eat. I was relieved not to see a monkey up there. I thought I detected an expression of sadistic pleasure on Cleopatra's face as she placed dish after dish on the table. Finally I said: 'I'm not going to be able to eat any more.' Cleopatra gave a brief, mirthless laugh as if she had won a victory. This was her revenge on the white tourists who came to her country. As I sat sullenly digesting my dinner, I saw her taking a tray of delicious-looking fruit through a door marked 'Employees Only'.

The bill (EC$57.15 – approximately £18) came, accompanied

by a guest book in which diners were encouraged to write their comments. 'This meal will be featured in my next book' read an entry from Washington DC. Mine too, I thought. Something had to be salvaged from the evening. Cleopatra stood over me as I wrote: 'Thank you for a wonderful dinner.' She read it, then gave a kind of snort and announced, in stentorian tones, that service and tax were included in the bill. I had seen neither a menu nor a price list all evening. Later that night in *Greetings*, the magazine put out by the Grenada Tourist Board, I found an advertisement for the restaurant which promised a twenty course dinner. I had got off lightly.

Back at the guesthouse, Rosemary was lying like a beached whale on a couch in front of the television watching something beamed in from Miami. Another guest, a Venezuelan 'business-man' whose business was not clear, sat in silence beside her. The reason for his long face soon became evident. Intending to go out for the evening, he had walked down the narrow track that led from Mamma's Lodge to Lagoon Road. Lagoon Road itself, though a busy thoroughfare linking the airport road to St George's, had no street lights. Caribbean nights tended to be very dark. The Venezuelan had got as far as the junction of the track and Lagoon Road when two men, brandishing cutlasses, had jumped him and relieved him of his watch and his money.

The next morning I met Selwyn Allberry. Allberry, an excit-able man of medium height and scrawny build with a goatee beard, occupied a couple of rooms on the lower ground floor of the hotel. There, amid a sea of newsprint and glue, he pro-duced, with the aid of a sleepy-looking young woman, a weekly free newspaper, the *Caribbean Echo*. The *Echo* (motto 'The West Indies Must Be West Indian') was 'Florida's Longest Reigning Caribbean Newspaper'; its main readership was actu-ally in Miami but Allberry, as editor, writer, owner and pub-lisher, did most of the creative work in Grenada, from whence he came. He claimed to have been secretary to Maurice Bishop's Marxist-Leninist New Jewel Movement ('JEWEL' standing for Joint Endeavour for Welfare, Education and Liberation) in its early days. The NJM came to a bloody end with the murder of Bishop and others six days before the United States' invasion of Grenada – and, even though he had become disillusioned with it (and perhaps its leaders with him), Allberry remained an old-style leftist and, as such, seemed to me a rather familiar and comforting figure.

It was the United States' invasion of Grenada (code name 'Urgent Fury' and, until the 1989 invasion of Panama, the largest military action carried out by the United States since the Vietnam War) on 25 October 1983 that put the island firmly on the world map. For the previous four and a half years, Grenada had been under the control of the People's Revolutionary Government (PRG), with Maurice Bishop at its head. The NJM had taken power in a bloodless coup in 1979, ousting the then-Prime Minister, Sir Eric Gairy, a former trade union leader and founder of the Grenada United Labour Party.

One of Gairy's more harmless eccentricities was an obsession with flying saucers and he is instantly recognisable in Peter Morgan's novel of 'traditional West Indian bacchanal politics', *A High Tide in the Caribbean*, where he appears as the Right Hon. Sir Matthew Ernest Richardson, Prime Minister of Chario, founder of the Chario United Field Workers Union, and a sincere believer 'in the existence of Unidentified Flying Objects'. But his style of government left something to be desired: 'Gairyism' was an unattractive blend of terror, corruption and buffoonery, and Gairy himself was in the habit, particularly after 1970, of dealing with any opposition or attempts at popular protest by unleashing the Mongoose Gang, his own personal army of thugs. Maurice Bishop's father, Rupert, was shot dead by the Mongoose Gang in a demonstration in 1974.

After this, Bishop's government could hardly have failed to be an improvement, but its strongly Marxist principles and close links with Cuba and Fidel Castro guaranteed that it was unlikely to meet with the approval of President Reagan. When an internal faction led by Bernard Coard, the Finance Minister, rose up and murdered Bishop and five of his closest associates, including his pregnant mistress, Jacqueline Creft, on 19 October 1983, the United States was happy to have an excuse to intervene.

Coard's hard-line group had taken control in the name of the Revolutionary Military Council, attempting to impose a total curfew throughout the island, forbidding people under pain of death to tend their crops or feed their animals. But their reign of terror was short-lived; it lasted only six days, and the arrival of six thousand US Marines was greeted with enthusiasm even by those who had supported the PRG. An American photographer who had covered the invasion told me that there seemed to be more troops – and journalists – than Grenadians on the island.

The United States justified the invasion on the following grounds: that US citizens were in danger (always a favourite), that Grenada's Governor-General had asked for help and that the Organisation of Eastern Caribbean States (OECS) which included all the islands from Grenada to Tortola, except Barbados, Anguilla, the French islands of Martinique, Guadeloupe – and its dependencies, the Dutch Antilles and the US Virgin Islands, was entitled to invite the Americans to intervene. The Prime Ministers of Barbados (then Tom Adams), St Lucia (John Compton) and Dominica (Dame Eugenia Charles) were the moving spirits in seeking help from the United States. Under Charles's chairmanship, the members of the OECS voted unanimously to establish a peace-keeping force to go into Grenada and to seek the assistance of friendly countries in mounting the force.

The show of popular support which greeted the invading force led, however, to a widespread, but not altogether accurate belief abroad that Bishop's government had been universally unpopular and his downfall, if not his actual death, had been welcomed. 'If Bishop had been alive, leading the people,' remarked Fidel Castro at the time of the invasion, 'it would have been very difficult for the United States to orchestrate the political aspects of its intervention.'

A poll carried out after Bishop's death found that two-thirds of Grenadians were in favour of Bishop's leadership; a slightly smaller number concluded that the PRG had always been popular. And Lord Melody, a calypsonian of the time, sang:

> Since the revolution
> We have a change in every direction
> Look around us and you will see
> The rise in our economy,
> It's a miracle, some people does say,
> Believe it or not we are on our way.

Still, I found a postcard, part of the 'I Love Grenada' series (with the word 'love' enclosed in a red heart), which was a photograph of a building literally covered in pro-US graffiti: 'THANK GOD FOR U.S. *and* CARIBBEAN HEROES OF FREEDOM. O GOD HELP + US. THANK YOU U.S.A. FOR LIBERATING US. K.G.B. *BEHAVE!*' I couldn't track down the building so I never discovered whether events had moved on and some new message was now in its place.

The invasion had a number of repercussions. For a start, the British were none too pleased at America's unilateral intervention in the affairs of a former British colony and member of the Commonwealth (Margaret Thatcher was not informed of the invasion until after the fact and the whole affair was presented in the British press as an insult to the Queen who remains the Head of State in Grenada). More importantly though, it enabled the United States to establish a presence in Grenada and gave rise to a number of expectations among the local population which have not been met. The feeling on the island seems to be that the invasion gave Reagan a much-needed boost at a difficult time ('Reagan used Grenada to divert attention from Lebanon' said Allberry) and the United States had failed to repay the courtesy. Anticipated aid had not been forthcoming. When the then-Secretary of State, George Shultz visited the island in 1984, he remarked – with spectacular insensitivity – 'It's a lovely piece of real estate'; but today Grenadians still have to travel to Barbados (an expensive little trip) to obtain a visa for the United States. In short, America has not proved itself to be the friend that Grenada hoped for.

I had an introduction to Mrs Lynn Creft, mother of Maurice Bishop's murdered girlfriend, Jacqueline; she was also a relation of Rosemary's. I went to call on her one hot afternoon. She lived high up in St George's in a tall house above a beauty salon. She took me along a narrow corridor into a big cool room. The house was very clean and tidy, with crocheted squares on the backs and arms of the chairs, but smelt faintly of damp or old age. On the walls and shelves, there were photographs of smiling black people of various ages in various situations – festive, sportive, formal – including a picture of a handsome young woman with a thoughtful expression wearing a scholastic gown and mortar board. In the next frame was a photograph of a boy of about fifteen. I sat down and said: 'Tell me about your daughter.' She looked embarrassed – embarrassed for me, I thought, for my bad manners.

I began again and asked about her childhood. Her face cleared. She had been brought up in the countryside the other side of the island, one of eight children. 'When I was a little girl, it was happy days, happy days,' she said and she began to describe an idyllic rural existence, a childhood of perfect simplicity and harmony, in which the trees groaned with mangos, coconuts, bananas and jackfruit and children ran around without fear or shoes, where no one was hungry or afraid, where your neighbours were your friends and people lived decent God-fearing lives and every day brought a new dawn.

But the bad days came. Jacqueline, the young woman in the photograph, had been Minister of Education in the revolutionary government and five months pregnant with her second child when she died. The boy was Vladimir, Jacqueline's son by Maurice Bishop. He had been six in 1984 and had had to be sent to Canada where he had been given Canadian nationality. Money was tight and Mrs Creft herself had had to leave Grenada and had worked in New York for some years, looking after an American woman suffering from Alzheimer's disease. Now things were different in Grenada. Single parents were hardly a novelty then but now even the schoolgirls in their uniforms, their hair neatly braided into cornrows, stood a good chance of becoming mothers before their fifteenth birthdays. 'You see a baby with a baby, a little girl with a bow just got a baby.' She told me that sixty per cent of the island's population was Roman Catholic but that this had next to no effect when it came to chastity and pre-marital sex. The Church's teaching which prohibits the use of contraception fell, however, on receptive ears and a widespread distaste for condoms meant that AIDS posed a real danger.

I told her that I was staying with Rosemary and she asked me to give her a message. Would she get her some special kind of crab from Carriacou (a neighbouring island) so that she could make 'crab-back'? She wasn't on such friendly terms with Cleopatra, whom she blamed for the death of Inslay Wardally: 'Patra bex [vex] she so, her heart pop.' Patra was one of a pair of twins, named to match. Her brother, Clio, oversaw the family business.

'Patra been with twelve men, been to England and she never get a baby – the devil!' Mrs Creft muttered angrily.

As I took my leave after a glass of juice and a large piece of cake, she said: 'Enjoy your escapade', meaning, I realised, my trip, and reminded me not to forget the crab. I walked slowly back down through the steep little lanes. The light was beginning to fade and the hills above the town grew velvety with the advance of evening. A translucent, almost-full moon glowed faintly through the soft blue of the nascent dusk. St George's, at any time of day, was ravishingly pretty. Now it was exquisite. The town rose steeply from the perfect horseshoe of the harbour and palm trees fluttered against the skyline. With its little houses clinging together on the hillside, it evoked the *chora* of a Greek island, except that there everything would have been dazzling white and the land exposed and parched like old bones. Here all was a lush green with the houses, an appealing mix of eighteenth-century French provincial and English Georgian architecture, washed in faded pastels, their roofs tiled a rusty red. Only the West Indian passion for slogans, either advertising or redolent of folk wisdom, betokened the twentieth century. I particularly liked one that read, 'What I am looking for is a blessing that is *not* in disguise.'

Down below, the looping promenade of the Carenage, dotted with souvenir shops selling spices and T-shirts, followed the curve of the bay. The clumsy bulk of the *Cunard Countess*, all the way from Nassau, dominated the harbour. From its deck came the unmistakable soft liquid tinkle of a steel band. Life as a party. White tourists danced while, on a lower deck, sparks – literally – flew. In the distance, the wailing siren of a fire engine began to compete with the steel band. The sea was by now rain-dark, pewter with flashes of petrol blue and a vast fluffy cloud, the soft pink-grey of a pigeon's breast, had settled on the crown of the hill. Just below the liner, floating on a surf-board, lay a black boy, his legs furiously bicycling in the air. As the sun finally slid into the water, the *Rhum Runner* came sailing in from a sunset cruise. The steel band gave way to reggae. The sparks went out of their own accord. The sirens died away. I went home and watched television with Rosemary.

The following morning, I went to the tourist office. Everyone, even old Mrs Creft, had appeared astonished when I expressed a desire to go to the country and I wanted to see whether there was anywhere I could stay if I were to go. There was a tall good-looking man in the tourist office, the statistical officer, who added unease to astonishment when I told him what I wanted to do. I was failing to conform to the norm. He was used to white tourists who came either from the cruise ships or on all-inclusive packages and rarely wanted to leave the protective confines of their resorts. I told him about Rosemary's Venezuelan guest and he looked even unhappier. I could understand his problem. Grenada, like all the small Caribbean islands, is heavily reliant on tourism. Sugar is finished and bananas soon will be. Grenada's spice industry could not begin to compete with Indonesia's so tourism remains the only viable source of income. And tourists are fickle and faint-hearted. Rumours of rising crime could send them scurrying to another sunny destination (earlier in the year the United States Information

Service had issued a travel advisory warning of rising crime in Barbados which had prompted the Bajan Minister of Tourism to counter: 'As a developing country dependent on the inflows from tourism to ensure our future progress, government views with the utmost seriousness any attempt to kill the goose that lays the golden egg.'). The statistical officer didn't want me to see or write about anything which might – even slightly – disrupt the myth of the Caribbean as an idyllic tourist destination: sun, sea, sand (and, for the more adventurous, sex). But it was becoming clearer by the minute that the kind of tourism promoted for the Caribbean could only lead to problems. *Far From Paradise: An Introduction to Caribbean Development*, published in 1990, cited 'resentment against the luxurious lifestyles of wealthy foreigners, an increase in prostitution and begging, exploitation of local workers by foreign-owned hotel chains, and an artificial rise in the price of land' as just some of the reasons why the sort of tourism in which the Caribbean specialised was not a good idea.

I had noticed, back in England, that advertisements for winter sun holidays in the Caribbean rarely featured black people – perhaps just a black hand proffering an exotic drink – and the islands were presented as largely uninhabited, subliminally encouraging a sort of Crusoe fantasy. Large numbers of cruise liners docked daily, disgorging hundreds, even thousands of tourists, who would wander up and down the Carenage, spending, at best, tiny sums of money on minute baskets of nutmeg, cloves and cinnamon, then returning to their ship for meals. This wasn't much use to the cottage industries or the local restaureurs and bar owners and it meant that the tourists and local people had very little contact. One of the aims of the NJM had been to develop the country's economy by introducing a 'new tourism' to reduce the role of private owners and foreign interests, which often went hand in hand. Local farmers had been encouraged to produce food for the tourist industry but, with the demise of Bishop and his government, all such idealistic schemes were consigned to the dustbin.

In a bookshop in town, I had found a geography book for

school children called *Caribbean Lands*, full of facts and figures about the region. In the chapter on the Eastern Caribbean states, there was a box headed: 'Comparisons and contrasts . . .', which seemed to sum up the problems of the Lesser Antilles.

Comparisons

All are small in area
All have small populations
All have only one major town
All have a tropical climate
All lack rich natural resources
All are short of capital for development
All have small internal markets
All import more than they export

Down at the port, I picked up a copy of the winter cruise list which gave details of all the ships docking at St George's between October and April. It ran to ten pages and carried the names of 258 boats. While many of them were yachts, there were also a number of cruise liners and, on one hideous day in January, nine were due in Grenada; they would disgorge some 4,500 passengers.

Young local males see the tourists arrive with their cameras, watches and white skins, and feel resentful. From this it is a short step to the cutlassed ambush on a dark corner of Lagoon Road. The cruise ship passengers are, on the whole, pretty safe, cocooned from the realities of Caribbean life on their floating rum punch palaces, but other white visitors might not be so lucky. All cats look grey in the dark.

In a narrow almost vertical street running up from Wharf Road round the corner from a restaurant called 'Delicious Landing' was the Grenada National Museum. At the entrance right by the ticket desk was a large – and fairly terrible – oil painting of a radiant young black woman, all teeth and curves: Jennifer Hosten, Miss World 1970, one Grenadian who had made it. I looked at a few photographs of the events of 1983, including one entitled 'Looting On The Carenage' and another of two white (male) West German journalists, one of them clad in a tiny swimsuit of the kind known improbably as a 'posing pouch'. There were three or four musket balls under a sign which read 'Relics of Our Colonial Past' and, under another notice saying 'And sometimes we find things we can't begin to understand – like this', lay a fossilised fish or snake. But the most striking exhibit was an announcement of a public auction:

> To Be Sold & Let
> By Public Auction
> On Monday 18th May 1829
> Under the Trees
> For Sale
> The Three Following
> SLAVES
> viz

HANNIBAL, about 30 Years old, an excellent House servant, of Good Character.
William, about 35 years old, a Labourer.
Nancy, an excellent House Servant and Nurse.
The MEN belonging to LEECH'S Estate and the WOMAN to Mrs D. SMIT.

Included in the same sale were 'Fine Rice, Grain, Paddy, Books, Muslin, Needles, Pins, Ribbons, etc.' and finally 'At One O'Clock, That Celebrated English Horse BLUCHER.' The words 'Blucher' and 'Slaves' were printed in exactly the same size type.

The slave trade was a direct result of the growing European demand for sugar and then tobacco. When Columbus made his second voyage to the Americas in 1493, he took with him sugar cane from the Canaries and, by 1516, the first sugar grown in the New World, in Santo Domingo, was shipped back to Spain.

Cultivation of both crops was initially done by white indentured labourers but, as the supply of these dried up, the workforce came increasingly to consist of black slaves.

John Hawkins, the first British slave trader, took the 'middle passage' in 1562. The 'middle passage' was the name given to the infamous route across the Atlantic, traversed by ships which transported slaves in unimaginably horrible conditions from West Africa to the West Indian plantations (Columbus, having set sail for India and mistaken his route, named the first land he encountered the West Indies – though with the decline of colonialism and the emergence of nationalism in the second half of the twentieth century, the term 'Caribbean' became preferable). The middle passage was the second leg of the slave ships' triangular voyage. The first leg was the journey from Europe to West Africa to acquire slaves and the triangle was completed when sugar was carried back to Europe.

By 1700 the slave trade was in full swing and, as a result, more than eleven million Africans arrived in the Americas, though this was still less than half the number who were actually enslaved in Africa. Of that twenty-four million or so, millions died en route to the African coast or on the slave ships. (By the end of the eighteenth century, British slave ships were losing roughly five per cent of their human cargoes. In 1788 Alexander Falconbridge, a surgeon in the slave trade, published *An Account of the Slave Trade on the Coast of Africa* in which he described conditions on board: 'The deck, that is the floor of their rooms, was so covered with blood and mucus which had proceeded from them in consequence of the flux that it resembled a slaughterhouse.')

The morning of my fortieth birthday dawned, like most Caribbean days, bright and clear. From my balcony I could see the brilliant reliable blue of the Caribbean sea and the yachts bobbing in the marina. Rosemary gave me a card which told me that I was a 'wondrous part of God's creation', that the 'most delicate and perfect flower, the most intricate, fragile leaf' was 'no more beautiful than the smile that lights your eyes and the goodness of your heart . . .' But I didn't get any presents. None of my family knew where I was. After breakfast, I caught a mini-bus – like the 'maxis' in Port of Spain but quieter – into town. This one was personalised to read 'AH MOSS D BUS' – whatever that meant. On the roadside opposite the post office was a large sign commemorating World AIDS Day, 1 December 1992 and saying in foot-high letters: 'AIDS is not who you are, is what you did.'

I went to visit my friend at the tourist office. He had thrown caution to the winds and was now prepared to recommend a small recently-opened hotel in a little town called Victoria, twenty miles or so from St George's. I thought that I would go there the following day. He had a birthday card for me as well, inscribed to 'A seemingly wonderful and very conscientious person – Lucretia.' I could have done without the 'seemingly'.

The day passed in a dream. I had thought that being forty would be somehow eventful, almost as if certain dread physical changes would take place on the day. I might become a werewolf or some dark creature of the night. Before I left England, I had been consumed with fear and unhappiness, not just about being forty but about what I had come to believe that it would mean: that I would never have children, that I would cease to be attractive, that the time of the possible would be lost to me forever, that my chance – for happiness, for love, for a certain kind of fulfilling and secure life – would be gone, that I would never be young again. It was all depressingly predictable but none the less real for that. I had begun – only partly in jest – to wish that I believed in reincarnation, so that I would have another chance, another chance to get it right. When I fell in love in New York, it came as a wonderful surprise. When he had put his arms around me in an apartment in wintry, downtown Manhattan, I had found that I had forgotten how to relax into an embrace. But, now in the sunny Caribbean on my fortieth birthday, the memory of that embrace gave me courage.

I took a bus back to Lagoon Road and descended into a cloud of marijuana smoke and the time-warp strains of 'Baby, Baby, It's a Wild World'. Up at the Lodge, Rosemary was, as ever, glued to the television which alternated, as her preferred form of entertainment, with a weekly tabloid from Miami which specialised in weird and wonderful picture stories ('Mermaid Found On Florida Beach'; 'Elvis On Mars'; 'Woman Gives Birth To Giant Eyeball' – my personal favourite). Today she was in a state of terrific excitement, her gargantuan frame wobbling like a jelly.

Between England and the Caribbean there was a four-hour time difference and the news from London was just hitting the island. In the normal course of events, little attention would have been paid in Grenada to developments in England, but today was special. The separation of the Prince and Princess of Wales had been announced in parliament that afternoon. Rosemary, who took a keen interest in the British royal family (she had already made me promise to send her a copy of *Diana – Her True Story*), was agog. There was a particular poignancy in hearing the news having just come from the post office where, among the collector's items, were stamps commemorating the Prince and Princess's tenth wedding anniversary. In Port of Spain, when Princess Anne's engagement had been announced, Gina had remarked: 'She got a man, he must be doing it good, he must be doing something right.'

Rosemary had a more romantic view of the British royal family and was depressed by the news of the split, blaming Charles and 'his dirty business'. She thought that he hadn't been treating Diana well and deserved to be left. However, she also believed that marriage was forever, not having tried it herself.

Allberry wanted me to write a short piece about my impressions of Grenada for his paper which had to go to press later that day. I said OK, and that I would go and think about it on the beach. So far I hadn't yet been to a beach in the Caribbean and every time I called New York or England, I was asked how brown I was and what was the swimming like.

I took a maxi to Grand Anse, the famous stretch of white sand that adorns the island's southwestern shores. The beach was picture-postcard lovely with its limpid turquoise waters, fine creamy sand and palm trees. From the terrace of one of the big resort hotels came the dulcet plink-plonk of a steel band. But Grand Anse was also disconcertingly big, with row after row of sunbathers spread out like goods on a market stall, and it was difficult, if not impossible, to be alone. Every minute or so, someone wanted to sell me something: souvenirs, beers, soft drinks, drugs. There was a black girl with a comb and a bag of little glass beads going from female tourist to female tourist offering to braid their hair in cornrows. Remembering the unfortunate appearance of the Dutch woman on the plane, I declined.

Months later, back in England, I read in the *Daily Express* under the headline 'Our Hell in Paradise', that it was on Grand Anse that four cricketers from the Pakistani cricket team, in Grenada for the West Indies tour, had been arrested, allegedly for possession of marijuana, with a couple of English women whom they had met there. Though almost everyone on the beach either was, or could have been, stoned out of their minds, the authorities decided to make an example of the foreigners and threw them in the cells for a night. Three of the players were allowed out on bail to take part in a match – which testifies to the Caribbean passion for cricket – and the charges were subsequently dropped. One of the English women was quoted as saying: 'People should know about this place and be very aware of what can happen to them. The next time we go on vacation we will go to Cornwall.'

Down in the sweltering basement office of the *Caribbean Echo*, Allberry, smoking like a chimney, was cutting and pasting copy with a cheerful disregard for straight lines and margins, while his assistant, from behind a cloud of insects and a thin ineffectual wisp of acrid smoke from a mosquito coil, typed up each new story for him to lay out. I sat down and tapped out my little piece as fast as I could. Allberry was holding the front page. Taking as my starting point the headline from the (Barbados) *Daily Nation* ('Barbados – "land of violence and hatred" '). I wrote a couple of brisk paragraphs on the urgent need for greater contact between the white tourists and the black locals if further crime and violence were to be avoided. I had been in Grenada for only a short time and was a little embarrassed by this presumption of authority, but Allberry professed himself delighted, saying that he would not touch the piece, that it was very rare for him not to edit, but this was such thoroughly professional work, that he was going to let it go in just as it was, with not a word changed.

As a reward, he proposed to take me on a tour of the island in his car the following day; he would deposit me in the evening at my new hotel in Victoria. He also said that it was all he could do to get the paper out on time, that he was terribly tired, having been woken by a woman who had knocked on his door at four in the morning, saying: 'Sir, do you need me?' He opened the door thinking – or so he claimed – that it was me but, seeing that it was definitely not, said 'Woman, go away. I'm sleeping and I have no money.'

Allberry's car was his pride and joy. It was a 1972 Triumph Spitfire convertible that had originally been red, but, somewhere along the line, had been repainted – as opposed to resprayed – white. The original red gave a rosy tinge to the amateurish white paint job. The leather seats were cracked and torn and the wood veneer dashboard parched and peeling from the tropical climate. But Allberry loved the car and, when it refused to start, he began to wring his hands, saying over and over again, with an agonised expression: 'It's so embarrassing.'

Eventually the ancient engine leapt to life, and we set off. We went first to the airport to collect a delivery of the *Caribbean Echo*; on our way we passed the US Embassy, situated strategically close to Point Salines. As he drove, Allberry discoursed breezily about Grenadian politics. Marxism, he said, was suitable for an industrial society but not for the Caribbean. In Bishop's time, members of the Politbureau had been forced to attend judo classes and there was no freedom of speech. When Bishop had advised him to leave Grenada, Allberry had fled the island in a barrel.

I remembered a senior government official in Cambodia,

who, when I had asked how socialism was faring there, said that she thought Cambodian people liked doing what they wanted. If Marxism was unsuitable for Cambodia, how much less suitable would it be for the *laissez-faire* society of the West Indies? Allberry blamed Maurice Bishop's downfall on his basically weak character and claimed that most Grenadians were still unaware that Bishop had been, in his words, a 'dummy'. He said that the current government, the National Democratic Congress, which had been in power since 1990, headed by Nicholas Braithwaite, was also very weak. Braithwaite, who had been chairman of the interim government which ran Grenada for a year after Bishop's murder, was a former teacher and administrator. Largely free of Gairyite taint, he had, like many middle-class Grenadians, supported Bishop in his moderate moves; this meant that he was considered a safe candidate – neither pro-Gairy, nor pro-Bishop, nor pro-US occupation forces. But now, according to Allberry, he had banned all books by Marx and Castro and had all but lost control of the country. Allberry said that, were there to be an election tomorrow, 'Uncle' Gairy, even though now blind, would win.

After we had been driving for a bit, up and down through spectacular tropical landscapes on terrible broken roads which would suddenly twist to reveal waterfalls of greenery, shot through with brilliant sunshine, Allberry turned the conversation to more personal matters. He wanted to know what I thought about relationships between black men and white women in general, and in particular between him and me. I said that I was all for relationships between consenting adults of any colour or creed but anything between him and me was out of the question because I loved another. This might well not have stopped me for long if I had found Allberry at all attractive but, as it was, his puny body, his scraggly goatee and his generally unkempt appearance (he told me that he hadn't brushed his hair for two days), were profoundly off-putting.

He was, however, extremely persistent. I didn't feel that I could simply tell him the truth – that I didn't find him attractive – because I was sure that he would think that it was because he was black. The only way that I would be certain to convince him that I wasn't discriminating against him was by sleeping with him. Or, if I was clever, by persuading him of my love for someone else. My lies – of necessity – grew more and more complicated and I found myself inventing a lengthy biography for my beloved. It made little difference. Allberry said blithely, with the confident air of a man whose logic was infallible, that the beloved would never know if I had an 'affair' in the Caribbean. I said that *I* would know that I had deceived him. Allberry wanted to know what the reaction of my lover would be to my infidelity. And on it went.

This was to be the pattern of all such conversations in the Caribbean. The notion of a conscience, particularly in sexual matters, appeared to be nonexistent. Or rather the idea that love and sex might be connected was alien. This was probably no different to attitudes in many other parts of the western world. The men here were just more honest about it – and more insistent. And they wanted me because I was white.

Around noon, we reached Grenville, the main town on the east coast of the island and a collection point for bananas, nutmeg and cocoa. It was a dusty, shabby place with the usual hole-in-the-wall rum shops and a number of listless and not particularly friendly men standing around. When I began to take a photograph of the nutmeg warehouse on Jubilee Street, one of them lurched towards me, shouting and waving his fist. We ate an indifferent fish-and-chip lunch in a little café called O'Draggs (Grenville, according to Allberry, was famous for its blackfish – a big fish which looks like a cross between a whale and a porpoise) while 'Young, Gifted and Black' played on the radio. Allberry was neither young, nor apparently very gifted, nor was he really black – more a sort of speckly brown like an egg. And Grenville did not strike me as the land of opportunity. It was here, in 1973, at the Sea Moon that the NJM had held a convention in which Gairy had been told to mend his ways – or else. As a result, Bishop and his followers had been beaten up and imprisoned, presumably by the Mongoose Gang. Allberry pointed out another house which had been the local headquarters of the NJM and, to please him, I photographed the steps leading up to the meeting-room. Now, only a couple of sallow dogs slunk behind a wire fence and a magnificent blue and yellow parrot cawed on a gatepost. On the way out of town we passed a man pushing a 40lb kingfish in a small cart. This was the high point of Grenville.

We pushed on to Sauteurs. Central and rural Grenada is astonishingly lovely and, as the midday sun weakened, the contrasts in the landscape became more pronounced. We seemed constantly to be either climbing or descending through banana and cocoa plantations, passing through tiny villages with houses in soft washed pastels, colours that only time and the constant washing and drying of the tropical rain and sun could achieve. The body of the land was draped in a great swathe of trees and shrubs: nutmeg, sapodilla, pawpaw, banana, coconut, the huge graceful fan of the traveller's tree, and ferns springing everywhere. There was every imaginable shade of green: sage, lime, apple, olive, avocado, emerald, green, green, green, all rendered polished and iridescent by the sunlight filtering through the leaves. The roads were narrow, winding and almost always very bad, with vast potholes which Allberry had to swerve to avoid. The little Triumph laboured terribly on the slopes and, at one point, cut out altogether and refused to start. Allberry, muttering 'Oh, this is so embarrassing', got out and peered under the bonnet. I was fairly certain that he had simply flooded the engine in his attempts to restart it but said nothing. Once it had rested for five minutes, it started again easily enough.

Morne des Sauteurs on the northern coast took its name from the mass suicide in 1651 of some forty Carib Indians who preferred to die rather than surrender to the French with whom they were battling for control of the island. The Caribs, whom the historian Père Du Tertre described as being well-formed, robust and the colour of 'cooked shrimps', were reputed to be energetic warriors and avid cannibals (this latter detail may well have been only a myth put about by the Arawaks and subsequently taken up by Columbus – the word *Carib* comes from the Spanish *caribe* meaning 'cannibal'; in their own language, they called themselves *Callinagoes* meaning 'the peaceful people'). They had succeeded in preventing both the British and the French from settling in Grenada but, in 1650, a French expedition from Martinique had landed and managed to establish an initial rapport with the natives. When relations soured, however, the French brought in reinforcements and massacred the entire Carib population.

Now Sauteurs seemed pleasant enough, with a few rum shops and grocery stores. There were signposts to Leaper's Hill: one, in addition to the directions, bore a four-leaf clover and a cheery exhortation 'To make the best better'; another had a gnomic figure dressed like Father Christmas pointing the way to 'CARIBS Leap, compliments E & F Supplies'.

In a playing-field below the thousand foot precipice from which the Caribs had leapt to their deaths there was the tail end of a fair. At a long table women were selling or dispensing fried chicken, rice and peas and other West Indian dishes. Most of the food had gone. The ground was strewn with beer cans and bits of greasy paper. An enormous stereo system with two loudspeakers, each the size of an elephant, belted out Christmas carols to a reggae beat. It was with a sudden jolt that I realised Christmas was only two weeks away. I had not only lost almost all sense of place – that is, I knew that I was in Grenada but I didn't really know where Grenada was – but I had also completely lost track of time. It was as if I were sleep-walking through the days.

I climbed up to the edge of the cliff and stared down at the rocks and the sea in to which the Caribs had flung themselves. Different species of cacti, cochineal, prickly pear and the tall fleshy phallic kind, all covered with vicious-looking spikes and festooned with strips of lavatory paper, grew in dangerous abundance on the rocks, themselves jagged enough. Below, the sea tossed and boiled. It was clear that the Caribs could not have hoped to survive and swim to safety. They would not have stood a chance. A lone donkey, grazing lugubriously, lifted his head as I walked past.

Driving out of Sauteurs, we passed a large white car coming

in the opposite direction. As it went by, Allberry recognised the driver as an old friend whom he had not seen in ages and turned round to follow him back into town. We all got out and repaired to a rum shop to celebrate the reunion. His friend, a delightful man called Albert Xavier, had been a journalist on a paper called *Torchlight* which had been forced to close under Bishop. Later he had been Herbert Blaize's ambassador to the UN. Blaize, whose New National Party came to power in 1984, had been Prime Minister after Bishop and had died in 1989. Xavier said, with a broad smile, that he was now *persona non grata* on the island, adding cheerfully that Grenada had gone 'from primitiveness to decadence without the benefit of civilisation in between' – a comment more commonly made about the United States.

As we continued towards Victoria, Allberry, fortified by the rum and his encounter with Xavier, began to fantasise about the kind of working future we could have together if only I would stay on in Grenada.

'We could rule the world,' he said, taking his hands off the wheel and waving them in the air. 'Through the power of the press, the world could be our oyster. You and me together, imagine what a combination.' Imagine. His idea was that we could transform the face of Grenadian politics by working together on a newspaper, presumably the *Caribbean Echo*; that my journalistic skills (of which he had an absurdly high opinion) and his local expertise would prove an irresistible force.

The light was fading as we drove on and the dusk threw a veil over the countryside. There were little houses half-concealed by branches hanging like giant eyelashes from the trees at the side of the road; dark faces gleaming softly like a reflection blurred in bronze on the narrow verandahs and child shadows playing in the dust. There were mangy dogs and scrawny chickens, all in a landscape so rich as to seem almost overripe. Here nature had a hand in every corner. We were driving through old plantation land: to our right, the Blair Atholl estate, the Samaritan estate, to our left Mt Rodney, Duquesne and Nonpareil, beautiful names and once ordered lands of plenty. There was something growing in every spare inch of ground and the fecundity was unnerving.

At Chantimelle, we stopped. I wanted to admire the setting sun and the view down to Duquesne Bay where straight tracks of red earth bisected the plantations and the soft uniformity of the vegetation was broken by the flash of an occasional tin roof. Allberry wanted to take a photograph of a mini-landslide, a piece of the hill that had fallen down on to the road some three weeks before and was still there. It had all but blocked the road and he was incensed that it had not yet been moved. He leapt out of the car, brandishing his camera, saying: 'I'm going to nail the government.'

Further on was a turning to a beach. In the half-light, it looked idyllic – nothing but palm trees and silver sand. At the entrance was a sign which read: 'But Do Not Commit Suicide.'

Finally we reached Victoria. It was dark and the little Victoria hotel was lit up like a Christmas tree. It was love at first sight. It turned out that I was the only guest in the place – a situation which Allberry did his best to remedy. There was piped muzak playing in the bar – 'Strangers in the Night', or something similar, which he interpreted as a sign. Our song, he said, so romantic. He couldn't possibly leave me here alone. Please, please, could he stay. But I longed to be alone and sent him on his way, after agreeing to photograph for the *Echo* a teachers' dinner that was to take place at the hotel that night.

Soon after he had left, my friend from the tourist office telephoned to check that I had arrived safely. It sounded as if he had reservations about Allberry.

'I can take care of myself, you know,' I said, 'I'm a big girl.'

'You certainly are,' he answered, 'a nice big girl.'

He was depressed, he said, because he had been refused a bank loan of EC$6000 to buy a new stereo. Sounding aggrieved and somewhat surprised, he added that the bank regarded this as a luxury item. However, he was prepared to bow to the will of a greater authority (God). I liked the contrast between his venality and his religion. On another occasion, one evening in the True Blue Inn out on Grenada's southern coast, he confided to me that he had lost his virginity to *two* Seventh Day Adventists.

I funked the teachers' dinner and went upstairs to bed after a solitary meal in the hotel dining-room. There were four men playing a desperate game of cards in a room down the corridor. I locked my door and fell asleep. All night long the sea crashed outside my window and all night long I tossed to the noise, waking, turning and falling back into a sleep beset by dreams. In the morning, the sea was a millpond. It had apparently been like that all night but underneath its calm surface the noise raged on, audible only in the dark when, because I couldn't see, other senses went into overdrive. There was a balcony running round the first floor of the hotel where my room was – and from it a beautiful view: to the left, a stretch of narrow sandy beach; to the right, dwarf cliffs, sprouting coconut palms and sprawling sea grape, dropped sharply to the sea. A church tower rose unexpectedly in the midst of all this greenery.

Victoria was scarcely more than a large village, with one main street running through it which led on to St George's. Open drains ran along the side of the road but it all appeared clean enough. The churches, of which there were at least seven, including Pentecostal, Anglican, Roman Catholic, Seventh Day Adventist, Church of Christ and a couple whose denomination I didn't get, lined the main street, one after another like pubs in Ireland. The Victoria Community Centre advertised a 'Yes Party Massive'.

'Come Alive This Saturday 12th Dec. D. J. Fowla will be mashing the Place Down for Only $3.00 Bar Solid Proceed in aid of Pan Symphony.'

I walked up and down the main street taking photographs. There was no shortage of subjects: in one front garden, a cactus had whole eggshells stuck on each spike. In another, the flowerbed was edged with a border of conch shells. Children in the kindergarten came to its door as I peered in. They were ridiculously sweet with their big brown eyes and curly heads. One wore a T-shirt saying: 'Correct Me With Love' – as if one could bear to do anything else. Pinned to the door was a picture of a cricketer missing a ball. The caption read: 'You can't score on drugs.' There were many places 'licenced to sell spiritous liquor'. At one end of the village, there was an exquisite little lagoon surrounded by palm trees and, on the other side of the road, off a track leading up towards the hills, there was a shack inhabited by a Rasta, who made crocheted things in the Rasta colours: green, yellow and red – belts, bags and huge caps like tea-cosies designed to accommodate the volume of dreadlocks; a predictable cloud of marijuana smoke hung in the air nearby. Later that morning, Swynton Fletcher, the proprietor of the hotel and of Fletcher's Shopping Complex across the street, took me on a tour of the cocoa station. Part of the old Diamond Estate, it had been built in 1774, some sixty years before the abolition of slavery, and the building, weathered and shabby, was still standing. Now the station produced around three thousand bags of cocoa beans a year. According to Mr Fletcher, Grenadian cocoa was the richest in the world and he said that Cadbury's bought it to mix with African cocoa which was much cheaper. First the beans were put in piles to 'sweat', then dried in big trays that slid in and out of the building like huge drawers, then put in sacks for shipping. The heaps of fermenting – or 'sweating' – beans gave off a sour smell, like ammonia. Upstairs, there were dozens of bags waiting to go. Mice or rats scampered around the floor and there was a barn owl perched on the rafters above.

We walked back towards the centre of town stopping to look at a ruined sugar mill. The tangle of vegetation that ran riot over the ancient machinery gave it a romantic air. Mr Fletcher was hoping to have it preserved as part of the national heritage and as a tourist attraction. He had spent twenty-five years working in England but had come home before the revolution. He didn't have much time for the present government but said that Gairy hadn't been all bad and that education had been much better under Bishop; for one thing, there had been more opportunities for people to go abroad to study.

On a street corner, we met his friend, Alec, who came with

us for a drink in a noisy bar. Alec was, to borrow a phrase from
C. L. R. James, 'as handsome a man as you would meet in a
day's journey'. He was tall and slim with fine features. He said
that it was his birthday, that he was sixty-five today. I couldn't
believe it and told him so. What did it matter, he asked with a
sideways glance, what was it to me? I said that I thought that
sixty-five was too old for me. Why he said, an old gun could
shoot just as well, the bullets went just as straight.

Like Mr Fletcher, Alec had spent years of his life in England.
He had gone there in 1951 at the age of twenty-four and worked
for British Rail earning £4 a week in the parcels office. He
described handling parcels in the snow, and talked nostalgically
about Euston, St Pancras, Marylebone and the girls from Sheffield. He had liked Wales: the Severn Bridge hadn't been built
then. His wife had died of leukaemia in England.

'I tend my garden,' he said, 'I live like the birds, take a little
honey here and there.'

We made a date for that evening and I went back to the hotel
and fell asleep, worn out by the heat, the noise and the rum. I
dreamt about Alec, that he refused to embrace me until I had
washed because I was dirty after being held by someone else. I
didn't know who that person was; Selwyn Allberry perhaps.
When I woke, the light outside had dropped. Instead, there was
a beautiful clear yellow sunset, darkening, as I watched, to
flame-orange and burning a slow fuse to the silky water. There
were fishing boats on the horizon and dark figures slipping
silently in and out of the sea which kept up a steady thunderous
roar. I heard a soft whistle and looked down to see Alec appearing out of the shadows below. He swung an elegant leg over
the fence and came up to my balcony. He said that the sea was
'doing its work', bringing the sand to cover the rocks and that,
in a few months, the whole beach would be sandy. When he
was a boy, they used to run races along this beach.

We walked down Victoria's main street to a rum shop. Alec
said that he bet that I couldn't drink the local rum as it should
be drunk. You ordered an eighth or a quarter which was poured
from a big bottle into a small one and then drank it in a tiny

glass with an inch of fiery white rum and an inch of water. You 'heaved back' and then were expected to collapse coughing. I got the hang of it immediately, and after four or five of these, Alec and I were getting on just fine. He said I reminded him of the girls in Sheffield.

We walked on up the hill in the moonlight past the Rasta's hut into the countryside. At the top of the hill, we stopped and looked around. The sky was very black against the clear bright moonlight and the night was warm and scented. The land lay, dark and secret, below us. I turned to face Alec and he took a step towards me. I couldn't read his expression. I hadn't known what I wanted from him or even that I wanted anything – though the dream in the afternoon should have warned me – but, in that instant, I knew and moved closer for him to kiss me. We stood there, kissing, close, till desire became imperative. I untied the sarong from my waist and spread it, like a sheet, on the grass. The ground was strangely comfortable and Alec was right. An old gun could shoot just as well.

3

Slow Boats to Carriacou, Union and Bequia

Oh, please, don't you rock my boat,
Don't rock my boat
'cos I don't want my boat to be rockin'
I like it, like it, like it like this . . .
(from 'Satisfy My Soul' by Bob Marley & the Wailers)

I got up early and caught a maxi down to the capital. Rosemary, with my luggage, was already on the deck of the *Alexia*, waiting to leave for the little island of Carriacou, one of Grenada's two dependencies (the other was Petit Martinique, a blob with only six hundred inhabitants some two hundred miles south of its larger French namesake). Allberry, in the Sprite, its engine idling, was waiting on the quay for the return of his camera. I was slightly surprised to see him: he had telephoned the previous evening as I was rushing out with Alec and had been very put-out that I wasn't coming back to Mamma's Lodge. He had said that he couldn't believe that I wasn't planning personally to return his camera, that it was most unprofessional, most unjournalistic. I had said that I would give it to Rosemary the next morning. The boat looked as though it was about to sail so we said a hasty, somewhat bitter, goodbye – his unfulfilled hopes and desires hung in the air like cobwebs – and I went aboard.

Rosemary, all set for a weekend with Errol, her lover, was magnificent in shiny black lycra leggings, a voluminous T-shirt supporting an American baseball team and a peaked cap from Puerto Rico. She said that she had a fiendish hangover from drinking too much white rum the night before while watching the cricket on television. There was no sign of Errol.

The deck was laden with huge bunches of bananas, sticks of sugar cane, sacks of coconuts, bottles of rum, cases of soft drinks, boxes of frozen chickens, everything imaginable. Rosemary, cursing Errol and her hangover in graphic terms, opted for a seat under the shelter. I preferred to stay in the open along with the cargo and watch St George's slowly disappear from sight. As we chugged north up the island's west coast, we passed Victoria and, like a lover nursing a secret passion, I craned to make out the outline of the little hotel, just recognisable by its balcony and the satellite dish. The boat was slow and, once we hit the open sea, the journey began to lose its novelty. I settled down against a stack of planks and started to read *A Handful of Dust*. Behind us the sea and sky formed a steel-grey wall.

About a third of the way to Carriacou, near the uninhabited islet of Diamond Island, there is a famously rough patch of sea. Both the island and the seas around it were known as 'Kick–'Em-Jenny' (from the French *cay qu'on gene*), but that day it was barely choppy and the 23–mile trip – all three and three-quarter hours of it – was monotonously uneventful, the only excitement provided by a school of porpoises and the shoals of little leaping fish. Frigatebirds – Man-o'-War or Hurricane birds, as they are sometimes called – their wings perpetually extended, swooped dramatically around the skies like dancers in some huge aerial ballet.

Finally we arrived at Carriacou, the largest of the Grenadines. Across the bay from the dock at Hillsborough, the island's tiny capital, is Sandy Island, an exquisite parcel of land, scarcely more than a handful of sand with a few palm trees, floating in the turquoise waters, the sort of thing that, given the right materials, a child might have made. Rosemary lumbered ashore and I followed, dazed by sun and sea and dragging my luggage behind me on a little trolley. Disembarking passengers are greeted by a weather-beaten sign erected by the Grenada Civic

Awareness Organisation (GCAO). This features a coat-of-arms with a kind of rat with a sweet expression and Grenada's national symbol, the rare Grenada dove, on either side of a heraldic shield and above the motto, 'Ever conscious of God, we aspire, build and advance as one people'. There follows a list of statistics: population, land area, geographical location, places of interest, hotels and the information that Carriacou is famous for 'Boat Building, Annual Regatta, and Big Drum Dance'. Along the waterfront I noticed a number of derelict buildings, their entrails gutted like fish by the last hurricane – or perhaps the one before; only the rough skeletons remained, bleached by the surf.

Reservations were supposed to have been made for us at Ade's Dream House by Rosemary's cousin who lived in Carriacou but it soon became clear that the message had somehow not got through. The front half of Ade's Dream House was a building-site and there was no room at the inn. The good news, though, was that Errol, having missed the boat, had arrived before us on a plane, and had made alternative arrangements. The bad news was that he was nowhere to be seen.

Suddenly, without warning, it began to pour with rain. The main street was full of potholes which immediately filled with yellow water. Rosemary and I, out looking for somewhere to have lunch and pacify our hangovers, got soaked. Lunch was a silent and unsatisfactory meal in a deserted restaurant. The Sands Guesthouse, where it seemed we were to stay, was a ten-minute-walk from town but it was quiet and clean and faced the sea. Its owner, a Mr McLoy or McLean, drove us there in his pick-up, showed us the facilities (spartan and spotless bathroom, kitchen and three bedrooms), then left. He was dour to the point of surliness and did not live in. Rosemary and I promptly went to bed.

When I woke up it was dark and Errol had put in an appearance. He was a small man, half the size of Rosemary, with a neat beard and a muscular, compact body. Rosemary had changed into a pair of white cycling shorts. Outside the night sky was filled with stars and there was a full moon but it somehow failed to penetrate the heavy blanket of dark which lay across the land. We hailed a passing mini-bus and rattled along an unlit road riddled with potholes through the pitch-black countryside to Tyrrel Bay. The bus pulled up by a small French restaurant and we went in. There were a few desultory white diners who turned to look at us and some soft music in the background. We sat down and Errol announced: 'We have come fo' de turtle dinners'.

Our French host, who was busy proffering menus which featured *tomates à la crème frâiche, rillettes avec cornichons, steack haché* and a host of other unlikely delicacies, looked mystified. I translated but it didn't help much. 'Pas de tortue,' he said emphatically. Errol insisted that he had telephoned through his order: two turtle dinners and one mutton. Eventually, with a sudden spurt of comprehension, the Frenchman pointed down the road to a noisy little shack blaring reggae music. That was the turtle-dinner establishment. There our carefully-ordered dinner consisted of vast platters of greyish turtle and mutton, in thick gravy, and a mountain of 'provisions' – yams, sweet potatoes, plantain. The turtle, which I had chosen back at the guesthouse – in a spirit of adventure rather than greed – was tasteless and heavy, definitely meaty rather than fishy, not at all like the 'unorthodox' dish described in a 1956 guidebook ('The stew made of fins is even more exciting; fins are also rubbed with rum and lime, then onions, green peppers, young papaw and hot sauce are added, and the whole is casseroled till cooked tender'). The others ate quickly and with apparent enjoyment and, in what seemed like minutes, we were back at the side of the road waiting for the bus home.

The darkness had an almost tangible quality, like a thick, soft, black cloth draped over the island. Sometimes, as the bus sped along, hurtling in and out of potholes with a careless disregard for the suspension and the passengers, we passed people walking by the side of the road. You couldn't tell if they were men or women or children: only their movements and the occasional flash of white teeth in a dark face revealed them as human.

In the bay opposite the guesthouse the *Sea Cloud*, like a

vision from an earlier age, stood at anchor. The brigantine, with its four masts and furled white sails, ablaze with lights, looked impossibly stately in comparison with humble little Carriacou. It was like looking at another world across a chasm of time and space, from the Third World to the First. I imagined the people on board, rich people, white people, drinking champagne, playing baccarat and roulette, wearing designer clothes, cruising through the Caribbean.

Inside, Rosemary had poured generous measures of Bailey's Irish Cream into tall glasses filled with ice. I fetched my radio and a pack of cards from my room and sat down to teach Errol a Patience that I had learnt one summer in the South of France, thirty years before. We too knew how to live.

The next morning when I got up, Errol was sitting at the table eating a breakfast of tinned, mashed corned beef and water biscuits washed down with tinned orange juice. Rosemary was lying in a heap on their bed wearing only a skirt. Later, after Errol had gone out, she said that she had ended up sleeping on the couch because, when she had attempted to touch Errol, he had hit her. And he had snored very loudly all night long. She also told me that Errol was married with five children – by three different women.

Outside it was a beautiful day and the island gleamed from the night's rain. At ten o'clock, Mr Jameson, a stocky man in his sixties with a strong barrel chest and a deep tan, came to take me for a tour of the island. He owned an estate that had once belonged to the family of a friend in England. We had spoken a couple of times on the telephone and I had assumed that he would be black. But his family were originally from Somerset and had come to Grenada towards the end of the last century and had bought my friend's family's estate in 1927. I had never met any white West Indians, descendants of the old plantocracy, and hadn't realised that a West Indian accent had nothing to do with colour.

I climbed into the front of his jeep. Two of his sons – men in their forties – were sitting in the back and we bumped along the road to Hillsborough to visit the museum. As we passed the graceful Anglican cathedral, I turned to admire it and Mr Jameson said that there were fifty-two Anglican churches on the island and that thirty-two sects were represented. Carriacou is an island with a total area of thirteen square miles and a population of under five thousand so this was quite a statistic. In the 1940s, there had been twelve hundred communicants at the Anglican church. Now there were only 250. This seemed less extraordinary. There were also over a hundred rum shops and apparently only one petrol station.

The museum was closed but Mr Jameson, clearly a man of some importance, produced a key from his pocket and unlocked the door. The museum was a model of organisation – unlike that in Grenada. Some Americans doing VSO, or something like it, had supervised its beginning. There was an exhibition of paintings by a local artist, Canute Caliste, and I bought one. It was a naïve painting – they all were – but this wasn't a Carriacou scene like all the others. It showed the devil with horns and a tail and scaly arms like a dragon and little devilish spurs on his ankles, holding a large fork in his right hand, all vivid reds and black. He had a messy red mouth and red eyes. 'The Devle in Heal Busy' was the title. It cost US$60 but it was worth it.

There was an excellent exhibit on the Caribs and the Arawaks who had come to Carriacou sometime soon after the birth of Jesus Christ from the Orinoco Basin in South America. The Arawaks, who were peaceable, had been driven out after several hundred years by the warlike Caribs who, despite their best efforts, were, in turn, all but exterminated by the Europeans. There was a chart which showed the movement of peoples from Africa to the Caribbean. Africans from Senegal, Gambia, Guinea-Bissau, Mali, Sierra Leone, Liberia, Ghana, Benin, Nigeria, Cameroon and the Congo, from the Ibo, Moko, Congo, Temne, Mandinka, Chamba and Kromanti tribes, had all been brought to the Caribbean in slave ships; their descendants lived and worked on Carriacou (Carriacou was also used as a staging-post where those slaves, who had survived the horrors of the 'middle passage', would be 'refreshed' by exercise and fresh fruit and fish before being 'oiled' for sale).

Though over twenty million Africans made the middle passage, I noticed the names which clutter the maps of the Caribbean are not theirs. As the names of the once-great estates of Carriacou testified, Britain and France still held nominal sovereignty: Dumfries, Craigston, Belair, Lauriston, Meldrum, Limlair, Beau Séjour, Mount Pleasant. A map of Carriacou dating from 1784 gave the acreage of the estates, as well as the names of the then-owners who were mainly Scottish with a sprinkling of French. In 1784, the entire island, with the exception of the strip of land on which Hillsborough was built, had been divided into estates, all owned by white foreigners. On the north-west coast of the island, between St Hilaire's Point and Tarlton's Point, was a little cove called Jew's Bay.

I had a girlfriend in London who had a thing for African men and I had noticed that they – and she – seemed to despise West Indians. I wondered whether it was because West Indians had been enslaved; they – the Africans – were the ones who had got away. The Martiniquais writer, Frantz Fanon, observed the exact opposite, writing of West Indians who joined the French Army and served in Africa before 1939:

> [T]he West Indian, not satisfied to be superior to the African, despised him and while the white man could allow himself certain liberties with the native, the West Indian absolutely could not. This was because, between whites and Africans, there was no need of a reminder; the difference stared one in the face. But what a catastrophe if the West Indian should suddenly be taken for an African!

And Trollope, writing in 1860, when the abolition of slavery was still within the living memories of most Afro-Caribbeans, commented that, 'The West Indian Negro knows nothing of Africa except that it is a term of reproach.'

But over the second half of the twentieth century there has been a change in West Indian attitudes towards Africa and Africans. In 1914, in Jamaica, Marcus Garvey founded the Universal Negro Improvement Association and, in 1919, *The Negro World* as its official organ. In it, he called for equal rights and economic independence for blacks and, although his success in his lifetime was limited and he was constantly persecuted, his insistence on the equality and dignity of black people set an important precedent. In the 1930s the Rastafarian movement (so named after Ras Tafari, the original name for the Emperor Hailie Selassie of Ethiopia who compared the 'heaven of Ethiopia' with the 'hell of Jamaica') originated in Jamaica where it remained a popular religious cult for forty years having little effect on the rest of the Caribbean. In the 1970s, though, its back-to-Africa message, coinciding with the aims of the Civil Rights and Black Power movements in the United States, achieved more widespread favour, helped, at least in part, by the rise to fame of Bob Marley.

Around the time that Rastafarianism was taking root in Jamaica, the Martiniquais poet, writer and politician Aimé Césaire co-founded the *négritude* movement, which called for a resurrection of black values – an 'Africa of the heart' and a 'heroic affirmation of blacks and their culture as other than the dominant Euro-American values that had enslaved and degraded them'. In his *Cahier d'un retour au pays natal*, the definitive expression of *négritude*, Césaire wrote: 'et aucune race possède le monopole de la beauté, de l'intelligence, de la force' ('and no race has the monopoly on beauty, intelligence, or strength').

Mr Jameson and I left the museum to drive on up to his estate. On the way out of town, he pointed out the hospital on the top of the hill – built there, he said, to escape the yellow fever and malaria in the low-lying swamps.

The estate lay to the north-east and the house itself was at the top of a hill commanding wonderful views over Sparrow Bay. The early eighteenth-century house built by my friend's ancestor had been destroyed by Hurricane Janet in 1955. It had been swept clean away so that only the foundations remained to form the basis of the present structure. Mrs Jameson showed me some drawings of the old building, which wasn't as grand as the term 'Great House' had led me to expect and looked, as far as I could make out, rather like the new house – a modest, but pleasant enough edifice with a beautiful, broad verandah running round it and a relaxed atmosphere of shabby, comfortable gentility.

Mr Jameson said that people tended to go into shock after a hurricane and stopped functioning. Unless they could be galvanised into action very soon after the event, nothing would happen and, very quickly, the ruined house, the tree across the road, the ravaged landscape would become the norm. This had clearly happened down in Hillsborough where many of the buildings still gaped to the elements.

The estate had originally spread over three hundred acres, but bits of it had been sold off to develop into holiday homes. It used to grow limes, sending gallons of lime-juice to Rose's in London but Mr Jameson had had to give this up in 1981. It just wasn't profitable enough and, under the PRG, they couldn't get people to bring in the crop. We sat on the big open terrace with its beautiful views to east and west and Mr Jameson gave me his views on the political situation past and present.

The PRG, he said, had attracted 'the young ones coming to manhood' but 'no one who has not lived under a Communist regime can imagine how bad it is'. He said that a third of Carriacou's small population had left the island during the New Jewel (PRG) revolutionary period and that the revolution had contributed to the closure of the lime business because estate owners couldn't get the men to work; they were too busy digging foxholes and manning the beaches because Reagan might be on his way. The police and the civil service had become demoralised; and the number of policemen had dropped from twelve hundred pre-PRG to a hundred and twenty by 1983 when Bishop was 'assassinated – or exterminated – depending on who you are talking to'.

It had been claimed that the American troops had been unaware of Carriacou's existence when they invaded Grenada. However, when the soldiers finally made it to the little island on 1 November 1983, they were welcomed by friendly natives bearing soft drinks and beer; later Thanksgiving dinners were organised to make them feel at home.

In the last election, 28.4 per cent of the population had voted for Gairy. 'People like positive action', Mr Jameson said, 'they would rather be ruled positively than not at all. The government now lacks direction. I've told the Prime Minister.' While he talked, his two sons sat in silence, as if they were still small boys. If I addressed them directly, they answered briefly and to the point, then fell silent. Mrs Jameson tried to join in the conversation but her husband was determined that this was his show – and his alone.

Outside, in the garden, there were huge lizards about six inches long and a big bush covered with lovely red flowers called Barbados Pride. By now the sun had, in Mr Jameson's phrase, 'cantered a bit' and it was very hot. I sat on the step watching the lizards while Mr Jameson went to fetch the jeep. He was going to the airport, to meet his eldest son who ran a hotel in Barbados, and he offered me a lift. As we drove, he began talking about his youngest son. He had apparently been due to go to Cambridge but just before leaving had broken two front teeth in an accident and said that his life was ruined and that he didn't want to go after all. Then he had become an airline pilot but now his marriage had broken up and he dabbled in journalism and Caribbean politics. His father wasn't very pleased with him. The eldest son, who was about to arrive, was much more satisfactory.

I said goodbye and got a lift along the coast to Tyrrel Bay from a couple of cheerful youths in a Suzuki jeep. By daylight, the island looked green and untouched, profoundly rural. There were few houses, few people, not much of anything. The little roads were barely more than tracks, untarmacked and potholed, forging their way through untrammelled vegetation. The muddy puddles glinted gold in the sunlight.

The French restaurant was empty and the *patron* was glad to talk to someone who spoke his language. He came from Sète in the south-east of France down the coast from Marseilles. He and his wife and nine-year-old daughter had been in Carriacou for two months. His [white] in-laws lived in Canouan, another of the Grenadines further up the chain. He said that it was much better here than in France but that it was difficult to get provisions for the restaurant. Supplies of cream, cheese and charcuterie, had to come from Martinique and they weren't able to grow their own vegetables because of the dry season, four months without any rain at all.

Back at the guesthouse, Rosemary, in yet another outfit (blue leggings and a T-shirt), was fuming on the verandah. I felt sorry for her, because she had clearly been looking forward to her romantic weekend, to spending time with Errol and he seemed to have behaved in the most casual and callous way. She went inside to lie down and Errol confided to me that he didn't really play around much and that anyhow it was all going to stop soon; that he thought he'd go off to Miami in a year or so – alone – and that, before he went, he thought he'd 'make another baby' with his wife. I went to my room and fell asleep, obscurely depressed by Rosemary's unhappiness, the messiness of their relationship, Mr Jameson's dogmatism and by Carriacou as a whole.

Months later back in England, I got a letter from Rosemary saying that, after the weekend, she had told Errol to find 'a new woman for 1993 because of his behaviour' and describing a telephonic run-in with Errol's wife – 'And to make matters worst on December 30th he gave me a call around midday, and his wife tipped toed into the living room and overheard his romantic words to me and took the telephone receiver away from him and start abusing me, she did not know whom he were speaking to but she may have overheard, and she fucked me with adjectives, but I did not answer, I just listen, so I am not sure if I am going to keep our romance alive, he got abuse as well, she told him she were going to mash his face up . . . So I am waiting to see if he will call me, after his wife carry on in that manner. Now if he really do call I will love him a little more, that shows he really wants me to be his woman. What she should understand, she have got the ring, I have the man . . .

he is handsome and very emotional. He needs loving and that is what he is getting from me . . .'

Rosemary was, I've come to think, a perfect illustration of what a woman I later met termed the 'fuck-so-sweet' syndrome. This woman told me the following story: she was waiting one day in the office of a lawyer. There was another woman there who was carrying on, crying and screaming about how terrible her man was: he took her money, he took the food, he ate the children's food, even the food for the baby. Finally she couldn't take it any more.

'Why do you put up with him?' she asked the other woman.

'Oh, man, he fuck so sweet,' came the answer.

Around dusk I was woken by a soft whisper, a voice saying 'Pat', as if through my open window but there was no one to be seen. Rosemary and Errol had left to catch the boat back to Grenada and the only other guests, a young English couple from Suffolk, were out. I went outside and walked round the house. The place was deserted. I must have been dreaming but it left me uneasy. I crossed the road to the sea and, with only the *Sea Cloud* as witness, took a quick dip. The water was cool and there was a perceptible tug of current under the surface.

Later that evening I walked along the dark, silent road to Hillsborough. It was a Sunday and the town was virtually dead. I doubted that Carriacou ever had much to offer in the way of nightlife. The only place open was a little bar called Billy's by the wharf and I went in to have a drink. 'There is no lending, only spending and depending' read a sign on the wall. I asked the old lady behind the bar whether she had ever been to Union, my next destination, and about an hour's boat ride away.

'No,' she said, 'I don't travel.'

I stayed there, drinking rum punch, for an hour or so and then, as she showed signs of closing up, walked home. A man, passing in the opposite direction, said softly:

'Hello, sweetie, needin' company tonight?'

I laughed and said: 'No, thank you.'

Further on where the road was at its darkest, I was surprised to feel my hands grabbed by three little girls. They had come from a tiny shack that I had noticed before because it had no electricity and was lit by flickering lamps. They belonged to a family of six children, all under eight. They wanted to plait my hair, they wanted my watch, my earrings. They insisted on walking with me back to the guesthouse, squabbling over who would hold my hands. When I kissed them goodnight, one of them said: 'You cut off your hair and give it to me.'

In the kitchen cupboard, I found a tin of alphabet soup which I put on the stove to heat, and a bottle of Sea Moss, a local drink, made on Carriacou by Capricorn Enterprises, which claimed to have aphrodisiac properties. The label, illustrated with a line drawing of a man putting his arm round a woman and squeezing her breasts, made good reading:

> Island Pride
> Double Trouble
> Double Trouble
> Sea Moss   Bois Bande
> Aphrodisia   Phallus
> Marina   Duratus
> Ready to Drink –
> Delicious with Evaporated Milk
> Wakes up the men! Invigorates the women!

I drank some of it. It tasted simultaneously seaweedy and sweet. I put the bottle back in the fridge and went to bed.

The boat to Union was due to leave sometime late morning – it was not clear exactly when but sometime between eleven and twelve. I woke early, after a night of somewhat shameful dreams for which the Sea Moss's reputed aphrodisiac properties could perhaps be blamed. The English couple were in the shower together for ages and eventually I went outside to pee in the scrubby, thorny garden. The sky was grey and overcast. I packed my bags and it started to pour with rain. The couple emerged from the shower and revealed that they both worked in local government in Ipswich and their passion was travel. They seemed to have been everywhere – from Tonga to Tanzania. The rain stopped and I walked into town for another look at the museum. It was closed and I went instead to telephone a friend in London. She chattered away about Christmas parties and who was seeing whom. It was strange to feel so utterly divorced from my old life, just not to care at all. I hung up with a sense of relief thinking, I'm never going back to England. Never. New York was another story.

By eleven, I was on the quay with my bags. The boat, the *Jaspar*, was much smaller than the one from Carriacou, just a 'bale' boat, with a hatch leading to a small hold, and barely room to swing a cat on deck. I stowed my luggage, and then went back to a bakery on the main street and bought a couple of hot dogs – I hadn't had breakfast – and settled down to wait over a beer in Billy's Bar. The second-in-command of the *Jaspar* had assured me that we would be leaving at noon but not before. As the captain himself was in Billy's with a woman on his arm and a child on his knee, I thought that I was unlikely to miss the boat.

Noon came and went and the loading of the *Jaspar* continued. Sugar, bananas, Dragon Stout, French brandy, on they all went. A good-looking Rasta with immaculate white teeth told me that it was really a smuggler's boat, 'official but not official'. He admired my necklace. It was made of beads in the Rasta colours and he told me I was a 'roots lady'. Further on up the street, there was a terrific noise coming from a van mounted with a loudspeaker but it was impossible to understand what was being said. The speaker could have been selling soap powder or exhorting people to join a political party. I asked someone what was going on. 'He preachin' de gospel.' Of course.

Down on the wharf, a party of young Swedes – two men and two women – were waiting to board the *Jaspar*. One of the men wore a T-shirt saying:

> Sweden – land of the Vikings
> I enjoy making model boats and drinking

He had put his expensive camera with its long lens under the T-shirt – presumably to protect it from the rain – and this created a bump like a misplaced erection. His golden legs were covered with thick, fair fuzz. The women, who were probably in their late teens or early twenties, had flawless bodies and immaculate young skin, with white blonde hair and pale blue eyes. They should have been beautiful, but their features were so ill-favoured that their lovely colouring and perfect bodies counted for nothing.

Just after two, the last passengers came aboard. A tiny baby, just a few weeks old, blinking and smelling of milk, was thrust into the hold along with the sacks of rice and sugar, the crates of beer and spirits, the passengers' luggage and seven adults. Its mother followed and settled down on a pile of cases, tucking the baby against her generous breasts where the milk had leaked a little, leaving a dark stain on her dress round her nipples. The second-in-command started to close the hatch and I climbed on deck, preferring the elements to claustrophobia. There were cockroaches, some four inches long, scuttling around. The last to board was a miserable-looking goat, dragged on by its owner. It, too, stayed on deck for the voyage, tethered to the side of the boat. Finally, at 2.15, in heavy rain, we set off.

As the rain eased, another passenger emerged from the hold. A disc-jockey from Union – a kid barely out of his teens dressed to kill, in jeans made of asymmetrical patches, carefully frayed at the edges, the latest fashion from Jamaica. He had his DJ name, Hammer, written on his jeans and shaved into his hair which was about an eighth of an inch long. His real name was Mark. He said they had no radio station on Union so he did live shows. I asked why dub, the monotonous, deafening, grinding music which had taken over from reggae, was so popular.

'Dub music rules today because that's what de youth want,' he said.

I was just passing through Union on my way to Bequia. The next boat left at dawn the following morning and, by the time I had gone through Customs and Immigration at the airport

(Union was part of St Vincent and the Grenadines and therefore another country), and found a bed for the night, it was after five.

The boat I was to take on to Bequia was unloading at dusk by the soft ochre bulk of the Revenue Office, and a cheerful procession of trucks, goats, dogs and people trooped down the gangway. But there were other more disturbing sights – like the mentally-retarded teenage girl, mocked and jeered at by little boys as she lurched along the street, and the man who cried out and fell into a ditch, twitching and moaning and frothing at the mouth; when I went into the rum shop and told the men sitting there that we must put a cork between his teeth to stop him swallowing his tongue, they laughed and said it was a 'rum fit', that he would be fine.

That night I slept in an enormous room above what passed for a department store and dreamt of the man in New York. I dreamt that he came to see me in England and that I took him to meet my oldest friend from school who lived in the country with her husband and five children. She said to him: 'I hear from Lucretia that you are coming to live in England.' He looked surprised, and I was furious with her for betraying my secret desires to him and mortified that he should know what they were.

It was dark when I got up and still dark down at the wharf. The dawn came up like a knife, red and bloody. In less than twenty minutes, it was daylight as if there had been no night. With the light came motion. A grey rubber Zodiac with a raucous outboard motor bounced across the bay shattering the silence and the glassy stillness of the water. Behind the little town, the side of the hill was soft, like moleskin, in the early light.

The *Snapper*, which had been lying alongside the quay all night like a large sleepy animal, was big and sprawling and untidy. In one corner of the wide deck, there were three large turtles lying on their backs, their front flippers sewn together with coarse thread, blood oozing from the holes. They were still alive and their eyes were open. It hurt to look at them and the memory of the turtle dinner rankled again. In another corner, some sheep and a goat were miserably tethered. To distract myself, I started to play with two little girls. They were on their way to St Vincent where they lived with their mother and father and umpteen siblings. A man with burgeoning dread-locks asked me why I wasn't getting off at Canouan (a tiny island with a population of under eight hundred described in one guidebook as like a 'Bacardi ad' island). I said I had to get to Bequia. He said that he had noticed that I hadn't been 'socialising' much except with the children.

'Are you afraid of challenges?' he asked with a leer.

I said I didn't think so.

The poor turtles remained a source of morbid fascination for everyone on board. A young woman, who could have been a tour guide, began explaining why they weren't suffering that much and I moved over to talk to her. She turned out to be a child psychologist from St Vincent who had trained in Canada and now worked with what she described as 'exceptionals' (an admirable, if rather too politically correct, term for mentally retarded children). She was also a devout Catholic. She said: 'I practise chastity otherwise I would have ten children.' I imagined her as a character in a Bateman cartoon – the only woman in the Caribbean to say 'No'. She gave me a lecture on the importance of natural things, of not putting chemicals into your body, but she was happy to accept two painkillers for her headache. She produced a little photograph album, full of pic-tures of her family, her church, herself on skis, with a snowman and with her boyfriend, Gary, who was in England. Gary was, she claimed, perfectly content with the chastity rule.

It took a long time to get to Bequia. Our speed averaged about four and a half miles an hour. With all the stops, delays, and the uncertain nature of the boats and the sea, the journey could take days. Yet Grenada and St Vincent were only about sixty miles apart. The Grenadines – 'Mot magique, presque divin, qui evoque à lui seul l'image d'un paradis retrouvé ou l'homme serait à nouveau libre et reconcilié avec la nature' –

comprised some six hundred islands, islets, cays and rocks, ideal for diving and drug-smuggling, but most of these were too small even to be noticeable. We stopped at Mayreau and then Canouan where the goat got off, and chugged past Mustique where the rich go for privacy.

The next stop was Port Elizabeth, Bequia. At last. The journey had taken five hours. I staggered off the boat and weaved along the pier and the waterfront, the ground shifting under my feet. The little guesthouse was mercifully only a hundred or so yards down the road above a bookshop. A woman with red hair and pale skin was lying reading a magazine on a couch on the balcony. She greeted me in a pronounced Irish accent and said that there was indeed a room for rent at EC$30 a night (about £5), a little one at the back, taken up almost entirely by a double bed.

The household seemed chaotic. From a room at the front came loud groans every few minutes. These emanated from the master of the house, Papa Mitch, a decrepit man in his eighties, bedridden from arthritis and toothless. His nephew was the Prime Minister of St Vincent and the Grenadines, James 'Son' Mitchell, whose constituency was Bequia and after whom the island airport was named. Bridget, the red-haired woman, was the estranged wife of one of the old man's sons, and she took me inside to meet her father-in-law. He lay in a darkened room, an electric fan revolving by his pillow, his shrivelled penis – which had been responsible for siring twenty-seven children by seven women – poking from the slit at the front of his pyjamas. Papa Mitch had clearly been something of a tyrant in his day. His youngest son, Alvin, who looked more North African than Negro, had been brought to live with his father at the age of three. Another son, Anthony, had been kidnapped from his mother in Barbados when he was only two. He didn't see her again, I was told, until he was seventeen.

I had one room, Bridget and her four-year-old daughter, Alicia, had another; two German girls were lodging in a third; Alvin had a fourth, and Alvin's Italian girlfriend, Daniella, who was visiting for six weeks from Bologna, where she ran an acrobatic dance school, had yet another. The place was like a rabbit warren, both poky and infinite. There was a small lavatory and a shower room which ran cold water stinking of sulphur. The main room was used as a thoroughfare and dumping ground, and the dog, a big sloppy friendly beast, slept there when he wasn't snoozing on the galvanised tin roof which stretched down from the verandah and served as a porch for the bookshop below. A notice tacked up outside the old man's room read:

> 1 person to lodge in a single room,
> 2 persons to lodge in a double room.
> Please avoid embarrassment.

A separate building, up some steps across the yard at the back, served as kitchen and dining-room and you had to fight your way through a jungle of laundry to get there. Everything was dusty and grimy and, if not actually broken, falling apart at the seams.

In many ways, the same could be said for Bequia – which the Caribs called the 'island of the clouds'. The house faced the town rubbish dump, under which could just be discerned a structure bearing the words 'Keep Bequia Clean'. There was the usual flotsam of empty bottles, tin cans and plastic bags floating in the sea, and on shore, the usual panoply of rusting metal, broken bits of motor vehicles and rotting vegetation. The whole place had a hippy feel to it, an anything-goes, who-cares-man, be-cool feel. Of the two German girls staying in the house, one had been sleeping with Alvin till his girlfriend arrived, and before her, he had shared his bed with a Greek girl from New York who had won a holiday with Dive Bequia. No one seemed much interested in the outside world.

I was in a bar one afternoon when the music finally stopped for a news bulletin from Barbados. The barman immediately got up and fiddled with the dials until he found another reggae station. The Bequians had other priorities. When I bought a pareo in a gift shop, the saleswoman said, 'You have good taste. Jerry Hall bought the same one last week.'

Bridget was glad to have someone to talk to. She had come out to the Caribbean from London six weeks earlier in a final, last-ditch attempt to make a go of her marriage. She hadn't seen Dennis, her husband, for two years. He was the second of the old man's twenty-seven children, one of the few who were legitimate, and a barrister in St Vincent; she had met him when he was called to the Bar in London. Three days after she got to St Vincent, his mother told her that he was living with another woman, a Mrs Sandiford, the ex-wife of a doctor. On her first night in Kingstown, Dennis left her after supper, saying that he had to go out. She didn't see him for three days.

I couldn't make Bridget out. She seemed nice enough, but naïve beyond belief. She kept saying, in her soft, lilting, Mullingar voice, 'I think Dennis accepts that the marriage is over.' I wanted to shake her and say, 'You idiot, if you wouldn't come out here before, if you haven't seen him for two years, and if he's living with another woman, then, of course, the marriage is over and he doesn't give a toss.' Their child was lovely, white as milk, with a mane of curly soft brown hair. You would never know that her daddy was a black man. Bridget had been six months pregnant when they married but she had still worn a white dress. Now she was going to family therapy – on her own – in Kensington.

One evening we went to a 'jump-up' along the coast at a smart hotel called the Plantation House. I found myself simultaneously attracted to and repelled by the place. The thought of the air-conditioning, the cleanliness and the tranquillity was agreeable, but I found it disturbing that the old plantation 'great houses' should be converted into absurdly expensive hotels for white tourists, staffed by blacks on low wages. Burning them to the ground almost seemed a healthier option.

But not all the tourists keep their distance, and the 'jump-up', which was open to everyone, was a good place to observe other forms of interaction between black and white. On the dance floor a slender Finnish woman with white-blonde hair whom I had seen that afternoon in a bar in town had twined herself like poison ivy round a young black boy. From behind she looked like a girl but, when you saw her face, it was clear that she was in her fifties. The boy looked about seventeen. As she ground her crotch against his, an expression of desperate yearning flooded her face. His face registered only grim concentration. Earlier, I had heard her laughing and complaining of 'another shitty day in Paradise'.

Bequia was, it appeared, a mecca for certain extremes of black/white relationships. I wasn't sure how much there was to choose between the 'exploitation' of the servants in the 'great house' hotels and that of the young black boys recruited, albeit willingly, to service older white women. The latter might involve pleasure but only the very naïve could fail to be aware of the disruptive potential of such liaisons, tapping, as they do, into an ancient and deep insecurity on the part of black men *vis à vis* white women – as Frantz Fanon wrote, 'I wish to be acknowledged not as *black* but as *white* ... who but a white woman can do this for me? By loving me she proves I am worthy of white love. I am loved like a white man ... When my restless hands caress those white breasts, they grasp white civilisation and dignity and make them mine' – to say nothing of the reciprocal fantasies that white women (and white men) might have about black men as lovers.

When, in England, I had told male friends that I was planning a trip to the Caribbean, the expressions of prurient complicity and nervousness which chased across their faces were a sight to behold.

A 1988 report by the Director of the Organisation of American States' Jamaica Office on the 'Socio-Economic and Cultural Impact of Tourism in the Caribbean' commented:

> Regarding the very delicate question of relationships between black local men and white female tourists, there is ambivalence as to whether these basically sexual relationships helped to improve race relations. My own observation is that in the context of Barbados, which remains very much a

71

plantation society in this regard, these relationships, although generally tolerated, have been frowned upon by the local population ...

Here in Bequia it was smiles all round – for the moment at least.

Bruno, a German from Hamburg, with whom Bridget had been dancing, wanted to know why the local (black) men seemed to favour white women and whether I thought the black women were jealous. I said I thought it probably had something to do with white women having been taboo for so long – forbidden fruit. I didn't know whether the black women were jealous – resigned more likely.

Like the German women at the guesthouse, Bruno and his friend (who spoke no English) were married but had come on holiday without their spouses. Bruno, a jolly man with a round face and a bald head, enjoyed dancing and went to dances three times a week.

'Here, in Bequia, dancing is the custom of the holidaymaker,' he announced with cheerful enthusiasm. He liked swimming too, and one day had spent eighteen hours swimming the six-mile stretch of sea that lay between Bequia and St Vincent. He came back by boat.

In Trinidad, Gina had told me that the mistake foreigners – Europeans and North Americans – make is to dance from the waist up, with their heads and shoulders, jiggling all over the place in a discombobulated fashion like puppets on strings. They danced, she said, with their brains and expected their bodies to get the message. But West Indians dance from the waist down using their pelvises, barely moving their feet, just the whole body, swaying, shaking, like trees in the wind, to the music. 'Wining', which was not unlike belly dancing, was the stroke (as opposed to step) of choice. Face to face, crotch to crotch in a rhythmic grind.

My partner was a man called Ivan, tall as a basketball player, a fisherman who said that he had caught a 50lb marlin that day.

I found that I was too hot and couldn't breathe if I had my face buried in his sweaty T-shirted chest so I turned round and he grabbed me by the waist from behind, never losing the rhythm for a second. Inside his jeans, he was hard as a rock. All the men were. I remembered going dancing in St Lucia and Virgin Gorda and noticing the same thing. But their excitement didn't appear to be overwhelming them. They weren't breathing heavily, or no more than the exertion of the dance would warrant. They weren't taking undue liberties. As the band played, you could almost feel the temperature rising. The music seemed intended specifically to up the ante, to generate more and more excitement and energy. Pump up the volume. And, when the band struck up Bob Marley's beautiful 'No Woman No Cry', the unofficial national anthem of the Caribbean, a kind of collective sigh of yearning and recognition and pleasure went up from the floor.

Port Elizabeth was a tiny town. Apart from the post office where there had been an official notice warning against catching turtles and a smattering of souvenir shops, there was little else. Along the road from the guesthouse is the beautiful church of St Mary The Virgin with Holy Cross, one of the early churches built by white settlers which have a grace and dignity lacking in more recent structures. It was light and airy with tall pillars supporting the high, beamed ceiling. The huge arched windows were open to the balmy Caribbean air. The pews were painted a soft pale blue which echoed the blue trim on the doors. A large oil painting of a black Virgin Mary seated on a throne of fluffy clouds, holding up a little sailing boat in one hand while a naked child with a halo of stars stretched out his hand for it, hung to one side of the altar. On the other side hung a painting of a man – also with negroid features and halo – dressed in a white robe and holding a palm, his feet surrounded by broken pottery, with waves crashing in the background.

One evening, I met a builder from Guyana, the former British colony on the edge of the South American mainland. Earlier that day I had – or so it had seemed at the time – nearly drowned in the waters off Princess Margaret beach. Taken unawares by a sudden huge wave – the Caribbean sea is full of treachery – I was knocked off my feet and sent spinning in a salty whirlpool; my lungs were bursting, ears hurting like hell, every orifice jammed with sand; when I finally crawled, panting and choking out of the sea, a pound of the stuff had settled in the crotch of my bathing suit, dragging it down around my knees. This brutal encounter with mortality left me shaken and exhausted. The house that evening was awash with lodgers and groupies, so I went into town for a quiet drink. But no sooner had I sat down than the local drunk or pervert – perhaps both – had materialised at my table and, despite a sign on the wall saying 'Put the brakes on foul speech', neither I nor the owner of the bar could shut him up.

Eventually, he was thrown out into the street where he continued to shout and gesticulate. It was during this that the Guyanese builder had asked me to join him and his mate; he was the foreman of a team constructing a restaurant ('Beautiful wood – all the way from Guyana') on top of a hill overlooking the bay. He invited me to come and inspect it and then began to talk about Guyana where, he claimed, I would never be bothered by hopeless drunks. He spoke with rum-warmed enthusiasm of the Amerindians, the Demerara river, the broad sweeps of savannah, the warmth of the people.

'In Guyana, they will kill you with their friendship.'

After a few more drinks, he turned philosophical.

'What I don't understand is why are they so damn happy here? Every day I ask myself, what have they got to be so happy about? I can't find an answer. I tell my son – he's twelve – it's a cruel world. It's a jungle out there, dog eat dog.'

When I got up the next day, Bridget said that she had dreamt that she strangled her husband's lover, Mrs Sandiford, who (in the dream), was white and had a child. I said that she was really strangling herself because she was angry with herself for being in this mess. She looked at me with big round eyes and said,

'Oh, you are clever. Do you really think that's what the dream means?'

The frog-like proprietor of the bookshop below the guest-house had suggested that I should walk across the island to Friendship Bay and one morning I left the house a little after seven. There was something rather wonderful about the idea that I could traverse Bequia on foot. It wasn't too hot yet, and the early morning was luminous and fresh. There were bursts of flowers everywhere, pale delicate papery Morning Glory trailing in among the ferns and the tamarind trees, the robust reds and yellows of the hibiscus and the poinsettia. The air was soft and clean. I walked for about an hour, climbing and then descending towards the brilliant curve of Friendship Bay. As I came over the hill, a little boy lying by the side of the road outside the Kingdom Hall of Jehovah Witnesses sat up and said: 'You want I sing you a song?' The harsh nasal bleats of the goats and sheep reminded me of the old man lying on his bed of pain back at the house, and across the valley came the faint sweet strains of a choir singing 'What a friend we have in Jesus/ All our sins and grief to bear . . .'

4

The Lights of Kingstown

Days I have held,
days I have lost
(from *Midsummer, Tobago* by Derek Walcott)

St Vincent, the 'mainland', was, according to the tourist brochure, 'exclusively Caribbean'. It also, so other less rosy-lensed
sources told me, had the distinction of being, after Haiti, the
poorest of the Caribbean islands with an annual GNP per capita
of $1,200, as well as massive unemployment; this made Mus-
tique's proximity and Grenadine status all the more distasteful.
People from other islands said that if Columbus were to come
back to the Caribbean, the only place that he would recognise
would be St Vincent – and that wasn't meant as a compliment.
The bartender in Union had come from St Vincent which he
had had to leave after he lost his job when the American-owned
'tennis factory' had been closed down. Sir Algernon Aspinall's
1907 pocket guide to the West Indies, describes St Vincent as
'one of the most prosperous of the West Indian islands'. But
times have clearly changed.

I came over from Bequia on a big fast boat, with Bridget and
Alicia. Bridget thought that she had better make a final stab at
sorting things out with Dennis. The journey took an hour and
Bequia had, in its laid-back way, been so tiring that we all lay
down and slept. We parted on the dock, arranging to meet at

The Lights of Kingstown

my hotel later, and I took a cab to the Cobblestone Inn which had been converted from an early nineteenth-century, stone-and-brick, sugar and arrowroot warehouse and was supposed to be the best in town. After the congenial squalor of Papa Mitch's place, I felt ready for a little luxury and this was a proper hotel with air-conditioning and hot water and telephones in the rooms. When I arrived, there was a mini-steel band – just four musicians – playing in the courtyard but the hotel, which was reached via some steep steps, seemed virtually empty. Its restaurant was closed for refurbishment, but down below was another bar and restaurant under separate management which, I had been told, was the place to meet local politicians and such journalists as there were. The cab driver asked about my plans. I hadn't really made any and didn't much want to until I had had a chance to look around. Gina had given me the telephone number of a friend of hers but otherwise I intended, as usual, to go with whatever turned up. After I had responded with a series of evasive answers, he twisted in his seat to look at me, saying with a look of cool disdain: 'My reasons for asking are purely commercial.'

Kingstown, the capital of St Vincent, was set in a shallow basin surrounded by green hills but that was about as far as its beauty went. It was far scruffier than St George's, and had none of the Grenadian capital's instant picturesque charm. The booklet put out by the Ministry of Tourism carried an article entitled 'Kingstown, A Special City'. It was difficult to recognise the city from Vivian Child's description. Here she is on the public library: The 'elegant Public Library . . . was built in 1909 by the generosity of Andrew Carnegie and can be glimpsed in the distance among its ornamental trees.' Indeed there would be no point in going any closer. A big square neo-classical building in a state of advanced decay, it appeared to be permanently closed with the glass in the windows long shattered and the door nailed firmly shut. Careful scrutiny did reveal some fine old buildings, mostly constructed of dark volcanic stone, not unlike the dour flinty stone of a Scottish manse, but the ciry as a whole gave off a sad air of dirt and decrepitude.

Outside the headquarters of the Salvation Army was a sign which read 'Serving St Vincent & the Grenadines with heart to God and Hand to Man'. Names like Da Silva, Gonsalves, Corea and Veira hung above the entrances of the seedy little shops, testifying to the passage of the Portuguese who had, in the 1840s, come up to the Caribbean from Brazil as indentured labourers. The narrow streets around the market, where you could buy face-cloths in Rasta colours and homemade tapes, stank of urine and excrement and the air was thick with flies. In front of the Supreme Court building was a War Memorial, known locally as the 'Iron Man', erected to the memory of the 'sons of St Vincent who gave their lives for king and country in the Great War 1914–1918'. There were thirty or so names engraved on the memorial and a drunk passed out at the foot of the statue. Nearby a man was urinating against a wall while a woman stood next to him. At first, I couldn't make out what he was doing so I stared for a minute longer than was wise. 'What you lookin' at?' he shouted angrily across the road and I moved on quickly.

Back at the hotel, the bar was empty except for a group of white West Indians, two men and two women, perched on stools. I went and sat in a corner to wait for Bridget.

'But, you know,' one of the men was saying loudly, 'they eat monkey brains. They put the monkey in a trap and they break off the top of his head and they eat them while he's still living – with a little salt maybe – that's our civilised brethren in New Guinea.'

'In New York the yuppie food is *sushi*,' said a woman.

Eventually Bridget and Alicia showed up, the child hot and whining, the mother dispirited. Her husband had showed neither signs of remorse nor a desire for reconciliation but had simply asked her what he had been expected to do (for sex, I think) during all those months and years while she was in England refusing to come out to the Caribbean. Besides, he said, he now had obligations to Mrs Sandiford. We sat there for an hour or so, Bridget going over the same ground again and again like a stuck record, myself nodding, smiling, commiserating, bored, deathly bored. The bar slowly filled up until Bridget glimpsed her husband through the window and rushed out to call him in. She wanted me to meet him and God knows I was curious enough.

Dennis was, in fact, a revelation. I don't know what I had been expecting. The old man had never uttered more than a groan, so I didn't know what he had to pass on to his sons. Alvin had seemed a charming but feckless character, lacking both education and ambition, and I had supposed, without really thinking about it, that Dennis, despite his profession, would be a kind of brawny beachcomber, all muscles and teeth and sex appeal. Instead he was a tall man in his early fifties, with a smooth coffee-coloured skin, a small soft mouth under a tidy moustache and a courteous self-deprecating manner, faintly tinged with irony. He was amusing, intelligent, cultivated and attractive. I no longer wondered what Bridget had seen in him. Rather, I wondered what he had seen in her. He had seen, of course, that she was white and, when they met, she must have had a soft, fresh Irish charm. But she could never have matched him intellectually and even now, watching them, you could sense a barely-contained impatience in him with her. In *Soul On Ice*, Eldridge Cleaver wrote: 'Ain't no such thing as an ugly white woman. A white woman is beautiful even if she is baldheaded and has only one tooth . . . it's not just the fact that she's a woman I love; I love her skin, her soft, smooth, white skin . . .'

I wondered – and this continued to intrigue me – about Dennis, and about other people whom I had met who had chosen to return to a tiny island once they had seen the world and all it had to offer. But perhaps it hadn't offered them all that much. The fact that it was difficult, if not impossible, to achieve anything unless you wanted to make a splash in local politics – apparently mattered less than the agreeable quality of island life and the fact that the island was 'home'. As the song goes,

I've got to go back home
This couldn't be my home
It must be somewhere else
Or I would kill myself
'Cos I can't get no clothes to wear
Can't get no food to eat
Can't get a job to get bread
That's why I got to go back home . . .
There is no gladness, nothing but sadness
Nothing like a future here . . .
That's why I got to, got to go back home
Even if I have to run . . .

V. S. Naipaul, whose low opinion of his Afro-Caribbean countrymen is no secret, has written that: 'History is built around achievement and creation; and nothing was created in the West Indies.' The high standard of twentieth-century Caribbean literary endeavour alone goes a long way to disproving the latter part of this statement, but achievement, other than on the cricket field, is more difficult. Size is a problem. The islands of the Lesser Antilles are so small and have such tiny populations – micro-countries, without oil or any other natural resources to give them power. But you could, if you were lucky, be a big fish in your native pond, an unlikely fate in England or the United States.

I wondered about the degree of racism that someone like Dennis – for all his charm and intelligence – might have experienced in England. (A recent study, commissioned by the Law Society, found that barristers' chambers discriminated against blacks in offering pupillages.) He had a white wife, a child and a distinguished profession – all in London, but still he had preferred to leave and come home to St Vincent. In reality, however, the returnees were in the minority and those who left, even to go only as far as another Caribbean island, often went without seeing their families and their native land for years at a time.

Dennis sat down between us and a couple of men who had

come in earlier and were sitting drinking Scotch and talking intently. He knew them and soon turned to join in their conversation. One was a white West Indian called Neville, who, with his dark hair and eyes, sensual face and big fleshy nose, looked Italian or Spanish. The other, whose name I didn't hear, was a tall, very black man who didn't talk much. Both men were active in the St Vincent Labour Party, of which James ('Son') Mitchell, the Prime Minister, had been a member until he formed the New Democratic Party in 1975. Now they were busy plotting to bring down Mitchell's NDP government – it had been in power since 1984.

When Bridget got up to take Alicia to the lavatory, I slid down the banquette to listen to them. The talk was all of 'Son' and his alleged iniquities. He was, they claimed, involved in all manner of corruption, bribe-taking and drug-running. They said that St Vincent was 'the heartbeat of the cocaine trade', that you could buy an American passport for $10,000 in Union, that anyone could buy a Vincentian passport from the Commissioner of Police at a price, that the NDP's 1989 election victory had been rigged ('Come election time, there's a lot of cement, blocks and lumber given out'), that 'Son' had spent $80m. travelling round the world. They said things got done much more quickly in the Grenadines, that the Prime Minister favoured Bequia, his constituency, where he controlled 'everything'.

They were particularly critical of the Ottley Hall development project, a scheme set up by Mitchell and a group of Italian investors to build a $75m. luxury shipyard marina to repair and refuel yachts on a piece of prime beach on the coast just up from Kingstown. The Grenadines offered some of the finest sailing in the Caribbean and the idea was that the marina would attract yachtsmen and encourage tourism (which was restricted by the airport's inability to accommodate large jet aircraft), but ordinary Vincentians were going to have to be taxed in order to repay almost half of the loan for this project, which would do nothing to improve their standard of living.

They said that *obeah* (from 'Obi', the Ashanti word for priest

– a superstition rather than a religious cult; an obeahman is believed to work spells) would be a big factor in the next election. The Governor-General, Sir David Jack (Knight Grand Cross of the Order of St Michael and St George), had – or so the local people believed – been 'struck down by the hand of the Lord three times' while attempting to deliver the 'Throne' speech at the House of Assembly. The first time was when he mentioned Ottley Hall in a speech, and the second one was too. It was, though, Mitchell they claimed, who was responsible for the destruction of the arrowroot industry and, when he closed its sugar factory, had reduced Georgetown (the second largest town on the island) to a ghost town. He had once accused Vincentians of 'having a breadfruit mentality', referring perhaps to the breadfruit tree in the Botanical Gardens which was a direct descendant of the original plant brought to the island in 1793 by Captain Bligh of the *Bounty*. It wasn't clear what he had meant but it was clear that he had not intended to flatter. (Mitchell seemed to believe that in St Vincent political messages were best conveyed through botany – he told his listeners in an Independence Day speech that 'the quality of our life depends on the quality of our bananas'.) On a more personal note, he was, the men said, very vindictive and never forgot an injury; he did not like black people (he himself was light-skinned and could almost pass for white); he had always been a loner and, they said, there was a streak of madness in him.

The afternoon sun faded as they talked and drank enormous quantities of Scotch, and the warm gold light of early evening began to filter through the windows of the bar. Bridget, who was supposed to be catching the 7 o'clock boat back to Bequia, started to mutter about staying over but I could see that it would be more fun without her. In a rather touching way, her husband's kinship to the Prime Minister was a source of pride to her, and she had been quietly horrified by the criticisms of him. She believed that Mitchell's position should have pro-tected him from attack. She felt that the views of Neville, the white West Indian, were unbalanced and, whereas I was keen to urge him on to further and further excesses, she thought – and said as much to me in a loud whisper – that what he had said virtually amounted to treason.

In Grenada Allberry had given me an introduction to the owner of the *Vincentian*, a local weekly. I had bought a stack of local papers earlier in the day and now asked my companions if they knew him – which, of course, they did. Everyone knew everyone. The *Vincentian* was anti-Mitchell and often attacked him and the government, in the fiery rebel-rousing manner of an Old-Testament prophet which Caribbean journalists favoured – many hours in church put to good use. The pro-Mitchell paper, *The News*, the only one rich enough to carry colour photographs, was described by Neville as a 'minefield of misinformation'. The third paper, *Unity* (motto: 'Behold, How Good And How Pleasant It Is For Brethren To Dwell Together IN *Unity*'), was the organ of the Movement for National Unity (Freedom and Development) and edited by a man called Cecil 'Blazer' Williams.

But newspapers in both Grenada and St Vincent were hardly calculated to inspire – though apparently they did often embarrass governments – which was frequently the only intention – and the journalism was often lively, if a little long-winded. Journalists in the Caribbean were big on rhetoric. There were no daily papers, except in Trinidad, Barbados and presumably Jamaica: according to Allberry, print and paper costs were too high for more than a weekly output. One weekly would inevitably be the mouthpiece of the government, another would express the views of the official opposition and the third would probably carry those of the unofficial opposition. They were invariably poorly printed on indifferent paper, and full of typographical errors; Caribbean papers, on the whole, carried next to no foreign news (unlike, for example, the English-language press in Thailand or Vietnam) and foreign papers weren't available, except for the more sensational ones from Miami, or the odd copy of the *News of the World*, or the *Sun*, which had somehow found its way across the Atlantic. There was, of course, local radio, which devoted many hours to death announcements, and advertisements of special offers and sea-sonal sales. There was sometimes local television – usually government-controlled and reluctant to give a voice to the opposition. All this conveyed a sense, not just of insularity, but also of isolation. No one knew. No one cared.

Bridget finally gathered herself and her daughter (by now replete with ice-cream and potato crisps), and set off to walk to the quay. Dennis, somewhat belatedly, leapt to his feet to escort them, promising to return as soon as possible so that we could all go out for dinner.

We drove out towards Villa, St Vincent's answer to Beverly Hills on the southern tip of the island, stopping *en route* to call on an older man who had been a minister in a previous Labour government. I couldn't see the point of the visit – we were there for barely five minutes – later I thought that they were just touching base. Neville's act – as it were – seemed to involve pretending to be a participant in some major conspiracy and perhaps this visit was part of that. As we left, he pulled a scarlet anthurium out of a vase in the hall and presented it to me with a bow.

Anthuriums are strange – a single prominent spine protrudes from the flower, which is shaped like a heart. The skin – or maybe flesh – of the flower is stretched taut and has a polished, waxy sheen to it. They look almost artificial and, when they die, you can hardly tell. They seem to petrify rather than to wilt. They make me slightly uneasy.

I can't remember where we had dinner – only that it was somewhere down by the sea. I certainly can't remember what we ate. I think the men drank yet more Scotch and perhaps I had a rum punch. I remember marvelling at how easy it was to be with them. I liked the casual blend of chivalry and chauvin-ism that was the hallmark of their behaviour towards me. I was allowed to be both one of the boys and, at the same time, treated like a princess.

I remember snatches of the conversation and Neville quoting Ralph Gonsalves, the leader of the Movement for National

Unity, on the subject of Mustique, where, he claimed, the mosquitoes and sandflies were the worst in the Caribbean and where the cheapest villas cost $3,500 a week to rent: 'Mustique is a state within a state, a blight on our national psyche, it is an open, festering wound that will soon require major surgery . . . We may have to sail over there one day . . .'.

At the airport in Union, I had seen the little planes of Mustique Airways taking off for Mustique but I didn't want to go there, however beautiful it might be. The idea that a Caribbean island could still be the property of a white foreigner was disturbing and I disliked even more what I had heard about – that the only local people who had right of residence were those who had come to the island before 1969, that black people weren't 'allowed' to be born or die on the island (pregnant women were sent off the island a couple of months before the baby was due). I disliked its elitism, its fabled exclusivity.

Mustique was bought in 1958 for £45,000 by a Scottish aristocrat, the Hon. Colin Tennant, who later became Lord Glenconner. Local gossip claimed that he used to order his servants to strip naked 'as they were born'; before he covered them from head to toe in gold paint.

Tennant had turned Mustique into a retreat for the rich and famous, a 'suntanned Chelsea-on-sea' as the *Daily Telegraph* put it. Princess Margaret, David Bowie and Mick Jagger all had, or have, houses there. 'I bought it for the beaches,' Tennant once said, 'I thought if everything in the rest of the world goes on strike, I'll have this island.' In the Seventies, however, he was forced to sell and it became the property of the Mustique Company. Then he turned his attention to another Windward island, St Lucia. Some years before, while visiting St Lucia, I had read in the local paper about a controversial scheme to develop a resort on the site of an old plantation named Jalousie (which, in French, means both 'jealousy' and the louvered shutters that you find in the tropics) at the foot of the Pitons, the two volcanic peaks at the southern tip of the island that are the symbol of the Windward Islands and, in the words of an official from the Organisation of American States (OAS), 'one of the most significant ecological and geological areas in the Caribbean'. Tennant had bought Jalousie in 1982 – 475 acres where Amerindian remains have since been found – then sold it to a group of Iranian developers, despite a number of local objections. 'He's just a vain old man buying attention' was one of the milder comments I heard.

Derek Walcott, the poet, who comes from St Lucia has written in the St Lucia *Star* that 'the Jalousie deal makes a whore of Fair Helen!' (St Lucia was known as the 'Helen of the West Indies', a reference to its beauty and the fact that it had changed hands fourteen times between the French and the British). 'To sell the Pitons is worse than prostitution,' Walcott wrote. 'Prostitution is a kind of slavery after all. It is usually a result of desperation. How desperate is St Lucia, to sell the Pitons, and which of these investors would dare propose these developments to his own native tribe?'

A United Nations proposal has called for the Pitons to be designated a World Heritage Site and an alternative scheme from OAS has suggested that a Pitons National Park be created, claiming that:

> The success of small hotels and guest houses, restaurants and other tourist related businesses ... would be doubtful in the absence of the Park. The proposed development of a large private hotel on the Jalousie Estate ... is incompatible with the overall concept of the Pitons National Park and could also hamper the conservation or preservation of the unique cultural and natural attractions of the area.

But, of course, the resort deal went ahead and in March 1992, the Jalousie Plantation opened, a place where only the very rich and very white are likely to stay; to add insult to injury, subsequent reports have claimed that it has not turned out to be what the very rich and very white hoped for.

Conversation at dinner turned to the writings of Nabokov and Dennis said that he had been so aroused by *Lolita* that, when he finished the book, he had had to masturbate. He started quoting: 'Lolita, fire of my loins ...' Earlier in the day I had seen a maxi-taxi called 'Lolita'.

Then Neville told a joke about three men. Two of them are arguing about whether the moon is more beautiful over Villa or over Argyle (a district on the Atlantic coast). They turn to the third man, who comes from Stubbs (a district between the two), and ask him to arbitrate. 'I'd like to help,' he says, 'but I'm from Stubbs.' That was the punchline, and they all laughed as if it was the funniest thing they had ever heard.

On the way back, Dennis dropped off at Mrs Sandiford's large house and the silent black man left us to walk home down a steep, narrow, bumpy, dark lane and Neville and I drove on towards the capital. As we rounded a curve, Neville stopped the car so that we could look down at the lights of Kingstown twinkling across the bay. It was dark inside the car but I could just make out his face. Earlier that afternoon I had telephoned the man in New York and, as usual, our conversation had left me with a languorous sense of well-being, not unlike being swathed in cashmere. That, and the evening's rum, and the good conversation and the warm light of admiration in the men's eyes had all done their bit.

The corner on which we had parked was hardly the ideal venue for necking and, after some time had elapsed and a number of cars had gone by, slowing down as they passed to peer through our windows, Neville started up the engine and drove on into town. I assumed that he would take me back to the hotel and was preparing to brazen it out in front of the desk clerk, but he drove instead to a huge deserted playing-field somewhere in the heart of Kingstown.

We stayed there for hours, parked right in the middle of the stadium or cricket pitch or whatever it was, making love – if it could be called that – in a nondescript uncomfortable modern car, starting, stopping, starting again. I felt no pain. When I lifted my head to look through the windscreen, I saw the ghostly outlines of buildings and very occasionally, the wan beam of a torch would falter across the ground. No one came near us. I doubt that I would have cared if they had. It was years since I had stayed up all night.

Neville had soft very fine black hair which curled close to his head. When he wore dark glasses, he looked like a Mafia hit-man. He was thin and seemed to need neither sleep nor food, only a more or less constant supply of Scotch and cigarettes. He said he couldn't drink rum for long, that, when they went out stirring up dissent in the villages, talking revolution throughout the night, if he drank rum, it would finish him off. He described himself as a 'man with a mission' and wanted to know if I knew anyone who could help him get guns. I didn't. I quite liked him, but I thought he was mad, a wild man. I couldn't believe that anyone would take him seriously. He claimed that Mitchell had tried to have him killed on more than one occasion. I had no way of knowing if this were true. His two main interests seemed to be sex and politics and he tackled them both with manic energy. Towards the former, he had a robust and graphic attitude ('rude' was how he put it) which combined appealingly with a sort of old-fashioned courtesy which had gone out in England in the late Sixties. I remembered an English friend describing opening the car door for a woman he was escorting to the cinema one evening. 'There's no need for that sort of behaviour,' she had said, briskly pushing his outstretched hand away.

It was rapidly becoming clear to me that West Indian men, black or white, were quite unlike the sort of men that I was used to. They combined ease and an immediacy about sexual matters which was incredibly relaxing, although there was a veneer of gallantry and romanticism which concealed a hard core of chauvinism.

Alec had not been the first black man whom I had slept with. That had happened some years before, on a press trip to the Cayman Islands, a haven of money-laundering and scuba diving. In England, the opportunity had simply never presented itself – I would have had to go out looking for it. On that trip to the Caymans, the handsome assistant manager of the hotel had been deputed to show the journalists the night spots, and one thing had led to another. My memory of that night, and the night which followed it has blurred with time. But I do remember him telling me that he could lose his job for fraternising so intimately with a guest. Even so, the experience – or more precisely, the fact of the experience – was like the loss of a second virginity. And, looking back, it seems to have been a kind of test that I had set myself. A rite of passage. But, while I was enormously relieved to discover that sleeping with a black man was not so very different from sleeping with a white man, I found it impossible to ignore the symbolism of the act. Every time I gave myself up to a black man's embrace, I felt as if I was committing a radical act – and I was. The sexual act functions on a lot of different levels, and inequality and difference between the sexes is never more apparent than during intercourse. With a racial dimension, the act of intercourse becomes even more charged.

In purely sexual terms, colour didn't seem to make any difference (despite the 'velvet skin' of which I had heard so much) and anyhow, the man in the Caymans or Alec could have been green for all I saw of their colour once we got close. If there was a difference, it was more *cultural* than *racial*. With West Indians I didn't feel judged and found wanting. Because sex appeared to be so casual, so much more spontaneous (rather, I imagine, as gay sex was supposed to be before AIDS), it didn't seem to carry with it the weighty implications demanded by more lengthy courtships; sex was part of life and a pleasure, and I found the absence of guilt refreshing. Male lust rarely felt threatening – and this was the reverse of what I had expected. If I wasn't in the mood, someone else would be. In the culture from which I had come, it was often hard to know which was worse, desire or lack of desire. Here, I felt, I could take it or leave it without fear of reprisal. I didn't know where that left 'falling in love', and I wasn't planning to find out.

West Indian men are notoriously irresponsible. One explanation proffered for their almost-universal failure to provide for their women and children is that during slavery, when children could be sold away from their parents, it was pointless and heart-breaking for men to develop a sense of responsibility – and this set an unfortunate precedent.

Later a West Indian woman told me that she thought the men were 'enjoying the effects of slavery too much'. The telling pronoun *for* as in 'have a baby *for* a man' seems to reveal perfectly everything I needed to know about the relationship between men and women. Men want women to have babies *for* them; women want to have babies *for* men – and that is as far as the contract goes. In Trinidad, Gina had told me: 'White people wait till they can afford a baby. Black people don't. If a black woman want to have a baby for a man, she don't care about anything.' Jamaica Kincaid, in her novel *Lucy*, sums it up: 'where I came from . . . Everybody knew that men have no morals, that they do not know how to behave, that they do not know how to treat other people.'

What West Indian men really like is to hang out with the boys. I remember a white woman telling me about the moment when she realised how much this was the case. It was one evening, after a long day by the sea followed by three hours in a bar, and she wanted to leave and go home to wash off the salt and sand, as did the small daughter of the man she was with. Eventually the child said, 'Dadda, why don't you take us home and then you can come back?'

'Nah,' he said with a grimace, 'All de fellars be gone den.' I never saw a West Indian man look at his watch, telephone his wife, tell anyone that he'd be late. They seemed to do exactly as they pleased. One West Indian woman in her early fifties told me that she was so fed-up with West Indian men that she had almost decided to give up sex but then she was told by a doctor that it was healthy to 'fuck through the menopause' so she thought she had better grin and bear it.

I knew, of course, that I was in a privileged position. I was white and I was moving on. I wasn't going to be left holding the baby.

The next day Neville took me out into the countryside, up to the Mesopotamia Valley and beyond. How it came to be named the Mesopotamia Valley is a mystery – unless it was because, as in the original Mesopotamia, it was where all the rivers came together. On Mondays and Tuesdays, women came to do their laundry in the waters of the Yambou, which tumbled down to the Atlantic over the rocks of the Yambou Gorge. Recently, three children had disappeared in the river and their bodies still hadn't been found.

A vast fecund basin formed by an extinct volcanic crater and surrounded by mountains – a land of milk and honey, bursting with nutmeg, cocoa, coconut, breadfruit, edoes, tannias and dasheen – the Mesopotamia valley was also the main banana-growing area on the island. Neville said that it was the most fertile stretch of land in all of the Caribbean islands. It had an obvious richness that took your breath away. As far as the eye could see, the land was yielding up its promise – there were bananas and banana plants everywhere.

Much of the best sugar-cane growing land on St Vincent was destroyed at the turn of the century by the eruption of the volcano Soufrière, which devastated nearly a third of the island and killed two thousand people. ('Soufrière' in French means 'sulphur mine' and it recurs as a place-name throughout the Lesser Antilles, most of which are volcanic in origin. Soufrière, which last erupted on Good Friday in 1979, and Mont Pelée in Martinique remain the only two active volcanoes in the Caribbean.) The sugar industry finally gave up the ghost in 1962 and the last surviving factory closing. Since the 1950s bananas have been the largest single export of the Windward Islands and, in the mid-1970s, they provided almost half of St Vincent's income. Two-thirds of the island is still devoted to banana cultivation and practically all of the bananas produced used to be exported to Britain.

The banana isn't really a tree; it is a large herb, perhaps the largest plant in existence without a wood stem. Depending on the species, it can grow to a height of twenty feet or more. What appears to be the trunk is in fact a firm mass of tightly wrapped leaf sheaves, which grow from an underground stem (rhizome). The fruit-growing 'tree' is grown from 'suckers' which, in their turn, grow from the parent plant and persist to maturity, which they reach after only nine months in rich soil. Each 'herb' bears a single flower head with about six to ten clusters or 'hands'. Each hand contains ten to twenty 'fingers' or bananas. The large, almost leathery, leaves of a banana plant arch upward and outward from a cluster of stems coming out of the ground. Female blossoms form at the end of each finger and the male flower is the large purple teardrop, the 'navel', which hangs down from the bunch. The 'navel' seems to act a bit like a placenta, feeding the bananas, but at a certain stage of development, it must be cut off so that the bananas can ripen, otherwise it consumes its own nourishment.

Bananas originated in south-east Asia more than four thousand years ago. They spread westward from Burma and India (where the Hindus believed them to be sacred to the goddess Kali). In the fifteenth century, they were growing in the Canary Islands and by the sixteenth century they had reached the West Indies. After the abolition of slavery in 1834, and the discovery in the nineteenth century that sugar beet could be grown, then processed, in Europe far more cheaply than sugar cane, the 'white gold' industry began to decline. The Windward Islands needed a new export crop. Bananas were chosen because most farmers could grow them; they could be grown on large estates or on tiny hillside plots. This flexibility is one of the main reasons for the current crisis; because they could yield a harvest as often as every week, they seemed to be the best possible cash crop.

An initial attempt to establish a banana industry in the Thirties failed, due to the onset of Panama disease, but, in 1953, a second attempt was successful. That year Geest (a British company set up by three Dutch brothers in the 1930s which has held onto its monopoly on the Windward Islands' bananas since the 1950s) took over the marketing of bananas from the islands. The so-called 'green gold' was good for Britain and a godsend for the islands. Bananas continued as the main agricultural crop of the Windward Islands; the industry has been further developed and has come to account for almost sixty per cent of the islands' export earnings. Bananas, in the Caribbean, have outlasted sugar, cotton and arrowroot.

The problem is that the Windward Islands are not really suited to agriculture. The soil is wonderfully rich but the land is difficult to negotiate, all hills and valleys, to say nothing of the risk of hurricanes, droughts and floods. The entire industry can be flattened overnight by a storm or hurricane – but only bananas can be replanted immediately, then, within a few months, exported.

Over the past five or so years, fierce competition from Latin America (where labour is cheaper – Latin America already has two-thirds of the world's banana market) has forced the banana producers of the Windward Islands into an increasingly tight corner; they can only hope to survive if their traditional markets continue to be assured. With the advent of the Single European Market in January 1993, the Caribbean banana's future looks increasingly uncertain. Latin America, which doesn't need the industry nearly as desperately as the Windward Islands, is ideally suited to banana-growing. Its vast plains can produce masses of fruit without problems and at a much lower labour cost. One plantation in Latin America can grow as many bananas as twenty thousand farmers in the islands.

The Germans, the largest consumers of bananas in Europe, have no historic ties with the Caribbean; along with Belgium, Holland and Denmark they would prefer to give direct aid to the islands rather than subsidise them by buying more expensive bananas. But John Compton, Prime Minister of St Lucia, dismisses this option as 'really beneath our dignity'. Only the bananas produced in the French islands of Martinique and Guadeloupe are secure, thanks to membership of the EEC.

Despite Mitchell's comment that 'the quality of our life depends on the quality of our bananas', he seems to be more supportive of the fishing industry in Bequia, saying recently to his constituents there, 'When bananas are gone, you'll still have fishing'. In St Vincent, tourism will be the new industry.

Geest delivered cargo to and collected bananas from the

Windward Islands every week. The boat got in early, usually around dawn; then the unloading and loading would begin. There would be queues of men looking to be taken on for a day's work as stevedores. People had to take work where they could find it. The three-quarters-mature bananas would have been packed into boxes by the growers on the plantations or in packing-stations round the island, trucked down from collection points to the weighbridge where they would be checked and then loaded into temperature-controlled containers deep in the hull of the boat and sent off to the ripening plants back in Britain.

Down by the quay in Kingstown where the bananas were loaded, there were banners proclaiming a 'Banana Week'. 'Join the MARCH for BANANAS! Rally in Support of the Banana Industry . . . BANANA IS EVERYBODYS BUSINESS.' That week's edition of *Unity* carried a poem entitled *Jumbie Leh Go* (a *jumbie* is the spirit of a dead family member or close friend, a sort of zombie without the horrific connotations). Its second verse went.

> Death not only rides
> A Pale White Horse
> But in its hand
> Is the Power of life and death.
> Its dagger of death
> Shows no mercy to sugar
> Milk will not be spared;
> And woe unto the living
> When banana is gone.

Lobbyists for the Caribbean banana producers warn of a potential complete breakdown of law and order, if the European consumers turn to Latin America. In this case, they say, all four Windward Islands but particularly St Vincent and the tiny Grenadines will be vulnerable to drug traffickers. Such political and economic stability as exists in the Windward Islands is largely thanks to the banana industry. As the calypsonian sings, 'My banana is it.'

Neville and I drove on from the Mesopotamia Valley through a succession of villages. In each one, there would be a rum shop or three, a tiny convenience store, a selection of churches. One village seemed curiously un-West Indian with its small grey flint church flanked by an orderly cottage garden such as I would expect to find in the depths of the English countryside stood in incongruous tranquillity. Only the rust-red, corrugated iron roof set it in context. The roads seemed slightly better than those in Grenada, though Neville assured me that they weren't, then pointed out that St Vincent was the only island which still could not be crossed by road. (This seemed to be at least partly because its interior mountain range was so steep – but the existence and condition of the roads were always a good guide to the state of a country's economy.) Rounding a bend, we came across four boys playing cricket and we stopped to watch them. The stumps were a cardboard box, the ball a tennis ball and the bat a piece of wood, but they played with absorption and absolute dedication.

After climbing through narrow lanes flanked with green fields of dasheen, we fetched up in Montreal, a large estate to the west of Mesopotamia.

St Vincent – along with Dominica – had remained a Carib stronghold until almost the end of the eighteenth century, long after its neighbours, St Lucia and Grenada, had been beaten into submission by either the French or English, or both. As a result, many Vincentians have traces of Carib in their physiognomy and the island itself has more Amerindian place-names than many of the other islands. Even so, a disproportionate number still hailed from the Old World. Today the most frequent reminder of the island's Carib past is a beer called Hairoun after the ancient Carib name for St Vincent (there are various spellings for and variations on this name, another was Youroumei, yet another Iouloumain). The beer's name, though, did not stop it being made by Germans who have a concession to produce it, and every other carbonated drink you can buy on St Vincent, including Guinness Stout and another beer called Eku. Hairoun was the Carib of St Vincent. All these beers tasted pretty much the same – refreshing but bland.

Anthuriums and other exotic flowers had once been cultivated commercially at Montreal and, though the whole place had now run wild, I could still see traces of once-orderly flowerbeds. We left the car in a clearing in front of an empty house and set off to walk through the bush. There were, as well as the rows of crimson and pink Anthuriums, ginger lilies, roses, breadfruit, 'ugli' trees (which bear a hybrid citrus fruit which is a cross between a grapefruit, an orange and a tangerine), pawpaw, nutmeg; tiny humming-birds hovered at the deep crimson throats of the hibiscus blooms, the petals crumpled like tissue paper; chameleons changed slow colour against the bark of the trees. Further on into this garden of Eden was a stream and a little cottage with the word 'Romance' inscribed in faded letters above the door. Neville shinned up an 'ugli' tree and picked one of the fruit. We sat down on the rickety wooden verandah, in the sunlight filtered through the hanging vegetation, and I took out my penknife and sliced through the knobbly skin. Inside the flesh was juicy and sweet.

Neville was in a strange, bitter mood. While Montreal filled me with a strange sense of nostalgia as well as delight at the abundance of nature – I wanted to play house in the cottage; I wanted never to leave. But it seemed to bring back the painful past to Neville. He cursed Mitchell for having ruined his dreams – whatever they had been, the overgrown gardens of Montreal somehow seemed to symbolise them. But, back at the car, he cheered up and handed me a fresh nutmeg straight from the tree, still encased in its scarlet filigree of mace, and a pink-red anthurium. The anthurium was, he commented, the colour of pussy, which he pronounced 'poossey', and informed me that the West Indian word for 'cunt' was 'cat'.

We left the gardens, and Neville's shattered hopes, behind and went to visit a man called Vincent Beache in a house high up a hill overlooking the sea. There was a splendid view and two or three chubby puppies with tiny sharp teeth rolling on the grass. I began a conversation with Mrs Beache's brother who was visiting from America, but Neville called me to come and talk to Beache. He was tall, distinguished and impressive, a former Minister of Agriculture, Trade and Industry, and the leader of the Opposition from 1984 to 1989; he had been replaced by another man who apparently wasn't doing a particularly good job. Some people, it seemed, wanted Beache back. It was still early afternoon, but bottles were produced and we drank huge glasses of Johnny Walker Black Label mixed with coconut water straight from a nut slashed open for the occasion. Neville seemed in part to be refuelling, rather like an aircraft in mid-flight, and, as soon as he had downed two or three drinks, it was time for us to go. It was another of those lightning, plotting visits.

We drove on, along the rugged Atlantic coast to Argyle. Argyle, named presumably for its resemblance to its Scottish namesake, was oddly pastoral, with cows grazing on short velvety grass. There was a church, in that same severe dark stone perched on a hill looking out towards the waves. The landscape seemed so unCaribbean that a single line of palm trees looked out of place. In front of the sea was a great wide stretch of savannah where Neville parked the car, then flung himself at me. There had been no warning, no build-up, no foreplay. When he gave me a moment to catch my breath, I commented on this. 'Ah,' he said, 'before I was working and you can't mix business and pleasure.'

The sea was too rough to swim in and I was nervous after having almost drowned in Bequia. We splashed around in the breakers while a car slowly circled on the savannah. It was a woman learning to drive. She wasn't much good and I kept thinking that she'd plunge off the grass into the sea.

The Labour Party Christmas Dinner took place that evening. I got dressed listening to a homemade tape I had bought in the market. It contained a reggae version of 'The Twelve Days of Christmas' with different words. It was badly made, all crackles

and background noise, and the words were difficult to understand, though it was clear that someone was having a hard time.

> . . . On the fourth day of Christmas, the people whisperin'
> I can't getta privacy and I don know what to really do
> On the fifth day of Christmas, I try and getta work
> Sweep out the office, mix little coffee
> And I just feelin little better now . . .
> On the nineth day of Christmas, things start lookin good
> Policeman start to beat I up and I don really do nothing . . .

The dinner was held at the Rotary Club. We left the car and
walked up a narrow alley. Suddenly Neville ducked through a
doorway, pulling me after him. It took me a moment to realise
where we were – in an enormous dark hall with rows of wooden
benches full of people all staring in front of them. Light and
noise came from one end of the hall. We were in a cinema,
having entered through the emergency exit. It was pretty basic:
the floor was stone, or dirt, and littered: the seats were hard,
but the screen was full-size; the audience seemed gripped and a
faint sweet smell of marijuana filled the air. I had no idea what
the film was. We sat down for a few minutes, then Neville leapt
to his feet and rushed out into the alley. He was one of the
most restless people I had ever met, always in need of a quick
fix. He said that when he was a boy, one person would pay for
a ticket and then let all his friends in through the back door.
He liked going to the cinema now, just going into the cinema,
as we had done, because it reminded him of being a kid. Dinner
was uneventful. The food was plain and plentiful, home-cooked
by the good ladies of the St Vincent Labour Party. The national
anthem of St Vincent was sung before we sat down. After we
had eaten, the present leader of the party, Stanley 'Stalky' John
stood up to make a speech. Halfway through Neville, predictably, had had enough, and we left.

Sunday in St Vincent is like Sunday everywhere in the Caribbean. Quiet, torpid, frugal. I overslept and missed the service
at St George's Cathedral. The restaurant downstairs was closed

with no regard for the hotel guests. Ditto the bar. It was 𝑝___
ing with rain. When it stopped around one, I set out to walk
to the Botanical Gardens. One of its main claims to fame is
Captain Bligh's breadfruit tree, and there was also a large *Spa-
chea perforata*, the Soufrière tree, one of only three of its kind
in the world. Legend has it that the tree was found on the slopes
of the Soufrière volcano before the 1812 eruption and it has not
been seen in the wild since (though assiduous botanists had
recently found it in Guyana).

The gardens were magnificent but I preferred the wilderness
of Montreal.

Walking back past murals which advocated safe sex – 'Don't
Take Chances with AIDS, Safe Sex, Protect Yourself' all in
different calligraphy – and advertisements for the St Vincent
carnival, I passed St Mary's Roman Catholic Cathedral, School
and Presbytery. The extraordinary jumble of blackened neo-
gothic buildings seemed like a Walt Disney variation of the
Tower of London. The original had been built in 1823, then
enlarged in 1877 and 1891 and finally renovated in the 1940s –
which might account for its architectural chaos.

Across the street, in serene contrast, stood the Anglican
Cathedral of St George, reflecting the uncluttered harmony of
the Church of England. This graceful, creamy Georgian edifice
was built in 1820, on the site of an earlier church which had
been destroyed by a hurricane in 1780. It had cost £47,000 to
build – which must have been a prodigious sum at the time;
£5,000 had been contributed by the British government from
the sale of Carib lands.

Unlike St Mary's, St George's was open and I went in. A
boy was practising 'While Shepherds Watched Their Flocks By
Night' on the organ and the familiar melody took me by surprise. I felt a sudden rush of homesickness. I walked round the
cathedral, looking at the tablets on the wall. The inscriptions
were long and eulogistic. Robert Cooper was 'most tenderly and
deservedly beloved by all his family and universally esteemed
by all who knew him'. Peter Hill was a 'most accomplished
gentleman, distinguished alike by polished manners and amiable

deportment in every social and domestic relation . . .' The 'irreparable loss' of Janet, the beloved and only child of John L. Morrin, who died aged eighteen, having been in St Vincent for a mere nine months and ten days, was commemorated by a marble tablet which depicted a mournful woman leaning on an urn and an inscription which began:

> Inexorable Death – Ah! Couldst thou not have spared
> The only pledge to pure affection given . . .

I particularly liked the memorial to John Roche Dasent, 'His Majesty's Attorney General for this island during the space of twenty-six years . . . While in the discharge of his duties . . . he was seized with a stroke of apoplexy, which, after a few hours of suspense, terminated fatally on the 15th of February A.D. 1832 and in the 56th year of his age. "In the midst of life we are in death".'

I left the Cathedral and walked on through the town. By now I was very hungry, but every restaurant, café or hole-in-the-wall eating-shop was closed, in respectful observance of the Lord's Day. Only the Kentucky Fried Chicken's emporium in all its red-and-white glory – the Colonel's distinctive features blazing forth like those of a consumer deity – was open. (From Penang to Puerto Rico, from Bangkok to Bermuda, from South Korea to Kingstown, the Colonel reigned supreme.) I had never before been in a situation where he was my only option, the offer I couldn't refuse. I swallowed my pride and went in. Dish of the day was spicy wings. Eating took only a matter of minutes ('fast food' is so called, not just because of the speed of service but also the speed of consumption – you simply want to appease the demon in your belly).

Afterwards, across the street from the South River which ran through town, I found a little bar and drank a couple of Hairouns to wash the taste of the wings out of my mouth. The Black Cat was pleasantly seedy. There were some boys playing pool in a back room and a loud reggae beat came from a tapedeck. Outside the riverbed was dry and clogged with garbage, a source of some complaint in the letters page of the *Vincentian*. Perhaps, at another, wetter time of year or in another life, it might have been transformed into the 'tumbling river' which the tourist board boasted about, but then, though, the tin cans, plastic bags, banana skins and coconut shells would have all been bobbing on the surface instead of wedged in among the bone-dry stones.

Neville was asleep in the lobby in front of the television when I got back to the hotel. He woke up and said that he wanted to watch the programme – something with Rowan Atkinson and Griff Rhys Jones, to the end. I went to my room and lay down on my bed to read. It had begun to rain again. Sometime later Neville appeared and we spent the afternoon, curled up like two kittens in a basket, cocooned from the weather and the outside world.

On my last night in St Vincent Neville took me out to Villa for dinner. The restaurant was by the sea and there was a cool breeze but I was tired and growing exhausted by Neville's constant carping about the island's politics. I asked if we could possibly talk about something else (by this, I meant, could *he* talk about something else – my contributions had of necessity been limited). There was a long silence. Conversation, it seemed, had to be for a purpose, to campaign, to convert, to complain, but it could not really be an exchange of information or of views. Neville knew almost nothing about me. How could he? He had never asked, and he perceived me only through the prism of his needs and desires. He kept saying how much he liked me, how he felt at ease with me – comfortable – and he certainly liked going to bed with me. But how could he fail to? There I was, apparently infinitely complaisant, both audience and mirror.

One evening we had been driving back from some remote corner of the island, on narrow winding roads through all those dark and secret little villages where all you saw was the flash of teeth and all you heard was an unintelligible greeting as you whizzed past. Somehow Neville had begun to talk about

Europe. The old world was finished, he said, the future lay with the new. And Germany. What, he wanted to know, was the point of Germany? Well, I said, Germany had produced many great writers – Goethe, Rilke, Mann, Nietzsche, to name but a few – and composers – Bach, Beethoven, Schubert, Strauss and so on. 'But they're all *dead!*' he said, as if that settled it.

Perhaps, given the nature of the history of the Caribbean, he didn't feel that the past had much to offer, but our conversation served to reveal a further incompatibility, a lack of common ground between us. However, I was moving on, and our fragile relationship was already slipping into the past.

5

The Weather Prophet

Many rivers to cross
But I can't seem to find my way over . . .
(from *Many Rivers* by Jimmy Cliff)

From the air Dominica was covered in dense vegetation and green, all green – what you could see of it. Only the narrow mud-red roads shiny with rain and the myriad soft brown rivers tumbling over black rocks varied Dominica's verdant colour scheme. The higher parts of the island were shrouded in cloud and cloud puffs lurked like thistledown in the valleys. Through the banana plantations – clearly identifiable from above – ran tracks of red dirt and occasionally you could see a small figure toiling under a load. Houses were few and far between except down by the coast. The sea was grey and a thick driving rain lashed the island. In the soft long grass next to the runway grew a few stray pink Convolvuli – as if to soften Dominica's forbidding face.

I hired a car and drove along a winding road, that looped and twisted like a snake *in extremis* over the mountains of central Dominica, to spend a night near Melville Hall, the international airport. My sister, Olivia, who was coming out to spend Christmas with me, was arriving there the following morning, rather than at Canefield, the little airport on the Caribbean coast to which I had come and which took small inter-island planes. It was by now high season and her ticket, which compelled her to spend a night in Barbados *en route*, had cost some terrifying sum of money, nearly a thousand pounds. As I drove, I listened to the radio. The show was in patois – or Creole – and seemed to be a series of death announcements. Words like *mort*, *aimé* and *famille* with a string of proper names, kept cropping up. Dominica, like St Lucia, had been French for years and still retained close links with that island. 'La Dominique et Sainte-Lucie, nous sommes comme des soeurs – sisters,' a man later told me. Then the radio switched to English.

> We don' want charity,
> Give us what we due

was how the song went.

Olivia was trying to put together a film of Patrick Leigh Fermor's only novel, *The Violins of Saint Jacques*, which, he said, was set in Dominica (a close reading actually suggests that Martinique and in particular the 1902 eruption of Mont Pelée formed the factual basis for the book) where he had also written parts of *The Traveller's Tree*. (The proprietor of the bookshop in Bequia had urged me, in reverential tones, to seek out the place where he had stayed and to see the desk at which he had done his writing.) And Jean Rhys had been born in Dominica in 1894. I wanted to see the island from which she had come and whose spirit lingered in her work – the place which had inspired *Wide Sargasso Sea*, her haunting and heartbreaking evocation of the early life of the first Mrs Rochester. I felt a sense of identification with Rhys whose problems seemed to have much the same causes as mine: men, money and drink. The Antiguan writer, Jamaica Kincaid, had once told me with a strange sort of sigh that her mother had been born in Roseau, the island's capital, and that she herself remembered standing in a river in Dominica and inhaling the scent of almonds.

A series of increasingly desperate telephone calls from Trinidad had secured accommodation overlooking the sea (not unreasonably Olivia wanted to get a suntan for her money) and it looked as if we were all set. Neither of us, however, had bothered to discover that Dominica had the highest rainfall of any Caribbean island (over 5000mm annually), was the largest and most mountainous of the Windward Islands (more rugged even than Switzerland), was the least developed (this was a bad thing only in so far as it meant fewer hotels and restaurants and less variety), and was *not* known for its beaches, which were of mainly black, volcanic sand. The booklet I picked up at Canefield when I arrived should have warned me:

> The Caribbean the way it used to be . . .
> Unspoilt . . . Undisturbed . . . Natural . . .
> Discover Dominica Nature Island of the Caribbean

This was Dominica's billing. And it was intended to stay that way. In the local paper an editorial proclaimed:

> The Time Is Approaching
> When More Visitors Will Be On Our Shores
> REMEMBER . . .
> A Helpful Hand . . .
> A Kind Word . . .
> A Thoughtful Act . . .
> All Can Ensure That Our Visitors Have
> The Vacation of a Life-time In Our Nature Isle.
> Let's All Play Our Part For Tourism.
> Take Care And Share:
> Tourism Is Everybody's Business.

And, if that wasn't enough, a sign on a massive rubbish bin read 'Keep The Fucking Place Clean'.

The central highlands of Dominica were formidable. To either side of the surprisingly good road (Dominica's Prime Minister, the idomitable Eugenia Charles, clearly had a better grip on the country's economy than other leaders in the Anglophone Caribbean), the rainforest stretched into infinity, dripping and dense. The mountains were not, by world standards, particularly high but they were very steep and, as the writer of *Caribbean Lands* put it: 'Remoteness in such a country is not a matter of distance but of difficulty of access.' Without a car, we would have been stuck.

The drive from Roseau across to the Atlantic coast was only about thirty miles but it took over two hours. I had booked into a hotel called the Floral Gardens near the Carib reserve – Dominica was the only island where there were any surviving Caribs – and along the coast from the relevant airport. On the edge of the rainforest, it was cool and damp. It continued to rain all night, a slow, steady drip. To an accompaniment of American country music, I ate a delicious dinner of lentil soup and freshwater crayfish, sharing a table with a young American who was spending his days hiking in the rainforest. Rather him than me.

Floral Gardens reminded me of a hotel called Ye Olde Smoke-house in Malaysia's Cameron Highlands. It had the same comforting and oddly colonial feel, the same anachronistic decor, flowered chintzes, polished brasses, a place where visiting botanists, and those in search of the particular sense of security that an interest in flora bestows, would feel at home. Of course, if you put your nose outdoors, the illusion was instantly dispelled as the jungle threatened to envelop everything. I went to my damp bed (mosquitoes the size of bats) and dreamt that I was furious with my mother.

Olivia arrived tired and tense – the London effect exacerbated by the interminable journey. Despite a restless night, I was in sunny form – the Caribbean effect. I couldn't face that winding central road across the island again and so we drove slowly along the coast road. For great stretches of land, there was no one to be seen. Dominica is both the largest and most sparsely populated of the Windward Islands with a population of only eighty-four thousand – as compared to over a hundred thousand in St Vincent and a hundred and fifty thousand in St Lucia. This is partly because of the sheer impenetrability of much of the terrain, most of which is forested. In Rhys's *Voyage In The*

Dark, the heroine talks of an island 'all crumpled into hills and mountains as you would crumple a piece of paper in your hand – rounded green hills and sharply-cut mountains'. This was Dominica. When Columbus described the island to Ferdinand and Isabella, he too was supposed to have taken a piece of paper and crumpled it in his hand. It had none of the immediate beauty of Grenada or St Vincent and even the villages seemed somehow to be turned in on themselves, closed, opaque. In Portsmouth, where we stopped for a drink, there was a sow the size of a rhinoceros on the beach and a faint smell of excrement in the air. We drove on to Roseau along the island's curving Caribbean coast. In 1936, when Rhys went back to Dominica, there was no road at all between the island's two principal towns 'as the two places detest each other and don't want one – that is so West Indian – everybody hates everybody else'. The whole journey took nearly three hours.

Roseau was a pretty, shabby little town, barely more than a village, of small painted wooden houses huddled higgledy-piggledy together, and flanked on one side by a broad river, the Roseau. There was one particular house that took my fancy: the stone or brick bottom half was painted scarlet and buttercup, the upper storey with its slatted wooden walls and verandah was green and blue, and the galvanise roof was the colour of burnt sienna. The Botanical Gardens had been badly damaged by Hurricane David in 1979 and compared poorly to those in St Vincent, but there was a massive banyan tree, its trunk the size of a small house. In some strange way, the roots, as well as being below ground, also hang down from the branches and there was a teenage girl swinging from them. I stopped to take a photograph and she said that, when she was small, she and her friends used to spend hours, hiding in the branches and swinging from the roots.

I wanted to see the house where Jean Rhys was born, now operating as Vena's Guesthouse, a rundown establishment attached to a restaurant called The World of Food. The large mango tree in the courtyard of The World of Food also claimed connections with the writer's family. Like all such places

(Pirandello's birthplace, Delius's grave, Henri Mouhot's tomb), it was curiously disappointing – unevocative, shabby and cramped. The restaurant too failed somewhat to live up to the promise of its name. There was no 'mountain chicken' on the menu that day and even had there been, I'm not convinced that Dominica's national dish – a large frog or *crapaud* – would have appealed. I bought a copy of the *New Chronicle*. 'Dear Aunt Kate,' began a letter on the problem page, 'I used to be ashamed of being a homosexual, but not any more. I see on the TV and hear on the radio that homosexuals have rights. They are allowed in the army. There are even priests who are homosexual. Right? So why do I feel so abnormal? Like some kind of freak? What can I do? – Confused.'

Aunt Kate's answer must have really made him feel better:

Dear Confused, Thank you for writing. Your feeling of abnormality is quite natural, because homosexuality is abnormal.

When God created this earth, he placed Adam and Eve in the garden. Had he ordained for man to be intimate with man, He would not have destroyed Sodom and Gomorrah for their homosexuality and other deviations. Seek proper counselling and recognise that a homosexual lifestyle is against God's law and nature.

At The Humming-bird Inn – which did indeed overlook the sea and the main Portsmouth-Roseau road but was nowhere near a beach or anywhere you could swim – the days passed easily enough. We got up, we had breakfast, we drove for miles to find somewhere to swim, we swam, we had lunch, we came home, we slept, we read – all in a state of suspended animation.

Most days and every night it rained. The other guests at The Humming-bird, a party of young German 'eco-tourists', set off after breakfast each morning in stout hiking boots and lederhosen and returned around six, ravenous. Over dinner (the inn operated a *demi-pension* plan and, as the nearest restaurant was miles away, we tended to eat there – the meals were excellent), they would ask us politely, while we devoured as much food as the cook was able to produce, if we had had a good day.

'Yes, thank you, and you?'

'Ja, it was very good,' this through a mouthful of christophine or plantain, 'but we did not see the parrot.' The parrot was the rare Sisserou parrot – *Amazona imperialis* – which is over 2ft high, has a purple-blue breast and head and is an endangered species. This failure was repeated every day and was a source of great disappointment to them. I myself was happy enough with the exquisite little humming-birds from which the inn took its name. They filled the garden, their tiny burnished bodies quivering as they hung almost motionless in the air, sipping the nectar from the hibiscus and Bougainvillaea that surrounded the house and sucking it up through their long beaks.

On Christmas Day I woke early with the traces of a hangover and period pains – six days early. We drove into Roseau to attend church. Olivia found the singing disappointing – I think she had hoped for something in the gospel tradition of the Deep South – but I found hearing 'O Little Town of Bethlehem' and 'Come All Ye Faithful' in this setting, with the windows flung open to let in the sweet Caribbean air, terrifically uplifting. The sermon was all about family values, about the importance of the family and of nurturing and protecting children. The prevalence of one-parent families and the traditional absence of fathers had the priest quoting the Barbadian writer George Lamming: 'My father who had only fathered the idea of me had left me the sole liability of my mother who had really fathered me.'

We had planned a picnic lunch up somewhere in the heart of the rainforest but, when Jeane Finucane suggested we come down to her brother's place, The Shipwreck, and see a West Indian Christmas, I thought we should go.

Jeane, a pretty, scatty woman, owned and ran The Humming-bird Inn. She had lived all over the world, in England, California, Ecuador, Tanzania, only to come home to Dominica. It was as if, having lived in the West Indies, it was impossible really to settle anywhere else. Nowhere would be as easy-going, nowhere would be as welcoming.

Some of the people at her brother's party had lived in England. One man had spent years working for a distinguished publishing house in London. I knew some people there and he was keen to hear the gossip, appearing nostalgic for the whole dreary set-up even though one of the senior editors had got drunk one night and hit him, calling him a 'lazy nigger'. He said that the man had apologised and all was forgiven and forgotten – but he remembered the night and the sequence of events as if it were yesterday. Another man had worked in Basildon in Essex where he held a senior position in some company. He said that he used to hear the other men saying, 'That black bastard's never in his office'.

Back at The Humming-bird, I lay on my bed, imbibing Dominica's damp melancholy and reading Agatha Christie's *A Caribbean Mystery*. In it, Miss Marple had been sent by a thoughtful nephew to the Caribbean to avoid the rigours of an English winter.

'Lovely and warm, yes – and *so* good for her rheumatism – and beautiful scenery, though perhaps – a trifle monotonous? So *many* palm trees.'

Christie had little time for Jews, who were often depicted as 'dope-fiends', and her recurrent anti-semitism is one of the most striking features of her novels. Her attitude towards black people lacked the same virulence, and I found myself wondering whether she had ever met a black person. There were almost no black people in *A Caribbean Mystery*, which was set on the fictional island of St Honoré, and only one who appeared as a character with a name and a function (a bit-player whose role was to attempt blackmail and be murdered for her pains). The rest were servants, wallpaper, background.

Though this was one of Christie's later novels, published in 1964, no racist cliché had been left untouched: the proud carriages of the natives (the result, no doubt, of years spent carrying loads on their heads); the innate sense of rhythm; the laziness ('worked like blacks, though that's an odd term to use out here, for blacks don't work themselves to death at all' '. . . Was looking at a fellow shinning up a coconut tree to get his break-fast, then he goes to sleep for the rest of the day...'); the relaxed attitude towards sexual relations and so on.

In an earlier novel, *The Hollow*, one of Christie's characters plans to ask the cook to make 'a really *rich* Nigger in his Shirt':

> 'A nigger in his shirt?' Inspector Grange had to break in.
> 'Chocolate, you know, and eggs – and then covered with whipped cream. Just the sort of sweet a foreigner would like for lunch.'

My aunt used to make this pudding but called it *négresse en chemise*. In a guide to erotic literature, I had come across an engraving entitled *nègre en chemise*. It showed a white woman being penetrated from behind by a rubbery-lipped black man with wild eyes and a huge penis. He was holding her arm out as if they were waltzing. The woman was naked except for a pair of high-heeled mules but the man wore a white shirt.

When I went into the kitchen in the early evening, I found Glenda, one of the women who worked there, barely able to move for pain. She was nineteen now, but she said that she had been racked with menstrual cramps from the age of fifteen. The doctor had told her that they would go away 'when she make a baby', but she didn't want to make a baby yet. Since she was clearly unable to work and Jeane was not yet back from the party, I offered to take her home. She lived further along the coast beyond the village of Massacre, named after some event so far back in Dominica's history that nobody now could tell me what had happened there (in fact, the massacre of some eighty Caribs by British troops in 1672), up a narrow almost vertical road, tarmacked but badly damaged and full of pot-holes. I drove as far as I could but, at a certain point, the road became virtually impassable. Glenda got out and said a cheerful thank you, leaving me to back the car in pitch-dark down an impossibly steep slope, as there was nowhere that I could turn. Back at the inn, Olivia was still lying down. There was no sign of Jeane who had promised to return by nine so that we could all go dancing. When she finally put in an appearance around midnight, we both felt too tired.

I was convinced – for some reason – that a proper understanding of the culture and customs of the Caribbean necessitated going out in the evening and staying up late (this belief only deserted me finally some months later well after midnight in a rowdy bar in Barbuda); accordingly, the following evening found us in the Sisserou Hotel some miles south of Roseau. I still hadn't got the measure of Dominica or I would have realised that I was doomed to late-night disappointment there. The Sisserou was a big characterless purpose-built place of the kind you find in socialist countries (or former socialist countries). There was a long buffet table laden with predictable dishes (salads, chicken wings, provisions) and a small steel band playing on a raised platform in one corner of a vast arena. Apart from a single white woman revolving dreamily on the dance floor while her elderly mother watched from the sidelines, the joint was not exactly jumping. We filled our plates, ordered a couple of rum punches and settled down to wait. Three-quarters of an hour later, nothing much had changed. The dancer, whose legs were encased in paisley leggings that made them look as if they were covered with tattoos, was still locked into her own private fantasy. She was actually hugging herself as she twisted and turned and there was something acutely painful about the look of naked longing on her face.

But the evening wasn't a complete waste of time. Just as we were thinking of leaving, a ripple of excitement, like the wind in the trees, ran through the room and Eugenia Charles walked in. Dominica's Prime Minister, the Caribbean's Iron Lady, was no beauty. Her long crimson evening-dress apart, she looked more like an elderly iguana than anything else – the same heavy-lidded gaze, the same greyish leathery skin, the same pouch beneath the chin, the same look of prehistoric cunning, the same darting concentration, simultaneously watchful and relaxed. I half-expected to see her tongue flicker between her lips.

But Charles, a lawyer from a wealthy land-owning family, the nearest thing that the Caribbean has to a black aristocracy, is the main reason why Dominica is unlike any other Anglophone Caribbean island. Though her enemies called her the 'mule' – educated at the Convent of the Order of the Faithful Virgins in Roseau, she had never married and had no children – the chaos, corruption and megalomania which had characterised the governments of the other English-speaking Caribbean countries since independence (especially the smaller ones) had, by and large, given Dominica a wide berth. Dominica was the only one of the former British colonies of the Lesser Antilles to be a fully independent member of the British Commonwealth, with a president, rather than the Queen of England, as Head of State. Charles's Dominica Freedom Party had been in power since 1980 and had brought a degree of stability and order, if not prosperity to the island (since 1979 three major hurricanes – David, Allen and Hugo – had devastated Dominica and the economy, never particularly thriving, had yet to recover). There were no rumours of gun-running, drug-smuggling and profiteering in Dominica. She might rule with an iron rod but Charles's Dominica was clean and seen to be clean, the roads were reasonable and the trains, were there any, would have run on time. (It remains to be seen whether, when Charles steps down at the next general election in 1995, Dominica's relative stability survives.)

This might also have something to do with the nature of Dominica itself. Like St Vincent, it was colonised late, remaining in Carib hands until the eighteenth century and then, like St Lucia, shuttling between the English and the French (Dominica is sandwiched between the French territories of Guadeloupe and Martinique and Creole is still widely spoken) for decades until possession was finally settled by the former in 1805. The inhospitable terrain would itself make smuggling or gun-running a tough proposition. People talk of Dominica as a 'dark place' (Jean Rhys wrote to Francis Wyndham in 1964: '. . . it is *dark* Dominica. Or was.'), where obeah is still much practised. Certainly, as we drove through the countryside, we would see strange little fetishes of shoes and other bits and pieces dangling from the telephone wires and telegraph poles. I asked someone what they were and the answer was typically vague. 'Maybe somebody lose them.'

The places had doom-laden names: Massacre, the Boiling Lake, the Valley of Desolation, Morne au Diables, Morne Diablotin (the French word for 'imp', also given to a now-extinct black-capped petrel), Point Des Fous. And the landscape, for all its lushness, was curiously bleak and forbidding. It was one of those landscapes that you had to have been born to. There was nothing easy about Dominica, nothing immediately charming, nothing accessible. Jean Rhys wrote: 'The black people have or had a good word for it – "she *magic* with him" or "he *magic* with her". Because you see, that's what it is. Not "Love" at all. There is too the magic of the place, which is not all lovely beaches or smiling people – it can be a very disturbing kind of beauty.'

To know Dominica may be to love her but it was getting to know her that presented problems. That said, it photographed marvellously – there was some luminous haunting quality in the light – and, if I didn't know better, I would think it the most marvellous place on earth.

Soon after that evening we moved to just outside Portsmouth at the north-west end of the island and rented a little wooden cottage on the beach. A neat border of conch shells divided the flowerbed from the black sand. It was better there but nothing would stop the rain. The rains came and how they came.

One day we drove over to the other side of the island to see the Caribs, stopping to give a lift to two women. They were Caribs and on their way back to the reserve. One was young and tall, the other old and small but their features revealed them immediately. Straight hair, straight noses, flat taut faces with high cheekbones, golden skin. Had they not told us when we reached the reserve, it would have been possible to drive straight through without noticing anything much. Only the sudden rash of little roadside stalls, selling the intricate black-and-brown basketware that the Caribs make, indicated that we had arrived.

Some two thousand Caribs live in this place, maintaining a degree of autonomy. They elect a chief every five years and have certain laws of their own which are supposed to be integrated into the laws of the island. No one who is not a member of the community is permitted to build a house in the reserve and, if a woman marries outside the community, she is no longer considered a Carib. However, if a strange woman marries into the community, she becomes Carib by virtue of having married a Carib. It was a chilling thought to realise that these pitifully few basket-weaving souls are all that remain of the once-powerful Caribs who had dominated the Caribbean for centuries.

I broke my sandal and took it into Portsmouth to be repaired. The shoe-mender lived behind a dressmaker's up a little track. His house was sea-green and full of shoes. Chickens lived underneath. He said he could mend the shoe and to come back in half an hour. To kill the time, I went for a walk round the town. The magistrates court, the police station, the sub-treasury and the post office were all housed in one long sugar-pink building. When I went back, the sandal was not ready. He told me to come back the next morning. The next day, the shoe-mender had gone. Over the next few days I tried several times to find him but he was never there and, though the woman in the dressmaker's shop told me that she knew the sandal was ready, I never saw him again and eventually abandoned the shoe.

One morning we took a boat trip up the Indian River (Dominica claimed to have 365 rivers, just as Antigua claimed to have 365 beaches – in each case, one for every day of the year). We floated up the brown water, with only the splash of the oars to break the silence. There was a smell of damp mud and a watery sunlight filtered through the leaves. The mangrove writhed silently in the shallows and, on the shore, a discarded snakeskin lay like a sinister evocation of mortality. 'Here he [the boa constrictor] change his skin,' said the boatman. There were young coconut trees and something called an elephant tree or creeper with leaves like elephant ears. A bridge called Monkey Bridge across which sugar cane used to be transported, lay in ruins, 'mashed up' in Hurricane David.

The boatman, a boy of nineteen called Ronnie, had been a child when Hurricane David had ravaged the island in 1979. 'You have to run for your life,' he said. He had hid in the Catholic Church in Portsmouth but a friend had not been so lucky. He had had his throat cut by a piece of flying galvanise, the edge of a tin roof that had come whizzing through the air and virtually decapitated him.

At dusk the trees were black against the slow burn of a pale orange sunset. I sat out on the little verandah watching the dove-grey clouds scuttle in the air, listening to the rush of the waves. Every silhouette stood clearly defined: the slender crescent of the new moon high in the baby-blue sky; the yachts with their tall masts; the palm trees like cardboard cut-outs; the feathery outline of another lower palm; the pier extending into the water now almost without colour – steely, opaque; the little wooden fence that marked the boundary of the property; the boys splashing in the surf that frothed in the shallows. A black bird catching a lizard in its beak and the lizard dropped like a stone to the ground. There was the sound of the crickets and the treefrogs and the birds and, in the distance, the thump of some heavy reggae. When it rained, the ground would hiss and steam, making a noise like a wet saucepan on a hot stove. Imagine being on a boat and seeing one of these islands for the first time. So green, so lush. You wouldn't know the hardships that it could bring. Columbus saw Dominica on a Sunday in 1493 and named it accordingly.

Sometimes the sun shone for just long enough for Olivia to feel sufficiently confident to install herself on the black sand beach but no sooner had she sat down than the heavens would open.

But mostly there was no sunshine. I lay on my bed and listened to the rain. All night long the crash of the breakers came every four seconds. In the morning, it might be clear for a bit and then the rain would start again, the whole sky clouding over so you couldn't even see the end of the island and the heavy rain gouged a track into the sand. I listened to the sound of the rain falling on the roof and the leaves. A sound of constant dampness. Dominica was slow, achingly unbearably slow. At night I heard a dog barking in the distance. In the morning there were pawprints in the sand. I drove into Portsmouth and asked a lady in a shop how long she thought the rain would last.

'Only God knows – he the weather prophet.'

6

Love in the Afternoon

Two white women travelling through Africa,
Find themselves in the hands of a cannibal head-hunter.
He cook up one and he eat one raw,
Them taste so good he wanted more, more
He want more
I envy the congo man
I wish it was me, I want to shake he hand
He eat until his stomach upset
And I never eat a white meat yet . . .
                    (from *Congo Man* by the Mighty Sparrow)

In the end the rain became intolerable so we went to Martinique
on the Caribbean Express, a big modern boat, a catamaran or a
jetcat, which flung itself at the waves, hitting them head-on
with a sickening – and sick-making – smack. At first, I stood
out on deck but the journey across the Martinique Passage was
horribly rough and I got soaked and then chilly. The St Lucia
Channel was even worse, according to a man standing next to
me, who described it as 'une armoire à glace' (literally 'a ward-
robe with a mirror' but used figuratively to mean 'a great hulk-
ing brute'). Downstairs in the cabin, people were groaning and
throwing up into plastic bags, and David Lynch's *Wild At Heart*
(dubbed into French – apart from the title which had evidently
defeated the translator forcing him to settle for *Sailor et Loula*)
was playing on the television screens. I had seen it before in a

cinema in London but, in this setting, it seemed particularly decadent.

From Portsmouth I had telephoned almost every hotel in Martinique's capital, Fort-de-France – or so it seemed – and they were all full up. Only the little Gommier had rooms and we could walk there from the port. The Gommier had evidently been flooded. Away from the entrance, the carpet had been taken up and great patches of damp streaked the walls. Gangs of mosquitoes lurked in corners and under the beds and my room smelt musty. Within minutes of arriving, the telephone rang. It was a friend of Neville's, a man called Roger Le Breton, and he was coming to collect us at four that afternoon to take us on a tour of the island.

Martinique, like most of the islands of the Lesser Antilles, had been the subject of constant dispute between the British and the French during the seventeenth, eighteenth and nineteenth centuries. The 1763 Treaty of Paris, which settled the Seven Years War, restored Martinique and Guadeloupe and its dependencies to France and awarded it St Lucia; the British agreed to be satisfied with Canada, the entire Ohio valley and much of French Hindustan. Today it is difficult to comprehend the rationale for this exchange, but such was the wealth generated for France by Martinique and Guadeloupe's sugar crop at the time that it made perfect sense. The fighting, however, continued for decades, with the British occupying Martinique on and off until 1814, when yet another Treaty of Paris once again restored Martinique and Guadeloupe to the French, this time at the expense of Tobago and St Lucia. Martinique and the Guadeloupe archipelago, which includes Grande-Terre, Basse-Terre (Guadeloupe), La Desirade, Les Saintes and Marie Galante, Saint-Barthélemy and the French half of Saint-Martin, started off as colonies in the eighteenth century, graduated to *départements-outre-mer* in 1946; (in Martinique, this was largely thanks to the efforts of the then-communist deputy of Fort-de-France, Aimé Césaire); they finally became fully-fledged *regions mono-départementales* in 1982.

This means that their citizens are French citizens, have French passports and the right to live and work in France. Approximately a quarter of a million people from the French Caribbean (including second-generation descendants) live in France which is known locally as the 'métropole'; Frenchmen or women from the 'métropole' are 'métropolitains'. The standard of living in the French Antilles is considerably higher than in the Anglophone Caribbean: the roads are generally very good, the food is immeasurably better and everything costs even more than it does elsewhere in the Caribbean. As French citizens, the natives of Martinique and Guadeloupe are entitled to financial help from the state and every day we saw long queues in the post office, people standing in line to collect their welfare payments. As a result, it could take up to an hour to buy a postage stamp and all the computers in the world did nothing to speed things up.

'Les Antilles furent pour la France la plus stimulante et la plus enrichissante des possessions' begins a history of Saint-Pierre, the former capital of Martinique. Once, that may have been the case. Now they are more likely to be regarded as a drain on the national purse – Valéry Giscard d'Estaing, the former French President, described them as 'the dancers of France', implying a frivolous subsidised existence, all rum and madras head-dresses. The French government offers tax incentives for French investors but except for a few hotel projects, there has been little interest, because the Antilles, with all their social programmes, are among the most expensive places in the Caribbean. The French state guarantees a minimum wage for both workers and the unemployed, health care, pensions and agricultural subsidies. France is keen to generate revenue by encouraging tourism to the Antilles but the islands are markedly free of the kind of luxury resorts which are liberally scattered throughout the English-speaking Caribbean, and which tourists have accordingly come to expect.

We still had some time to spare before Le Breton was due so we went to have a look at Fort-de-France. Outside it was at least not raining and it was pleasant to be once more in a big modern city. There were shops full of designer clothes and pavement cafés and *pharmacies* and little bars selling *apéritifs* and Bière Lorraine ('. . . specialement etudiée pour le climat tropical . . .') and copies of *France-Antilles* and *Paris-Turf* which brought the racing news – all the way from Vincennes. *France-Antilles*, for all its sophisticated presentation, still had its heart in the Caribbean: 'Le Cycliste M'a Sodomisé' ran one headline.

In the Savane, the public gardens in the centre of town, stood a white marble statue of the Empress Josephine, the gift of Napoleon III. Her rounded figure was swathed in the graceful dress of her time, one hand rested on her heart, the other on a medallion of Napoleon I, but her head had long been decapitated by the 'indépendantistes' who sought to sever the ties that bound Martinique to France. The independence movement was relatively small – only a fraction of the population supported it.

Josephine was born in 1763 at Trois-Islets in the south of the island, but she returned to Martinique only once after her first marriage to Alexandre de Beauharnais and took no interest in its fate. Napoleon vetoed public references to her childhood though he is supposed to have said to her when he first brought her to live at the Tuîleries, 'There, little Creole! You now have the chance to sleep in the bed of your masters.'

The remark may have been intended as humorous but even Napoleon cannot have failed to be aware that dozens of slave women were sleeping in their masters' beds, sometimes willingly, sometimes not. Today's Martiniquans regard their famous countrywoman with a somewhat jaundiced eye – not least because she was held responsible for the return of slavery; after the French Revolution in 1789, slavery was briefly abolished in February 1794 but, with the British occupation, it continued as before; it was officially reinstated in 1802 when Napoleon came to power and the colony was restored to French control – there is no evidence that Josephine played a part in its reinstatement. Complete indifference to the slaves' fate seems most likely to have been the Empress's stance. Napoleon himself would have needed no encouragement. His views were well known. Reproached for the reintroduction of slavery, he said: 'Je suis pour les blancs parce que je suis blanc: je n'ai que cette seule raison à donner, et c'est la bonne . . .' and on another occasion, 'La question n'est pas de savoir s'il est bon d'abolir l'esclavage, mais s'il est bon d'abolir la liberté dans le partie libre de St Dominigue . . .'

At one corner of the Savane was a small open-air theatre named after Frantz Fanon. Opposite, in another corner, was the Bibliothèque Schoelcher named after Victor Schoelcher, the French abolitionist who brought about the final abolition of slavery in the French Antilles in 1848.

The work of Henri Picq, the library was originally displayed along with the Eiffel Tower at the Paris exhibition of 1889, where it contained the stands of exhibiters from the French Antilles. It was subsequently dismantled and transported to Fort-de-France in 1893, where it was reconstructed to house the library of ten thousand books which Schoelcher had given to Martinique. A wonderful and astonishing building, it was vaguely reminiscent of the Brighton Pavilion. The top half is made largely of metal topped with a cupola, all reposing on a base of stone painted in alternating rows of terracotta and cream; into one row are carved the names of noted prophets and protagonists of abolition (Toussaint-L'Ouverture, Clavière, Brissot, Clarkson, Wilberforce, Raynall, Condorcet, Remusat and others), interposed with decorative art nouveau friezes; the whole is inset with a series of arched panelled windows. I thought it extremely pretty.

Schoelcher, who had been Under-Secretary for the Colonies as well as President of the Commission on Slavery, was a major presence in the French Antilles. As well as the library, streets and squares, even a whole prosperous little suburb of Fort-de-France, are named after the man. In the garden in front of the Palais de Justice stood a statue of Schoelcher, his arm round the shoulders of a slave child whose chains had been severed. The inscription underneath read:

NULLE TERRE FRANCAISE
NE PEUT PLUS PORTER D'ESCLAVES

Although slavery in the French islands was deemed not to be as harsh as that in the British (the French conceded that slaves were also human beings and devised a *Code Noir*, the articles of which included one which forbade the breaking up of slave families: the selling of members of slave families to different buyers was not prohibited by the English); but the French did not actually abolish slavery until 1848, fifteen years after the British had done so. Four years later, Napoleon III issued an edict which permitted planters to buy African *engagés* (contract labourers from Senegal); this violated the spirit, if not the letter, of emancipation – as did the use of indentured workers from the Indian sub-continent. That traffic endured for eight years and was only brought to an end around 1860 after complaints from the British. Yet, as far as I know, not one of the Anglophone islands has anywhere named Wilberforce. There the memory of slavery is still too bitter and only fit to be preserved in the former 'great' houses that now serve as luxury hotels.

But the French clearly see nothing contradictory in all these monuments. It is all part of the glory of France: those whose forefathers had imposed slavery now feel it appropriate both to congratulate themselves for having abolished it and to remind the natives that they had done so. And, as those natives are simultaneously West Indian and the descendants of slaves *and* French with all that that betokens, they have inevitably experienced confusion, almost an identity crisis.

This is one problem that West Indians from the Anglophone islands have not had to face as, even when the islands were colonies, they were never encouraged to regard themselves as Englishmen and, having now been roundly rejected by the mother country, could now at least pretend to sit back and comfortably loathe their former colonial masters. Martiniquans would often refer to someone from Dominica or St Lucia as 'un Anglais', apparently unaware that, while Britain had been touted as a model of civilisation, the standard to which West Indians were encouraged to aspire, there has never been any real suggestion that they could truly consider themselves British.

Whatever its legal status, Martinique remains ultimately a possession of France. Dependency, and the resultant gratitude that it demands, never makes for easy relations. The Martiniquan, not daring to cut the umbilical cord, desperately simulating a Frenchness that could only ever be, at best, artificial, is locked into a mutual conspiracy in which the sins of the 'father' are not only not visited on the 'son' but were apparently forgotten and forgiven. By making Martinique French, the French sought to wipe out the past and by accepting the 'gift' of Frenchness, the Martiniquan has agreed that the past no longer matters.

But perhaps the good roads, the first-class hospitals and schools, the fresh cheeses and fine wines, the bold, twentieth-century skyline of Fort-de-France – all these and more are adequate compensation for the psychic disorder of the French West Indian. I couldn't tell.

Le Breton, a former customs inspector, was an elderly man of medium height with a totally bald head, blue-green eyes and a compact chunky body like a teddy bear. He looked fit and strong and was apparently devoted to the feckless Neville whom he described as 'un fou'.

'Ah, Neville, ils aiment les femmes,' he said, sighing at the folly of it.

We got into his car, Olivia in the back, me in front, and sped off in the direction of the north of the island. Le Breton, as I was to discover over the following days, had a passion for graveyards and he took us straight to the town of Saint-Pierre which lies on the northern Caribbean coast in the shadow of the still-active volcano of Mont Pelée.

In a sense, Saint-Pierre is one huge graveyard. Until the beginning of the century, it had been not only the economic and social capital of Martinique and indeed of the whole French West Indies but also, but all accounts, a city of infinite charm and beauty. It was known then as the 'Paris of the West Indies' and the 'Pearl of the Antilles' (to add to all the other 'Pearls' strewn throughout the colonial world: Saigon, Penang, etc . . .

A contemporary account records that:

The picturesque situation of the city, with the gay costumes of the natives, gives the place a decidedly operatic appearance. The climate is almost perfect . . . As do all the colonial capitals of the French, St Pierre followed as closely as the steamers and mails would permit the customs and fashions of Paris. At the Hotel des Bains, at the 'absinthe hour', one might always find a gathering of young men of the town, who sat sipping their liqueurs and chatting gaily.

Early in 1902, Mont Pelée began to show signs of activity. A foul smell of sulphur filled the surrounding air. Farm animals showed signs of distress, birds ceased to sing and left the trees that shaded the sides of the volcano. Snakes deserted the slopes of the mountain. In late April, the volcano grew more lively and in early May, the inhabitants of Le Prêcheur and Ste Philomene were forced to take refuge in Saint-Pierre from a torrent of hot ash. For reasons for which there appears to be no satisfactory explanation, the situation was still not perceived as serious.

On 8 May 1902, just after eight o'clock in the morning, Mont Pelée erupted and within minutes, the entire town of Saint-Pierre was enveloped in a fierce cloud of fiery vapour and its inhabitants and visitors, numbering some thirty thousand people were killed. These included the governor of Martinique, Monsieur Mouttet, and his wife, who had come up from Fort-de-France to reassure the citizens of Saint-Pierre that there was no real danger, the United States Consul to Saint-Pierre and his family and the daughter of the Italian Consul to Barbados who happened to be visiting the town. Saint-Pierre literally ceased to exist. The sole survivor was a man called Cyparis who, protected by the thick walls of the jail in which he was a prisoner, spent three days waiting to be discovered. Later, Cyparis joined a circus where his act consisted of exhibiting the scars of the burns that he had suffered in the eruption. ('Roll Up! Roll Up! Come and see the man who has known the end of the world! His body bears the burns of hell!')

Some twenty-nine boats, plus numerous small fishing craft were also destroyed. In a matter of minutes the 'pearl of the Antillies' had become the 'Pompeii of modern times'.

In ruined St Pierre a myriad of dead were left entombed in fiery lava and grey volcanic ash, while the few trembling fugitives wandered homeless and hopeless, with bereavement tugging at their heart-strings and famine dogging their errant footsteps . . . St Pierre today is a vast charnel house.

The details that survive from contemporary accounts of the tragedy are heartbreaking; poignant cameos of death and destruction: a group of children found locked in each other's arms; the charred remains of a woman, with a silk handkerchief unburned and in perfect condition held to her lips; a brilliantly-coloured bird dead on the floor of its cage; the only living thing a solitary ox, thin as a skeleton, found wandering through the wreckage; a child with a piece of bread in his hand, the imprint of his teeth still on it; in the cathedral, a small chalice full of communion wafers, not one of them scorched. All the bodies were naked save for their shoes, the clothes having literally been blasted off them.

We wandered through the cemetery. Here, unlike in the English-speaking Caribbean, where the stones are as weathered and mossy as in a Somerset graveyard, the tombs were white, the older ones marble, the newer ones covered in shiny tiles such as you might find in a public lavatory. They lay in orderly rows separated by cement paths. Nothing grew anywhere. It was a totally urban graveyard. The iron railings that surrounded the larger ones were frequently twisted and bent out of shape but the tombs themselves were mostly in good order, almost all adorned with vases of, mainly artificial, flowers and inscribed with modest expressions of affection: an open book made of some sort of ceramic announced that, 'Le temps qui efface tout n'efface pas le souvenir.' The bones of those victims of the eruption who had not been buried beneath layers of lava had been collected together and placed in a large ossuary, above which stood a statue of Christ crucified, His mother weeping at the foot of the cross. Behind His extended arms, the jungle reared up the hillside. And in front, like a barrier between the town and the palpable reality of death, stood the cathedral. Rebuilt on the site of the original edifice, parts of which had survived the eruption, it was a solid uncompromising building, planted squarely on the ground, seemingly determined to withstand further disasters.

The remains of old Saint-Pierre lay on the outskirts of the new town. From these it was possible to reconstruct the thriving metropolis that had once been. The ruined fort, the pitiful remnants of the chapel of the bishopric and the broad sweep of the splendid double staircase that was all that was left of the theatre which had doubled as an opera house and was modelled on the theatre of Bordeaux and capable of holding 800 spectators (in a town that now did not even boast a cinema), all testified to an infinitely more splendid past.

But, over the past ninety years, a new town had grown up, a town of wooden houses and verandahs with iron railings and soft tropical tints, faded eau-de-nils and bleached pinks and oranges, the colours of the nascent sunset that now suffused the bay of Saint-Pierre. 'Un histoire d'amour entre le ciel et la mer' was one of the current slogans of the Martinique tourist authority and there was some truth in it. Modern Saint-Pierre may have lacked the magnificence of the past but it had its own charm. As we drove away, Olivia, who was very taken with the town, noticed a ramshackle turquoise and white building by the sea. Called La Vague, it claimed to be a hotel-restaurant and had a sign outside depicting a mermaid into whose stomach was set a blackboard on which to write the *plat du jour*. Olivia thought that it might be a nice place to stay.

On the way back to Fort-de-France, we stopped in Schoelcher at the house of one of Le Breton's neighbours who invited us to stay for dinner. Our host, Bertrand, was a *fonctionnaire*, a little balding man who looked like a frog – full of self-importance with glasses and bulging eyes. While we waited for the other guests, Roger made drinks.

The best rum of the Caribbean is supposed to come from Martinique and there are rituals to its drinking which are far more elaborate and formal than anything in the English-speaking islands. It has an almost symbolic quality, like rice or bread, deriving from the fact that Martinique's fortunes were based on sugar and sugar cane. More than half the rum produced in Martinique is drunk on the island. There are three grades: *agricole* or *blanc*, the white rum which the purists drink and which has a strong, slightly chemical smell; *vieux*, which is rum that has been aged in wood for a number of years (the price and quality depend on the length of time) – it looks and tastes rather like brandy; *paille*, which has also spent some time in a cask and is straw-coloured. The classic way to take rum is as a *petit punch* or *ti punch* in Creole (pronounced 'paunsh' with the 'ch' soft and liquid), straight, with just a little sugar or sugar-cane syrup and a squeeze of fresh lime. Ice is optional and not really authentic. *Ti punch* has an unmistakable smell and taste – simultaneously sweet and sour and powerful enough to bring tears to your eyes. Made right, it can be the best drink in the world and compared to it the *planteurs* (rum with fruit juice) which are drunk throughout the Anglophone islands seem insipid by comparison. If you ask for *un punch* in a bar or restaurant, the bottle and a bowl of brown sugar is brought to your table and you serve yourself. There are all sorts of nicknames for *ti punch*: *un feu*; *un péte pieds* (meaning to stub your toe); *ti sec* (without syrup or lime). The fishermen who get up at three in the morning sometimes take a *décollage* (lift-off) of absinthe before going out.

Roger made *ti punchs* of *vieux*. Bertrand busied himself in the kitchen. The other guests arrived and we sat down to eat at a long table outside. The guests were two couples: a fat young politician, based in Guyane, with a *métropolitaine* girlfriend and a slim black man with an attractive, heavily pregnant wife. Her name was Odile, and she had pale creamy skin like a camellia and markedly African features. I was reminded of Eric Williams' comment: 'Prospective brides looked for light-skinned men. They pray for "light" children, who might marry white. Expectant mothers abstain from coffee and chocolate. As the saying goes in Martinique, one who has reached the dining room should not go back to the kitchen.' He was writing in 1942. I wondered how much had changed. I asked her what she planned to call the baby. She said that they hadn't decided, but definitely not Josephine. Le Breton was in lively form – the effects of a succession of *ti punches* – and speaking Creole. Neither Olivia nor I could understand a word, but the others laughed a lot.

The next morning Bertrand arrived at the Gommier to take us on a tour of the south. The motorway ran swiftly and efficiently through fields of waving sugar cane. We stopped at Trois-Islets, the birthplace of the Empress Josephine. Notre Dame de la Délivrance, the church where she had been baptised, had a wooden ceiling painted a beautiful duck-egg blue and hung with chandeliers. On the wall was a stone tablet inscribed with the words 'Marie Rose Josephine Tascher de la Pagerie 27 Juillet 1763'. Her mother's tomb lay nearby, her name and dates dwarfed by the inscription that read 'Mère de SA MAJESTE L'IMPERATRICE Des FRANCAIS'. Josephine's former home has become a museum which that day was closed. Opposite the modest dwelling, originally the kitchen of the 'great' house which had been destroyed by a cyclone, were the ruins of a *sucrerie*. The surrounding countryside was dominated by a huge golf-course, 'le golf de l'Imperatrice'. There were hotels and restaurants everywhere. Here was the heart of Martinique's tourist trade, rooted in the legend of a woman who had done nothing for her country, whose memory was locally reviled and whom Napoleon had discarded because of her inability to bear him children. (When Madame de Staël asked Napoleon what kind of women he preferred, he replied: 'The kind who have lots of children'.) Once again the *métropolitains* were having the best of both worlds.

Away from the brooding presence of Mont Pelée, the atmosphere had a kind of febrile, fun-fair gaiety with families picnicking on the beach, small children with buckets and spades building sand-castles, and camp-sites full of caravans and trailers. The air was thick with the scent of pine needles and meat grilling on barbecues.

We ate a delicious and expensive fish lunch somewhere outside by the sea and then went to swim from a crowded beach on which French women with tiny, pert breasts sunbathed topless. The religious-inspired *pudeur* of the Anglophone islands, where Christianity had dictated that nudity was provocative and offensive (a modesty that had no apparent effect on the sexual mores of the people), seemed to have no place here. Nonetheless, I was startled by a postcard which depicted a woman's buttocks naked but for a strip of material in the cleft, both cheeks coated in sand: the caption read 'Martinique – Sea, Sex and . . . Sand'. Another card showed a handsome black man surrounded by white women in bikinis. 'Séduction Tropicale . . . Vacances Inoubliables'. But most extraordinary of all was a drawing of three black women wearing only hats and boots, cutting sugar cane with machetes. The apparent juxtaposition of sex and slavery (for that is still the strongest association of sugar cane) seemed almost surreal.

In the restaurant we noticed a middle-aged solitary, white woman, very plain, wearing glasses and a sort of cotton romper suit with palm trees and the words 'Barbados – Island in the Sun' printed all over it. She had overdone the sunbathing and her back was covered in little strips of burnt skin which she kept reaching up to peel off. 'Les métropolitains sont partout,' said Bertrand, in a tone which was at once aggrieved and complacent.

Bertrand asked what we were doing for New Year's Eve, which was that evening. Although we had left Dominica because we had thought that it would be fun to spend New Year's Eve in Martinique, we hadn't thought much beyond that. If we had had any ideas at all, it was that we would wander the streets of Fort-de-France and see what happened. I said as much to Bertrand. This was clearly unsatisfactory. The idea that we were not going to be properly entertained was more than he could bear. He had been invited to the house of some friends. He would telephone them and see if he could bring us. Nothing that I could say – Olivia was leaving all the talking to me – would deflect him. His friends said that unfortunately they could not accommodate two more people, so Bertrand determined that we would all three spend New Year's Eve together at his house. I couldn't work out what his motives were – national pride, hospitality, lust, pity – but it was impossible to sway his resolve. Olivia looked increasingly unhappy at the prospect of the evening ahead but I could see no way out. Suggestions that we might go out for dinner fell on deaf ears. Everywhere, he explained, would have been booked up for weeks. That was the way things were done. He wouldn't hear of us spending the evening alone, or rather, without him. I knew when I was beaten.

And it did turn out to be a nightmarish and interminable evening. Dinner consisted of a massive block of *foie gras*, easily enough to feed ten people, washed down with champagne, followed by a huge dish of *confit de canard* and fried potatoes with red wine, served chilled according to the local custom. Bertrand talked incessantly, alternating between fierce nationalism (*métropolitain* rather than Martiniquais) and open lechery. In his flirtatiousness he seemed not to discriminate between us. At first he appeared to favour Olivia, who is younger than me, but then, as she grew more silent, less and less able – or perhaps less willing – to appreciate his sallies, he turned his attentions and pop-eyed gaze towards me. When he saw me in my bathing-suit with my long legs, he said he found the thought of making love with such a woman very exciting. At another stage in the evening, he began to recount his memories of Britain. He had once stayed with a family somewhere in the south of England – somewhere like Guildford or Dorking. The man was an engineer and used to take him to the pub where Bertrand would watch him drink five or six pints of beer. Meals would consist of Bertrand wondering how to get peas onto his fork.

The child in the house, a boy called Andrew, kept feeling Bertrand's hair. Though this may have been bad manners, it seemed hardly surprising that Bertrand would have been an object of curiosity to a small child in England twenty years ago.

Everywhere I had travelled in South-East Asia, adults, as well as children, would stroke or pinch my white skin and I never thought anything of it. But I had begun to understand that if you were black, or even partly-black, you were likely to feel a whole range of undreamt-of – by a white person – fears and sensitivities. After all, in the British Caribbean, it used to be the case that automatic freedom was granted to slaves who had been legally designated white; legal whiteness was available to a *mustee* (the child of a quadroon or pure Amerindian and white man). One way, therefore, of attaining freedom was literally to breed out the 'African blood' over a series of generations. There is an old French maxim which states that 'colour is wedded to slavery; nothing can render the slave the equal of his master'. Frantz Fanon coined the term 'lactification' – the desire for whiteness. (In Barbados, however, no one of known negroid ancestry, no matter how remote, could be considered white with respect to social or legal status.)

Bertrand was light-skinned but not white, and this was a further source of touchiness. When I wondered aloud whether Le Breton, with his pale skin and his blue-green eyes, was a *béké* (a word which originally meant the white elite, the plantocracy, and is now used to mean their descendants), Bertrand, clearly irritated, said, 'Non, c'est un métisse comme moi.' I could see that I would soon become an expert on these subtleties of colour and shade. Naipaul, visiting Martinique in 1960, wrote that:

> One of the futile skills unconsciously acquired by anyone who has grown up in the West Indies is the ability to distinguish persons of Negro ancestry. I thought I possessed this skill to a reasonable degree until I went to Martinique. Time and time again I was told that a white-skinned, light-eyed, straight-haired person . . . was really 'coloured'.

Thirty years later this remains unchanged.

The superiority of the French way of life over that of the English is always a favourite theme with mainland French people; but it was surprising and seemed somehow particularly sad to hear this dreary old ritual in the Caribbean. And Bertrand was slightly ridiculous, and a little sad too – caught between two cultures, neither one thing nor the other, and struggling with the effort of being French. I said that I found it difficult to regard Martinique as a part of France (as opposed to French) when geographically it was so distanced. 'What on earth do you mean?' he said, 'we're only eight hours from Paris by plane.'

The illusion of proximity is fostered by both the *métropolitains* and the Martiniquans. A postcard showing a stout black woman with a straw hat and spectacles carried on the reverse side a wealth of information about Martinique including the news that it was 'A 8 heures d'avion de Paris' and had a temperature of 28°C 'toute l'année' unlike, say, Neuilly which, according to the daily weather reports, was currently buried in snow.

The evening wore on and on. While I listened to Bertrand talk, Olivia curled up on the sofa and went to sleep. I found and put on an old record of Serge Reggiani singing Georges Moustaki's 'Ma Solitude' which brought back memories of a boy I had known a long time ago in Greece when I was sixteen and still a virgin. He had seemed very sophisticated at the time, too sophisticated to be interested in me, but ten years later we met again and had a brief, torrid, and not altogether healthy, affair. He had had a kind of furious vitality which I had found irresistible. As Bertrand tried to embrace me, I looked surreptitiously at my watch. It was after three. Time for bed. Alone. The next day we moved to Saint-Pierre.

La Vague stood by the side of the main road which ran from Saint-Pierre to Fort-de-France, facing an exquisite reconstruction of the nineteenth-century *bourse*, which had been destroyed in the eruption; it was destined to become a museum but had yet to be completed. La Vague was a long white two-storey colonial-style building with window-frames and doors picked out in a pale turquoise-green. The ground floor contained a vast bar-room with a bar which ran from one end of the room halfway to the other, and a pool-table; adjacent was a dining-room which stretched out over the beach; behind were kitchens and store-rooms. Upstairs, there were some five or six rooms to let, offices, and more store-rooms. The bedrooms were hardly luxurious, with mattresses like sponges and only cold water in the derelict little bathrooms. But we didn't mind. There was something about La Vague which we immediately recognised and warmed to. It wasn't exactly that it was welcoming, more that it was *sympathique*. We agreed that Olivia, who had to leave in a couple of days, should have the better and bigger room, which had a balcony and looked out to sea. My small room overlooked the *bourse*; I arranged to change rooms after Olivia had left for London.

The *patron*, Rico, was a small man with dark foxy Indian good looks. His wife, or girlfriend, was called Rose-Helène, a light-skinned Afro-Caribbean, slender and elegant. They were friendly enough but in a cool somewhat distant way as if waiting to see whether we were their sort of people. The restaurant did most of its business at midday, catering to the passing tourists, and then closed for the afternoon between four and seven; but the bar stayed open late into the night with a hardcore of regulars, who came to play pool, drink and talk. As a result, Rico and Rose-Helène who lived on the premises in a room next to Olivia's, often didn't get up till after nine-thirty, and the main doors remained closed till eleven or so. If you wanted breakfast, you had to wait for it or go out. We both had keys to the outside door.

The days were pleasant enough. It rained much less in Martinique and somehow even the rain seemed less wet. We fell into a comfortable routine, more at ease with each other and our surroundings than we had been in Dominica. While I explored the town and the nearby countryside, Olivia would take her book and go and sunbathe on the black sand beach in front of La Vague. The beach was covered with tiny fragments of broken glass and china, presumably from the eruption, all now polished by decades of tides – jewel-like, so that, in certain lights, the sand took on a faint iridescent shimmer. The water was warm without being soupy and there was a discernible undertow, which gave you something to work against when swimming.

Several times Le Breton drove up from Schoelcher and took me out in his car. I began to get a sense of the size of Martinique; it was by far the largest of the Lesser Antilles, and it was the first island which felt to me like a proper country. You could go from one end to another, from Grand' Rivière in the north to Sainte-Anne in the south, in a day, but it was a long and tiring drive and the north/south divide was noticeable. The north was more interesting, more varied, more dramatic and much less cultivated and industrialised. We would circumvent the great mist-shrouded bulge of Mont Pelée exploring cemeteries, ruined plantation houses, '*les wuines*' (in Creole 'r' is pronounced 'w'), and far-flung villages where the palm trees against the skyline were twisted and bent by the winds; we drove through small towns with wonderful names like Ajoupa-Bouillon, where I saw a dwarf standing by the roadside, Morne Rouge, where the elite of old Saint-Pierre used to go to escape the heat of the summer months, and Macouba. André Breton, who visited Martinique in 1941 *en route* to New York, wrote a prose poem called *La carte de l'île* which is just a list of Martiniquais place-names: La Jambette, Favorite, Trou-au-Chat, Pointe La Rose, Semaphore de la Demarche, Pointe du Diable, Brin d'Amour, Passe du Sans-Souci, Piton Creve-Coeur, Île du Loup-Garou, and so on. Apart from the bleakness that the constant lashing of the Atlantic engendered, there was a resilience to these stark little settlements that was moving, a gritty reality which was at odds with the prevalent images of a benign sun-kissed Caribbean.

It is doubtless the spirit of these hardy enclaves that has ensured the survival and popularity of cock-fighting in Martinique. Every Sunday afternoon between November and April you could go to a *pitt*, often sponsored or owned by one of the big distilleries, and watch the birds tear away at each other. You could also see fights between mongoose and snakes. In the north of Vietnam near Halong Bay I had met an old man who had fought with the French against the Vietminh and had an enormous bird, somewhat denuded of feathers, that was his pride and joy and a source of considerable income. It was strange to cross the world and find the same passion for this cruel sport. I asked Le Breton if we could go to a *pitt* and see a cock-fight but he refused to take me and the *pitt* in Saint-Pierre was closed.

Every town, however small, had its *mairie* and its *centre culturel*. In Macouba, the church had a beamed vaulted ceiling and nine fat women were kneeling and saying the rosary. In the graveyard the vases of artificial flowers had been knocked sideways by the wind and, in a deserted funfair, dodgem cars stood waiting in rows like an army of huge mechanical insects. In Grand' Rivière on the far northern corner of the wind-battered Atlantic coast a BMW had crashed and gone off the road into the river. There was the usual crowd of puzzled-looking people standing around and wondering how to rescue the car. The cemetery lay high up overlooking the sea. You could stand among the crowded graves and see the Atlantic boiling below. I looked down at it and told Le Breton how rough the crossing had been. 'Tu aurais te casser les reins [you must have broken your kidneys] avec ce bateau,' he said.

In the cemetery in Basse-Pointe we saw the tombs of some of the twenty-five thousand or so indentured Indian labourers who had been brought to Martinique to work in the plantations after the abolition of slavery. Scores of Rengassamys, Ramakas and Sooprayens, all the way from towns like Pondicherry, Karaikal and Mahé in former French Hindustan, looked out, liquid-eyed and sombre, from the black-and-white photographs which adorned almost every tomb. Le Breton recognised one. 'Mon ami mort, il jouait le violon,' he said, before skipping on to examine another inscription. 'Jusqu'à present il fait pleurer encore les gens – il était si gentil' read the simple and touching epitaph of one R. Theolade (1924–1979). And then there were the memorials to those who had perished thousands of miles away – in Cantho (Cochin-Chine), Haiphong (Tonkin), Larbese (Algerie) – fighting in the colonial wars of their masters, and long lists of those who died in the 1914–1918 war. My favourite of the little towns in the heart of the rainforest was Fonds St Denis, with its terraces and houses clinging like ivy to the side of the mountain. Outside the terracotta-coloured *mairie*, built in the Thirties, was a tiny war memorial honouring, amongst others, two soldiers killed in Indochina; inside the church, dedicated to the Immaculate Conception, a beautiful rehearsal for sung mass was in progress.

Even wrapped in a thick fog, its summit impossible to discern, from every angle the volcano dominated the landscape and in its foothills, the rainforest glowed and dripped. Aimé Césaire saw himself as a 'volcanic' personality, likening himself to Mont Pelée, but it has a force and a presence that he could not have hoped to match. Le Breton called her 'Madame' Pelée. 'Elle est effrayante,' he said. In the dense humidity, steam rose from the tarmacked roads. To either side stretched a tangled mass of avocado trees, their branches heavy with huge shiny green globes; tall feathery ferns – *fougères royales*; wild orchids; swaying rows of giant bamboo; acres of pineapples; and bananas as far as the eye could see, all wrapped in blue plastic to protect the fruit. We left the tarmac for steep little red-dirt tracks that cut through the vast reaches of banana plantations. Down below in the valley, there was a *rhumerie*, a distillery, and a strong sweet smell filled the damp air.

As the days went by, we got to know the regulars at La Vague. There was Theodore – Theo – Rico's best friend and his partner in a fruit juice business; he was a neat handsome man, with skin the colour of walnuts and a brilliant smile under his moustache, who worked as a nurse in the hospital; he had an exquisite little 'soft-haired' daughter called Ornella whom he sometimes brought with him. Then there was Alix, who had been a soldier on the Côte d'Ivoire, where he had a 'wife' and daughter; Sans-Pêché, whose real name was Marie, but they called him *Sans-Pêché*, meaning 'without sin' or just Pêché; Dolly, who had some Indian blood and drank too much and brought his sleepy little son called Lionel; Emile who quoted Sartre and had hot angry eyes – he was usually rather drunk and spoiling for a fight, and Jean-Robert, an elderly white man, a *béké*.

In the evening, at least three or four of them would always be there, playing pool, drinking and talking. Rico and Rose-Helène rarely bothered to serve their friends who would go behind the bar or into the big cooler and help themselves. It was rather like a club, intimate and a little exclusive, and strangers who strayed into the bar rarely stayed long.

One night, Theo and a colleague from the hospital asked us to come with them to hear some *zouk*. I was all for going out, especially if it involved dancing, but Olivia didn't want to, so we stayed in the bar instead. It was a long evening. Every time we tried to go to bed, someone bought us another drink. Alix had his eye on Olivia but she preferred Rico and Rose-Helène was ever-present. Emile got very drunk and tried to get first me, then Olivia, to sleep with him. He didn't care which of us it was. When we declined, he became abusive, then coarse, and the evening ended on a sour note.

Olivia's plane home was to leave early in the morning and we decided to spend the night before her departure in Fort-de-France. Theo offered to drive us down to the city. On the way, he said, he intended to visit his son (he had two children, each by a different woman) in Morne Rouge; from there we took *la route de la Trace* to Fort-de-France. The *route de la Trace* wound through the rainforest and the central mountainous mass of the north of the island: it was, according to Le Breton, known as *la route de la propreté* because it was so clean. By daylight, by all accounts, it was a spectacular drive, but in the dark and driving rain, I felt hideously sick and scared. Theo drove fast round the hairpin bends, braking and accelerating. I couldn't see more than a couple of feet in front of us. Ever since Bertrand's New Year's Eve dinner I had been feeling faintly sick and exhausted and this drive seemed like the last straw. Theo agreed that the road was 'très sinueuse' but didn't slow down.

I felt bereft after Olivia had gone and I had forgotten how to be alone. I spent the next morning wandering around Fort-de-France, window-shopping and brooding, then returned to Saint-Pierre. That night I slept in the room that looked out to sea. The bed faced the window and I left the shutters open so I could see the sky and the moon. All night long there was a terrific storm. The raindrops fell like small pebbles on the corrugated iron roof of the balcony and the sound of voices floated up from the bar below. I woke at two and again at three and saw the bright moon high in a midnight-blue sky. In the morning, there was a watery rainbow over the bay and three drowned cockroaches on my bathroom floor. But my New Year's Eve hangover had finally dissipated.

Most mornings there was a market in Saint-Pierre. I loved the market. I loved the stalls of fruit and vegetables: avocados, mangos, papaya, limes, oranges, tangerines, pineapples, bananas, coconuts, lettuces, tomatoes, potatoes, yams, christophine, fiery little *piments*. I loved the tin basins of fish and live lobster and octopus fresh from the sea, sometimes sold straight off one of the fishing-boats that you could see creeping in at dawn – if you were awake. I loved the buckets of Anthuriums and lilies, the great bunches of Bird of Paradise flowers and torch ginger. I loved the sticks of cinnamon and vanilla and the fat cigars of cocoa and the mounds of rusty spices and the bottles and jars of homemade pickles and jams and spicy sauces – it was impossible to resist the *purée de piment*, the *confiture des tomates*, the home-ground *colombo* (a mixture of spices used for curry). I couldn't cook at La Vague but I bought them all. I loved the van full of baskets from Dominica and the pick-up truck, whose owner would slash open coconuts with a machete. Before I had come to the Caribbean, I had hated the smell of coconut. Now I couldn't get enough of it. I loved the old woman who sold pots and huge wooden spoons with long sharp handles ('big enough to dispatch a werewolf' a friend in Antigua said later when he saw the one I had bought), and unguents and potions in pretty glass bottles. I even loved the meat stalls with their glistening ribbons of offal and marbled slabs of beef. I loved the fat *vendeuses* in their madras cotton skirts and straw hats who hated having their photograph taken. Some of the older ones wore turbans, tied with a jaunty bow in front, the only time I ever saw traditional costume. In Fort-de-France you could buy a card which showed all the different ways of tying the turban: each style had a different meaning; one indicated that you were unavailable, others indicated varying degrees of availability. Le Breton had told me that Martiniquais women were 'très coquettes, quelque fois trop', and this business with the turban seemed to support his claim.

The morning after Olivia had left, there was as usual no sign of the lunchtime waitress, Ghislaine, and therefore no chance of breakfast so I went to the market. When I came back, with an armful of white lilies for Rose-Helène, Theo was waiting for me.

We drove up to Le Prêcheur where Madame de Maintenon, Louis XIV's long-term mistress and eventual wife, had lived for seven years as a child. In the main square there were three large bronze bells; the middle one had been given to the people of Le Prêcheur by the 'Sun King' at the request of Madame de Maintenon; there was also a sign which read:

Ici s'écoula
L'enfance de
Francoise d'Aubigne
qui devait être
Madame de Maintenon
Epouse de Louis XIV

We parked the car further on and walked through the forest down to a remote beach. It was raining slightly and the ground was muddy and slippery. I took off my shoes and Theo draped an arm round my shoulder, grazing my breast. The beach was beautiful and deserted with black sand and huge round boulders. It was raining hard by now and my dress was soaked through. We walked to the far end, away from the forest, and undressed. I hadn't brought a bathing-suit or even a towel so I swam in my underpants. Two young white couples arrived with a big picnic ice-chest and installed themselves under a tree, some way from us, near the path. They took off all their clothes and ran into the warm water, shrieking and splashing each other. The rain kept on coming down, big drops pitting the surface of the sea. Theo dived under and grabbed me from below. When he came up for air, he kissed me. I wrapped my legs round his waist, weightless in the salty water – you could stay in this buoyant sea for hours before you began to tire or chill; Paul Valéry called swimming 'fornication avec l'onde'.

We had no towels and my dress was damp; it clung clammily to me as we retraced our steps through the wood. By the time we got back to Le Prêcheur I was drier and we went to have lunch in a little restaurant called L'Etoile du Nord. We were the only customers and the *patron* seemed disappointed that we did not want dessert. After we had finished, I asked Theo what we were going to do now.

'On va faire l'amour,' said Theo.

'Où?'

He had the keys to the house of some friends who were away in France. He was feeding their cats. He said we would go there.

Theo had been pursuing me in a polite but determined way for several days and I still wasn't sure what, if anything, I wanted to do about it – though a strange feeling of lethargy or impotence had come over me. In a way I felt that I didn't really care what happened. I was happy to leave it to fate. But, on the way to Le Prêcheur – both as a delaying tactic and out of real interest – I had asked about Ornella's mother, with whom he lived in Case-Pilote, about ten miles from Saint-Pierre; I had asked how she would feel if he were unfaithful to her. He replied blithely that she would never know. Though family relationships in the French Caribbean seemed to be more orderly (for want of a better word) than in the English-speaking islands (people had fewer children preferring, according to Bertrand, to save up for a house or a car), the same apparent ease about sexual matters prevailed – as well as the same careless disregard for women's feelings. I had rarely seen any women in the bar of La Vague – Rose-Helène was the obvious exception and she and Rico had no children; the men came and went as they pleased.

Theo's friend's house was in the heart of the rainforest, high up in the mountains near the 1930s observatory which faced – and observed – the volcano. We took a short cut along a steep, narrow, bumpy road full of pot-holes and loose stones. On either side tall grass and bamboo pressed in. The jungle hissed and steamed and gave off a warm rich scent, redolent of fecundity and rotting vegetation. The greenness was overpowering.

Suddenly, Theo made a sharp left turn up into a driveway so steep as to be almost vertical. I got out of the car, narrowly avoiding a mass of cowpats; startled by our arrival, the animal responsible blundered off into the bush and we went into the house. As the door opened, I heard a screech and a bundle of matted fur flashed past, disappearing into the shrubs by the front door. The house belonged to two *métropolitain* psychiatrists who worked at the mental hospital at Colson and had gone back to France for a couple of months. Their cats appeared to have become completely feral.

The house was an amazing mess. It looked as if the doctors had been called away at a moment's notice – presumably not the case. There were open books, papers strewn everywhere, dirty glasses and dishes in the sink, damp towels on the floor of the bathroom, clothes on the backs of chairs. No attempt had been made to pack up the place and, were it not for the quantity of dirt, you would have thought that its occupants had gone out for the afternoon. There were cockroaches on the floors and fleas in the sofa. Jagged, empty tins of cat food littered the kitchen floor. Theo made no comment – I suppose he was used, and therefore oblivious, to it, but found a bottle of white rum in a cupboard and poured a couple of drinks.

The bed in the back room had escaped the worst because it had a mosquito net draped over it which must have prevented the cats from lying on it. Moving as if in a trance, I found some clean sheets in among the clothes and put them on the bed. Then I undressed and lay down, covering myself with a sheet.

When we got up, it was late afternoon and the rain had cleared. Out of the corner of one eye I had watched the light mellow as the afternoon drew in. We seemed to have spent hours exploring a changing landscape of flesh and bone and muscle, time-travelling in a zone in which colours vary and intensify, where textures roughen and grow silky, where reality is suspended and where all is clouded by desire. I felt refreshed and alert, languorous and ravenous.

I opened the French windows and stepped out on to the verandah. It was like standing on the edge of a cliff. The hillside fell away below, down to a valley throbbing with plant life. The observatory, like an Art Deco space station, twinkled on the next hill. There was a soft breeze. The light was soft and luminous, greenish-yellow after the rain. The green of the hillside and the ferns and the palms had intensified and threw the red of the stray hibiscus blooms into brilliant relief. The birdsong seemed sweeter, louder, somehow more penetrating. A tall, single coconut palm towered over the others, solitary against the skyline.

I had not forgotten about falling in love in New York – or anyhow not completely. But inevitably, as the weeks went by, and with each new encounter, the memory receded, lost its depth. Looking back, that first intense exchange in New York fuelled all those that had followed; it had coloured them scarlet, given them, in Jamaica Kincaid's vivid phrase, a 'wanton hue'.

That evening, sitting in the bar at La Vague, dreamy and so relaxed that I felt as if I didn't have a single bone in my body, I fell into conversation with one of the *habitués*, Jean-Robert, the old *béké*. When he heard that I had spent time in Indo-China, and knew Vietnam he became very excited. He had fought at Dien Bien Phu (which is also the name given by Martiniquais fishermen to fishing spots that were out of sight of land). Jean-Robert's time in Vietnam (which he persisted in calling Indochina) had clearly shaped the course of his subsequent life. He had fallen in love with a Vietnamese woman who had disappeared in the post-Dien Bien Phu chaos. He said that he had looked for her everywhere in Hanoi but he never found her again. In 1949 a bullet had grazed his head and he had lain for twenty-four hours in a paddy field. That wound had healed, but the pain of his lost love had never abated. He said that he had never really been able to love another woman and that, were he to find her again, even though they were both over sixty, he would marry her tomorrow. His subsequent revelation that he had a three-year-old daughter by *une femme coolie*, half his age, whom he did not want to marry because he feared that, in years to come, he would be unable to 'satisfy' her and that she would be unfaithful to him, did nothing to mar the romance of his story.

Jean-Robert was not a typical *béké*. Most of them lived on the other side of the island in splendid isolation on the Atlantic coast between le Vauclin and le François. They still controlled more than half the commerce in Martinique (and more than a quarter in Guadeloupe), and this power enabled them to maintain a way of life that, as much as possible, resembled the good old days. In their Creole mansions on big estates surrounded by high walls, they kept themselves to themselves.

In the past, it was the *békés* who had argued most forcefully for separation from France – not so much out of a desire for a specifically Martiniquais identity, but because independence would free them from French control and from the effects of Schoelcher and his like, whose efforts to abolish slavery infuriated and dismayed them.

Jean-Robert may not have been typical but he still retained some *béké* attitudes. He quoted to me the old Creole adage 'Si pa ni blanc y pa ni negre', and it was clear that he regarded the men in the bar as essentially lecherous adolescents.

Of course, if there had been no whites in Martinique, there would have been no blacks but, as a justification of slavery, this hardly stood up. But the saying perfectly illustrates the strong sense of possessiveness which the *békés* feel for the island. It is,

I imagine, comparable to the way that the Boers feel about South Africa.

We sat and talked all evening, moving from Vietnam to the subject of the insatiable, and apparently indiscriminate desire, of black men for white women. He told me that it didn't matter whether or not I was beautiful, it didn't matter if I didn't look my age, what really interested Martiniquan men was that I was a white woman. I said that I thought that this was a bit sad but also that it was true. I asked him what local women thought about it. He said that they tended to ignore it because they had their men at home and they knew that sooner or later the white women would leave.

That night there was another rainstorm. I slept fitfully, occasionally waking to see the opaline moon through the clouds – cameos from the afternoon flashed before my mind's eye like scenes from a movie. In the morning, there were scores of drowned cockroaches on the stairs and my back ached. I found Rico and asked him to put a board under the mattress.

After breakfast I walked to the Gauguin museum in Le Carbet. Le Carbet is a pretty little town a few miles down the coast towards Fort-de-France and is where Columbus was supposed to have landed in 1502; it is also where Gauguin spent some months painting, in 1887 – about four years before he went to Tahiti. Accompanied by his friend, the painter Charles Laval, he had arrived in Martinique penniless. Both men had had to sell their watches, and even then they had only enough money to rent what Gauguin described in a letter to his wife as 'une case à negres'. But it seems to have been idyllic: 'Un paradis ... La mer bordée de cocotiers ... des arbres fruitiers de toutes espèces ... La nature la plus riche, le climat chaud mais avec une intermittence de fraîcheur ...' From Le Carbet he wrote to a friend, the painter Emile Bernard, that 'L'avenir est aux peintres des tropiques ...' and to the critic Charles Morice that 'L'experience que j'ai faite à la Martinique est decisive.' Martinique seems to have paved the way to Tahiti.

The museum was nothing special – Gauguin's Martinique paintings have all been shipped off to museums or private collec-

tions in Europe or North America and only indifferent repro-
ductions (which did, however, reveal a landscape little changed
since the nineteenth century) were on display. But Le Carbet
itself was charming. A sign – 'COIFFEUR Joseph LE CUR-
IEUX' – marked the entrance to the town, which is set back
from the main road and the coast, concealed by a long shell-
pink building that looked like a school. If you were driving
through at speed, you would never know that there was anything to see. Untouched by the eruption that had devastated
Saint-Pierre, little one-storey wooden houses, such as Gauguin
himself might have rented, line the narrow back streets. They
looked picturesque enough, but shabby, with peeling paint and
patched doors and windows.

Over the days which followed I continued my explorations of
northern Martinique, and Theo and I continued our exploration
of each other. I learned the odd fact here and there about him:
he was one of ten children whose mother had died of kidney
failure, aged forty-five, doubtless worn-out by childbirth. She
had met his father when she was sixteen. Theo was twelve at
the time of her death and he had assuaged his grief by writing
poetry about her. He was forty now and had been married once
– to the mother of his son, Manuel. Ornella's mother was only
twenty-four and he had no plans to marry her. He was very
athletic and went jogging – which he called 'footing' – every
morning. He was methodical, orderly and quite conventional –
he disliked it when, one day, I painted Ornella's fingernails red
and let her put on some of my lipstick. I thought it made her
look like a beautiful little gypsy, but perhaps that was exactly
what he objected to. He had modest political and commercial
ambitions. He thought that Martinique had been psychically
damaged by its dependence on France, but that its people had
become too soft to be prepared to work as hard as independence
would require. One day we drove out to the Atlantic coast,
stopping briefly in Le Lorrain, where his father had been born,
to call on one of his sisters. She wasn't home, but Clarice, her
dreamy, leggy, fifteen-year-old daughter, was asleep on the sofa,

a copy of Camus' *L'Etranger* lying open on the floor. She woke up and offered us drinks. Her ambition was to become a pathologist. We drove on down the coast through Marigot and Sainte-Anne, never losing sight of the Atlantic which flung itself at the shore as if in a fury. We stopped in Tartane, a fishing village formerly favoured by smugglers and the only settlement on the Caravelle Peninsula. There, too, the beach was wild and windy. Even Theo, a strong swimmer who had once spent six hours in the water after the boat he was in had capsized, conceded that it was 'trop mouvementé pour l'amour'.

After lunch, we set off for the ravaged house in the mountains. The drive seemed interminable though astonishingly beautiful. The road zig-zagged round tiny hairpin bends, cutting like pinking shears through gorges brimming with ferns and palms and slashed by the torrents of waterfalls which tumbled to the roadside. Against this impressive and oppressive backdrop of nature, little houses perched on the mountainside and wayside shrines to the Virgin and St Bernadette of Lourdes seemed forlorn and insignificant. Each new vista was more breathtaking than the one before and the whole expedition was fuelled by an almost-painful sense of urgency, of mounting desire. But, when we finally got there, it was nearly five o'clock and Theo had to leave almost immediately for a meeting of Médecins-du-Monde in Fort-de-France.

The squalor of the house seemed, if anything, more pronounced, more extreme. The cats, wild and terrified, scattered as we came in, sending books and papers flying and fleeing through a high open window. Theo opened a couple of tins of cat food with a huge knife and shook the contents into bowls on the floor. A couple of cockroaches scuttled forward.

In this instance, I thought, it had been better to travel hopefully than to arrive, and maybe it was a mistake to try and repeat the magic of our first encounter. But it didn't really matter. Even this too-brief, somewhat unsatisfactory, exchange served to deepen our intimacy, to confirm that we were indeed lovers.

Through my association with Theo, I seemed to have been

accepted into the fraternity of La Vague. I felt able to go behind the bar and help myself. I felt at home. At the weekend there had been a party for Alix's birthday up at a house which Rico owned in Le Prêcheur. It was on the Caribbean coast, and overlooked a long stretch of empty beach. We had gone swimming and then sat down to a late lunch, or early dinner, of roast sucking pig; Dolly, who had cooked it, proudly displayed it – curled up in its pan like a sleeping baby in a basket. As the sun fell into the sea with a final burst of scarlet, I walked along the beach; the sand was moist and gritty between my toes, the salt tightened my skin and the blissful warm air suffused every fibre of my body with a sense of well-being. It seemed to me that I felt better in the Caribbean than I had ever felt in my life.

Sunset comes early in the tropics and by six it was dark. The men started to sing and make music, improvising with bottles and cutlery and a couple of big drums that had appeared from inside the house. They sang songs that I had never heard before, songs from an unknown childhood. They sang and played for over an hour and when they had finished, someone found a Mighty Sparrow tape and we started dancing to a song called 'Man Will Survive'. No one except me understood the English words – 'The name of the game is survival . . .' – but somehow their meaning shone through to us all.

On the morning of my last day in Saint-Pierre, I woke at dawn. I had stayed up late talking and drinking, and the combination of whisky, wine and rum – as well as lack of sleep – had left me feeling fragile. The early morning sea was glassy and the little fishing-boats were trailing in after the night's work. I didn't want to leave. But I packed and sat down to wait for Theo, who had taken the key to the outside door when he left the previous evening. I couldn't get out without the key.

Theo arrived and we spent a last half-hour in bed. Then, while I checked the room one more time, he went to find me a taxi. When he came back, he brought me a necklace made of brown seeds which he had bought in the market. I put it round my neck and, clutching a bottle of rum that Rico and Rose-

Helène had given me as a farewell present, said goodbye to La Vague and the north.

Le Breton had promised to take me to see some fishermen friends of his in the south of the island. The taxi deposited me at his house in Anse Madame near Schoelcher and we drove on from there.

Le Breton's friends lived in Anses d'Arlets, a fishing village which looked out towards Le Diamant, an inhospitable mass of sheer volcanic rock, 176m high and with a circumference of not quite one mile, rearing abruptly up from the St Lucia Channel, approximately a mile from the Martiniquan coast. British seamen had christened it Diamond Rock because of its shape – pointed, faceted, like some gargantuan eighteen-carat stone, and because, 'when the sun struck its salt-encrusted surface from a certain angle, the whole rock sparkled like a fine-cut gem against the blue backcloth of the sky and sea'. During the Anglo-French wars of the early nineteenth century, the rock became somewhat improbably – albeit imaginatively – a British 'battleship', HM sloop-of-war *Diamond Rock*, under the command of Commodore (later Admiral) Sir Samuel Hood. The enterprise was so successful that, supported from St Lucia, the batteries and signal station established on Diamond Rock in January 1804, closed Fort Royal (later Fort-de-France), the principal French base in the West Indies, for eighteen months to all save the smallest vessels.

It had been no easy task to establish the base. A contemporary account records that: 'The surface of the Diamond absorbed the sun's rays until it became untouchable and only the constant dousing of men, tools and the rock face with sea water, supplied by a bucket chain made the effort [of shaping a footpath up the cliff] possible.' There was also the 'nauseating stench of bat-dung' from the rock's traditional inhabitants and the constant danger posed by the *fer-de-lance*, the deadly poisonous snake which had been imported to Martinique (and St Lucia) as a deterrent to would be runaway slaves; it had somehow found its way across the sea to Diamond Rock. (The *fer-de-lance* eventually became so prevalent that mongooses were imported to kill the snakes; they in their turn multiplied with such abandon that today they are one of the few wild mammals in the Lesser Antilles.) But the absence of swamp land in which mosquitoes could breed meant that the hospital established on the rock was so healthy – 'most excellent and well-aired' – that the sick and wounded were sent there instead of to Barbados or to Antigua.

Cannons and other weapons and supplies, including fresh water, had to be hauled to the top of the rock from boats tossing on the sea below, and for well over a year some two hundred sailors endured what one might imagine to have been a hellish existence. But they apparently enjoyed it. They could go ashore for what came to be known during the Vietnam war as 'r & r' – or alternatively 'i & i' (intoxication and intercourse). Canoes from Martinique crept over almost every night bringing fresh fish, turtle meat and fruit. In addition to the scrub and cacti with which the rock was covered, there was also, as Captain Boswall recorded in *The Capture of Diamond Rock*, published in 1833,

> an abundance of thick, broad-leaved grass, well adapted for making straw hats for the seamen . . . There was also growing on the rock . . . an excellent substitute for spinach, called by the natives *calallo*; it is much the shape of the large common dock-leaf, and turned out a most useful vegetable . . . the calallo, when boiled in large quantities and served out daily, put a stop to a heavy sick-list of scurvy cases.

And, too, the sailors had their daily grog ration.

Johannes Eckstein, an artist of German origin, who spent six weeks on the rock, wrote in a letter to a friend in England:

> A bottle of Madeira or claret follows dinner; we drink to the remembrance of our friends in England . . . warmed by the genial bowl, we shake hands, bid goodnight, retire upon the dried grass and, rolled in blankets, sleep shuts our weary

eyelids, while neither fear nor uneasiness intrudes on our repose. At night, the continual roaring of the sea below is only interrupted by the replies of watching sentinels, or the scream of the tropic bird... I behold the starry face of the heavens as I lean on my elbow, the sea stretching before me her immeasurable blue domain...

In June 1805, the French re-captured Le Diamant and the great adventure was over. Le Diamant returned to being the 'most formidable and desolate place on earth'. But its memory lives on: today there is a military base opposite it and British ships still salute when they sail past.

Hilaire, the man whom we had come to see, was out when we arrived, though a bevy of female relations were scrubbing sea urchins and extracting their eggs, which, smoked, could fetch a great deal of money in the market. Rather than hang around waiting until he returned, Le Breton decided that we should take a drive through the surrounding countryside. Away from the coconut-fringed shore where the little *gommiers* in their brilliant blues and reds and yellows were beached in rows, and the fishing-nets and *casiers*, constructed like grotesque crinolines of chicken wire and bamboo, lay like giant spiders' webs across the sand, the landscape was curiously pastoral, with gentle green downs cropped close by grazing cattle.

We stopped for a minute or two at the entrance to an enormous estate called *Charmeuse*, all fenced in. Le Breton was in his element, discovering plants he claimed never to have seen before, skipping through the flower-carpeted meadows like a mountain goat. He was an enthusiastic botanist and curiously agile for such a solid man. He was always clambering to seemingly inaccessible spots to reach a plant from which he wanted to take a cutting. His little house in Anse Madame was already brimming with successfully transplanted cuttings, culled from remote corners of Martinique, and lovingly tended in jam jars and old tin cans. He had been left a widower some years before after a long and evidently unhappy marriage in which his only child had died; now he lavished the love and attention which he might have reserved for children or lovers on his plants and his dog.

At the highest point of Morne Blanc, we stopped. It was already past noon and the sun was blazing over the countryside. Le Breton went off to inspect a rare orchid. I began to pick my way through the vegetation to look down at the view – rolling acres of green merging with the brilliant blue of the Caribbean sea, infinitesimal fragmented points of light, like shards of glass dancing on the surface. Suddenly I heard a loud irate buzzing and almost simultaneously felt a sharp pain in my forehead. I let out a shriek and closed my eyes. When I opened them again, a minute later, I saw Le Breton running down the track, pursued by a large black-and-white striped insect. In response to my cries he had come back and the infuriated insect – I must have disturbed its nest – had turned on him. He was frantically waving his hands round his head, trying to deflect its angry attacks. At last, it flew off with a final furious buzz; Le Breton walked back to me and broke off a piece of aloe and put it on the swelling that had begun to blossom above my eyes. The cool sticky green gel oozed from the plant like pus from a wound.

Back down at the shore, Hilaire had returned and brought grey weather with him. At first, he said that it was too rough to go out at all. Then he changed his mind and said that we could go and see if he had caught anything in his lobster pots but that it was far too rough to go close to Le Diamant. Le Breton didn't want to risk it so I went alone, with Hilaire and an old boy who had only a couple of stumpy yellow teeth in his mouth and looked a bit simple. The boat was called *Dieu est mon chemin* and was little more than a rowing-boat with an outboard motor at one end. A thin, hard rain was falling and each drop felt like the cruel stab of a dentist's drill. The boat went quite fast, bumping over the waves. The first lobster pot we found was empty, the second contained a few bedraggled fish and some strands of seaweed, but the third proved a pot of gold. As the *nasse* surfaced, almost as if it were an omen, sunshine broke through the cloud and bathed the sea in light.

Inside the pot, were forty lobster. Both fishermen, literally, started to jump for joy, clapping their hands, embracing each other, and me.

'C'est de l'or,' said Hilaire.

They sorted out the catch, keeping the twenty-three biggest crustaceans, and throwing back the rest to grow to maturity. In high spirits, we chugged back towards the brooding bulk of Le Diamant.

Up close the rock seemed even more god-forsaken than it had appeared from the shore. The sides were craggy and almost vertical, every foothold sprouting a lethal growth of cactus; only low-lying scrub was hardy enough to survive on its bleak surface. All around the sea foamed and boiled. Gulls and frigate birds wheeled in the air. Burned by the sun, battered by the wind, soaked by the rain, an enforced sojourn on it wouldn't have been my idea of fun, but the British sailors must have been hardier than me. Hilaire said that he had once spent a night there because he wanted to see whether, at night, it was hot or cold. It was, he said, very cold.

On the way back to Anse d'Arlets, Hilaire dived overboard to collect a white sea urchin. As he surfaced, brandishing the spiky albino in his hand, a larger boat approached us. I had noticed that we seemed to be drifting towards the rocks and had been wondering, in a rather dreamy way, whether I should do anything about it – dive into the water, shout, seize the tiller. Hilaire, suddenly seeing imminent disaster, yelled at the old man in Creole; the old man grabbed the throttle and opened it wide. And the little boat leapt forward, up the side of the bigger boat's wash wave. We hovered on top for a second, then dropped like a stone. As we fell, I flew up in the air and landed with a massive thud in a heap on the floor of the boat, all the breath knocked from my body.

The old man was distraught and kept apologising in broken French. Hilaire was furious, at the near-destruction of his boat and his guest. And I was in agony, huge bruises welling on my arms and thighs. Fortunately nothing, including my camera, appeared to be broken and, after a few glasses of rum back at

Hilaire's house, the pain receded in a haze of alcohol and hospitality. Hilaire's wife, a massive woman with a sweet toothless smile, grilled four or five of the lobsters and, in the late afternoon, we sat down to a feast. After the lobster we ate a *court-bouillon de poisson* – *dorade*, pronounced *dawade* – sea bream – poached with spices, tomato and lime. Bottle after bottle of rum and chilled red wine appeared before us and it was nearly dark when we left – Le Breton for Anse Madame and me for a farewell dinner with Bertrand, the pop-eyed *fonctionnaire*.

I would have preferred to spend my last night with Theo, and he with me, but, by the time we both admitted to this desire, I was already committed to Bertrand.

7

The Island of Beautiful Waters

She knows you become exhausted in the tropics, you lose
momentum, you become comatose and demoralized. The
main thing is to keep going.

(from *Bodily Harm* by Margaret Atwood)

The other evening I dreamed of islands greener than
dreams ...

(from *Seamarks* by Saint-John Perse)

By the time I reached Guadeloupe early the next day I was so
stiff I could barely move. The traffic into Pointe-à-Pitre from
the airport was solid and the taxi driver became near-hysterical:
'La vie n'est pas facile. Pour gagner sa vie, il faut se battre,' he
said over and over again, as the jam grew worse – then, despair-
ingly: 'C'est un catastrophe, c'est un catastrophe.'

I got him to go via American Express. I wanted to see if there
was any mail from New York. There wasn't. The window of
the travel agency which had the American Express franchise
was filled with a poster which advertised the services of AOM
(Air Outre-Mer). 'Tous Les Jours Vers Paris Pour Retrouver
Ceux Qu'on Aime'; it featured a good-looking black couple;
embracing, apparently in ecstasies at the good news.

I checked into the Bougaineville hotel – depressing, expensive,
smelling of mildew – went to bed and slept for five hours.
When I woke it was afternoon and I was thirsty. In the market,

sacks of spices were displayed on long tables under a green corrugated iron roof supported by thin pillars. There were fruit and vegetables and flowers as well but the spices seemed to be the main attraction. Well-built women in madras frocks and turbans seized tourists – or anyone white – by the arm, whispering 'Doudou, viens voir des épices. Viens voir. Doudou, seulement pour le plaisir des yeux.' Le Breton and the fisherman in Martinique had said that 'doudou' was a term of particular endearment, that it was 'plus profond que chéri' and it implied a special closeness. This had given me a secret, warm feeling when I thought of Theo who had used it in moments of extreme intimacy; but it clearly didn't have that significance here. Over the cries of the market-women 'A Whiter Shade of Pale' blared from a nearby loudspeaker, triggering some long-forgotten memory of smoking dope at a party in Notting Hill in the Sixties. In a tourist shop, I heard one assistant say to another: 'On va s'amuser aujourd'hui.'

'Avec les Americans?'

'Non, avec les voleurs.'

I turned down a side street, and asked for a beer in a bar. In Guadeloupe the local brew is *Corsaire* – *blond* or *brun*. The family who ran the bar seemed strange. The proprietor who came from Marseilles, and was of Corsican origin, and his wife, from near the French Swiss border, were short, stumpy and overweight, with squashed-in faces and blurred features. Their children, aged sixteen, fourteen, twelve and ten, had inherited their characteristics; they appeared simultaneously mentally retarded and physically advanced. Even the ten-year-old playing with her Barbie and Ken dolls had little budding breasts under her T-shirt. They were, though, all perfectly friendly and the fourteen-year-old girl told me in lengthy detail the plots of two French films about Vietnam, *L'Amant* and *Indochine*. On the shelf over the bar there was a bottle of electric-blue liquid. I asked what it was. It turned out to be yet another *punch* and they gave me a glass. Its colour had no noticeable effect on its taste.

Guadeloupe is regarded as Martinique's poor relation (and in reality, it is much poorer, though both islands have the same number of unemployed – mostly young men); it is an unsophisticated country bumpkin – as it were, boring Belgium to Martinique's dazzling France. But I preferred Pointe-à-Pitre to Fort-de-France – though the latter is generally considered the more beautiful city. Pointe-à-Pitre has a beautiful central square, the Place de la Victoire – named after the victory won in 1794 against the English by Victor Hugues, the Jacobin governor of Guadeloupe, intimate of Robespierre, who conducted a reign of terror in Pointe-à-Pitre, guillotining eight hundred and sixty-five Royalist Creoles who had sided with the British. Unlike the Savane in Fort-de-France, it did not appear to be haunted by junkies and winos, and men who urinated openly in flowerbeds.

On one side of the quadrangle was the port, *la Darse*, with a flurry of ferries to the islands and stalls selling souvenirs and spices; on another was the *sous-prefecture*, a long shabby white building with blue shutters, and an apricot-pink Deco cinema called the Renaissance. The remaining two sides were filled with little restaurants and cafés; there was a Vietnamese restaurant, Kim, highly recommended in all the guidebooks but apparently long closed, despite, on the pavement outside, a metal cut-out of an Oriental girl in swirling robes claiming that the restaurant was 'ouvert le midi'; there was La Maison de Marie-Galante, an allegedly, charming hotel (also talked up in guidebooks, also closed), and a newsagent where I bought a copy of the *International Herald Tribune* and a disposable cigarette lighter, inscribed with the words 'l'île aux belles eaux' which was what 'Karukera', the Carib name for Guadeloupe meant; (Columbus had named the island 'Santa Maria de Guadalupe de Estremadura' which was soon shortened to Guadeloupe); finally, there was the Normandie, a long, bar-restaurant which offered an 'Apéritif Musical tous les soirs' – outside there were crowds of happy-looking young people sitting on the broad pavement.

I ate a pizza down by the port and arranged with the waiter, Abdul (who came from Djibouti) that he would show me the nightspots when he finished work at ten that evening – an arrangement I failed to keep, on grounds of fatigue.

As I walked up the Rue Frébault to an early evening screening of Roman Polanski's *Bitter Moon* (not at the Renaissance, but at the town's other, less architecturally distinguished, cinema), I looked at the discreet name-tags above each doorbell: Oncle Sam, Cabinet International D'Investigations Detective Privé; Marie-Ande Albane, Psychologue Clinicien – Psychotherapeute Sexologue; the Academie d'Hotesses Euro-Caribeennes. In Pointe-à–Pitre, it seemed, every problem had a solution.

A shop called Home Sweet Home – La Boutique Anglaise displayed in its window a statue of a young black boy with a toothpaste grin, cut-off trousers, bare feet and a jockey cap holding the British flag. I had seen such statues before – in Paris – but it was no easier to like them there. All over South-east Asia, you used to be able to buy a toothpaste called 'Darkie' with a sort of black-and-white minstrel character on the tube; they recently changed the name to 'Darlie'. There was, too, the usual array of hairdressers: Coiffure Dames – Soins, Trèsses Africaines, Défrisage – Tissage.

The women in Guadeloupe, as in Martinique, are on the whole smaller and thinner than those in the English-speaking islands (which must be something to do with diet), though there were occasional massive exceptions. They are also neater and more elegant, like their 'métro' cousins, and their hair has inevitably been treated in some way. In comparison, the tourists in their shorts and T-shirts looked under-dressed and sloppy.

Earlier in the afternoon, I had met a Guadeloupean woman in a shoe shop. She looked terrific, wearing a leopard-skin print vest with shoestring straps, a long tight skirt and bronze shoes with very high heels, a gold chain round her ankle, several gold chains round her neck, and gold earrings. She was trying to decide between a pair of high black suede shoes with curved heels and diamanté trim and a pair of purple leather stilettos with bows at the heel. The heels on both pairs of shoes were about five inches high. She wanted, she said, something to go with an outfit that she planned to wear at a gala – a black mini-dress with sheer black stockings. In the end, unable to make up her mind, she bought both pairs.

After the movie, I came out into the silent town. Suddenly, as if there were a train approaching, I heard a low rumble which grew to a roar. The streets, which minutes before had been deserted, were now thronged with people dressed in white, their black faces coated in white powder or flour, running, and dancing and shouting and blowing whistles. I was enveloped in loud music – drums, tambourines – it was something elemental rather than electronic. I was forced back, pressed into the side of a building, as a large blonde doll, all dimples and curls – the sort of thing little girls dream of – was carried past on a cross, high above everyone's heads. There was no other white person in sight and I felt afraid, as disturbed as if I were inadvertently witnessing something illegal or deviant. They ran on, like a train rushing through a station without stopping, followed by urgent boys on roller-skates; then, as the sound of their passage died away, the streets fell silent again.

That night I dreamt – not of the man in New York, not of Neville or Theo – but of an old lover to whom I had been attached for years. We had parted the previous summer and I hadn't seen him since. He had taken up with a movie star – a meeting of projections.

I dreamt that he and another man were both dating a woman I knew, an editor at *Vogue*. He had also, it turned out, slept with my sister Olivia, though somehow that mattered less to me. In the dream, which seemed interminable and endlessly painful, Olivia and I were getting ready for a party at which both these men and the woman whom they were dating would be. Olivia was fussing endlessly about which dress to wear. At the party, I told my lover – my ex-lover – that I was upset. I had a whole list of complaints; that he had never taken me dancing was one. At some point, I hit him very hard. At the same time the other man seemed to be telling me about some pills he was taking to remain young. Forever young. Just before

I finally woke, I said to my lover – my ex-lover – 'Look, you broke my heart. You broke it in Sicily. Look at it. It's broken.'

The next day, Sunday, passed in a daze of pain (from my boat bruises) and misery (from my dream). I visited the basilica of Saint-Pierre, the lack-lustre interior of which (wrought-iron pillars supporting some kind of gallery) failed to live up to the promise of its large, cheerful Latin-American façade. There was no service in progress, though pinned up on a noticeboard was a long list of names of people for whom masses were to be said. The whole church was filled with bunch after bunch of pale Anthuriums. Once more in the sunlight, I watched a mother and tiny daughter out for a walk. They were wearing identical dresses which stuck out sharply from their waists in a froth of petticoats: one wore sugar pink, the other ice blue – colours of an unequivocal clarity which only nylon can ensure.

Back at the hotel I met an old Frenchman, whose quivering hands were covered in liver spots. He shook his head at me gloomily and said, 'Mais c'est une ville morte.' And it was true. Everything was closed: shops, restaurants, cafés, the market. The doors were barred, the shuttered buildings seemed blind and there was almost no one on the streets. Perhaps everyone was at home with their families eating Sunday lunch.

The following morning, before taking the ferry to Marie-Galante, I went to the beauty parlour. The beautician, a substantial woman with spectacles and a large mole on her chin, wore a low-cut, black velvet evening-gown and displayed an impressive cleavage. The client before me was a black man who, she told me, had his beard waxed once a month in order to avoid shaving. Then she applied a softening mask which had to stay on for about an hour and, mask in place, he sat in the reception area and played with her little blond son while she attended to me. As she peeled and plucked, she discoursed briskly on the independence movement. According to her, it was only those who had lived for a long time in the *métropole* who wanted Guadeloupe to be independent. They married Europeans, then returned to Guadeloupe and they were pleasurably surprised to see how the country had advanced during their absence. They wanted independence. Everyone else was apparently more realistic.

Beautified, I emerged on to the baking streets and set off to visit the Schoelcher museum. Like Bibliothèque Schoelcher in Fort-de-France, it had been specially built to house the great man's collection; in Guadeloupe it was artifacts rather than books. Tucked behind a green wrought-iron gate, and set in a palm-filled garden, complete with fountain and statue of Victor Hugues with his pants down and sitting on what appeared to be some kind of lavatory, the museum looked like a private house. It was a pretty *hôtel particulier*, painted a dusty rose-pink, with the windows and mouldings picked out in cream, and an elegant double staircase leading up to the front door. The exhibits were a mixed bag and included a collection of fine porcelain (Schoelcher's father had been a Parisian porcelain manufacturer), a death mask of Dante, a metal collar weighing four and a half kilos and a repulsive engraving of a man as a pig. Incongruous piped music filled the air (it wasn't until I was about to leave that I identified it as the theme from *The Thomas Crown Affair*).

I was going to Marie-Galante – a small, virtually round, island devoted to the cultivation of sugar cane, some twenty-five miles from the mainland – at the suggestion of Abdul, the waiter from Djibouti. He said that it was very unspoiled, 'très tranquille, vraiment Creole'. There was, however, nothing tranquil about the crossing. The sea was very rough, there were huge waves, and the boat, a sort of catamaran, like that I had taken from Dominica to Martinique, had (despite its state-of-the-art appearance) sprung a leak just over my seat. I was still too bruised from my last sea outing to risk another fall, so I sat rigid in my wet seat, feeling violently sick and longing for the crossing to end.

Saint-Louis, Marie-Galante's second port, is a one-horse town. Its only hotel, Le Salut, lies within easy walking distance of the quay, its view of the sea obscured by the *hôtel-de-ville*. There was room there, plenty of it. The only other guest was an elderly French scientist, who was studying the flora and fauna of Marie-Galante. He was on his eighteenth visit and was still finding new species. The manager, Johnny, a young man with wide, startled eyes like a fawn, showed me to a corner room on the top floor. It was simple, clean and pretty and I liked it very much. A broad balcony ran round the hotel and, from it, I could observe the comings and goings of Saint-Louis.

The quay led directly into one of the two main roads which ran through the town, past two or three grocery stores, a couple of small restaurants, the post office, the school and a large unfinished sports stadium, then on up into the hills which lay between Saint-Louis and Capesterre on the Atlantic coast. The other road, parallel to the sea, ran past Le Salut, the police station and the *hôtel-de-ville*, then on past a few rum shops and restaurants – one, Chez Raoul, looked a cut above the rest.

In the gaps between the buildings, you could see the sea – limpid, molten. Both roads led, more or less directly, to the island's capital, Grand-Bourg, merging just before the sugar-cane factory. From the sea front, the town rose in a gentle slope to a grid of residential streets, to which the inhabitants of Saint-Louis presumably retreated at night. To the uninitiated, every street looked the same: Rue Martin Luther King might as well have been Rue John Kennedy. From my terrace, I could see across the galvanise rooftops to the fields of sugar cane beyond. I walked up the road to one of the restaurants.

Over lunch I got into conversation with a Rasta who wanted to show me the sights; he said that I simply had to get up at dawn to see the sunrise at Capesterre; a Swiss, sitting at the next table, offered to come and give me a massage – for my bruises. He had been a long-distance lorry driver and said that he had made a lot of money on the stock exchange. One day, in Basle, the Swiss said, he was on his motorbike with his daughter riding pillion. As he was going through a green light at a crossroads, an Englishman in a car jumped a red light and hit him full on. He lay in the road for two hours and then spent the next forty-eight in a coma. This had taken place eighteen months ago and he had never been right since; his back and his legs pained him constantly, he had lost his memory, he had epileptic fits. The insurance company refused to pay up, because its doctor said that he had been ill (perhaps epileptic) before the accident. He had had to sell his lorry, his car and his motorbike – he could no longer drive; his marriage had broken up. In the winter, when the weather was cold, his legs refused to work so he had to go to the sun. He had come to Marie-Galante to fish. He kept his watch set at Swiss time because he said that time meant nothing in the Antilles. He said that the people in Marie-Galante didn't know how lucky they were – they got all this money from France, and sometimes they were so insolent.

As the evening drew in and the light turned soft and rosy, the hills around seemed to glow, then blur – and then seemed to almost pulsate. Across from the parking-lot, which flanked the hotel, loud reggae music burst suddenly from a little house. With a fast gear change, a battered red car pulled into the lot and a black man got out and crossed the road to Chez Raoul. He unlocked its door, disappeared inside and, minutes later, it lit up and music exploded from it; later that evening I took Johnny there for dinner.

The owner of Chez Raoul was Johnny's cousin. He had been born in Marie-Galante, in what was now his restaurant, but his mother had taken him to Toulon at the age of seven months. As a result of that, Raoul spoke French with a strong – and to me almost incomprehensible – Provençal accent. People whose first language was Creole (divine gurgling) had a sort of nasal timbre but Raoul was just gruff; he spoke almost no Creole. He was thirty-seven and had been back in Marie-Galante for ten years. When he had returned the family house was in ruins; he had had to rebuild the whole thing. He seemed to me to be different from other Caribbean men. Perhaps it was something to do with having grown up in France which gave him an edge over other local people, but I think he had something less easily definable. I suppose he was 'cool' – both aloof and hip. He made no effort to please and he rationed his somewhat ferocious charm – which, when he chose to exercise it, could be consider-

163

able. He was medium height, dark-skinned, but not black, black. He had small ears without lobes, a gap between his front teeth and his skull seemed to flow into his neck, which flowed into his body. He was slender, but intensely muscular, and moved like a big cat, seemingly utterly relaxed.

His restaurant was beautiful, it had a white tiled floor and a ceiling of split bamboo; it was surrounded by wooden shutters which could be propped open on bamboo poles so that the dining room gave immediately onto the beach; a hammock swung between two palm trees; beyond it was the sea. Saint-Louis faced west, and at sunset the water was bathed in gold. When it was dark the single lamp-post at the end of the quay cast a slender column of pale light across to the shore. Johnny and I were the only customers. There was a small, steel-grey, tabby cat prowling around. Raoul shooed it away roughly. When I protested, he said, 'Ne t'inquiète pas. Je ne frappe pas les femmes.' We ate some swordfish in a sauce of cream and sage and, when we had finished, we all climbed into Raoul's battered red car and drove through the starry night down to Grand-Bourg.

El Moana, a pizzeria-cum-bar, run by a *métropolitain* with a weak, amiable face, was full. A Frenchman covered with tattoos leant against the bar and a black woman called Nicole with a rat's-tail of a plait, wearing sexy shorts was speaking French with an accent which I couldn't place. I asked her where she came from. And she said Paris, New York, London – and now she was in Marie-Galante.

It was late when we got back to Saint-Louis. As I started up the stairs to my room, Johnny grabbed my arm, saying surely I didn't plan to leave him all on his own. I freed myself – said I most certainly was – and locked my door behind me.

The next day when I went to the beach, Johnny followed me in his jeep, but after I let him know how much this irritated me, he stopped – or seemed to stop – wanting to know my every movement. But he was a strange man and for long periods of time, the hotel was locked up with no one around even to answer the telephone. One afternoon he told me that he didn't like most people, then said: 'Can I ask you something?'

'Yes, of course.'

'You seem very nice and you appear to get on with everybody. Are you really like that or is it just because of your work?'

I didn't know what to tell him. I didn't know the answer myself.

By daylight, Grand-Bourg was just another dusty Caribbean town. Many of its older buildings had been destroyed by a fire in 1901 and, on the whole, the architecture was nondescript. Fortunately, the church, Notre Dame de Marie-Galante, has survived. Built in 1827, it has a vaulted wooden ceiling painted a bright sky-blue – almost the colour of the punch in Pointe-à-Pitre – and an elaborate marble altar with a bas-relief of the Last Supper. The stained glass windows are modern and, I thought, ugly. A long street full of shabby shops, selling shoes and postcards, and bolts of cloth, ran from the steps of the church past the little market down to the port. A building with wooden shutters and a cool interior was the domain of the *Ecrivain Public*, a Frenchwoman, who was open for business from eight to twelve, Monday to Friday, and on Saturday *sur rendez-vous*. The *Ecrivain public* wrote letters for people, mainly business letters, but she also helped with contracts and other legal matters. The *hôtel-de-ville*, a white Thirties' building, was in a pretty tree-lined square with benches for old men to doze on; there were three or four palatial *pharmacies*, all plate-glass and chrome, full of homoeopathic remedies for disorders of the blood and liver; there were also an astonishing number of elegant little restaurants. In the market I heard a woman say, 'J'ai perdu tout mon espoir.'

In Saint-Louis I met a couple of French students, Rashid and Fred. They had taken a year off from their studies to work for a fisherman from Les Saintes and were trying to save enough money to get to Venezuela. But their wages depended on the daily catch and I doubted that they would manage it. Rashid, a

Kabyle originally from Algeria, was dark, deeply-tanned and handsome in a flashy James Dean way. He was twenty-two, a business student. Fred, aged twenty, had ginger hair bleached almost white and skin that couldn't take the sun. Rashid was the leader, the one with more confidence. They were very nice, very young and had beautiful manners. I asked them if I could go fishing with them one morning and they said that they would have to ask the *patron*. That evening they came to the hotel and said that their *patron* wanted to meet me.

The fisherman, Gerard, was white, a *Saintois*, a descendant of the Les Saintes Breton fishermen who rarely marry outside their race and colour. (The rocky, arid terrain of Les Saintes had prohibited the cultivation of sugar cane and there had therefore been no need for slaves.) Gerard said that his grandmother had been black but, looking at his blue eyes and straw-coloured hair, you could not tell. He was in his late forties, though years of exposure to the sun, wind and sea had made him look older. He had been fishing off Marie-Galante for twenty-five years. But the water round Les Saintes was now, he said, all fished out; from Tuesday to Saturday he fished off Marie-Galante, then returned to his wife and family in Les Saintes for long weekends; he had built a house with twenty-five rooms there, which he ran as a hotel. His brother operated a boat shuttle service between Les Saintes and Trois Rivières in Basse-Terre. He said he had five children – all of them, according to him, splendid-looking, particularly the girls – 'Je fais des très belles nanas' he boasted; but he had never once been around for one of his wife's *accouchements*. Grizzled, bearded, muscular, with legs like tree trunks, he sat at the table in his little wooden shack, a bottle of the lethal 65% proof Père Labat white rum of the island in front of him. We had a couple of drinks and he said that I could go with them the following morning. He also said that I must have been very beautiful when I was young and that he wished he had known me then.

When the alarm went off at a quarter to five, the sky outside was as black as could be. I dressed, and, just before five, walked along the sleeping road to Gerard's house. There wasn't a soul about. The faint roar of a motorcycle in the distance, the sounds of dogs barking and cocks crowing, the pink plastic leg of a doll abandoned in the dirt, were the only evidence of life.

Gerard was up and ready and suggested that we go and get a cup of coffee in town. There was no sign of the boys, so we walked back down the road; behind the hills, towards Capesterre; a faint luminous glow was already beginning to colour the sky.

In the little café opposite the market there were already a couple of customers downing a quick *décollage* before setting out to sea. As I drank my coffee, black, strong and sweet, Raoul's brother, Baptiste, came in for a quick early-morning jolt of rum. He had the sore red eyes of a heavy drinker – what is known as a 'rumbo' in the English islands.

Back at the shack, the boys, yawning, stumbling and rubbing their eyes, were as ready to go as they would ever be. We waded through the tide, then set out in two boats: Gerard, the two students and two young, local, black men in one; a tall slim black, named Lytho, and me in the other. Gerard, in a battered sombrero and oil-stained polo shirt, his waist cinched with a broad leather belt, looked like a pirate. Lytho, in a wetsuit with a balaclava hood, looked like a Martian.

Fishing requires patience. That soon became clear. We motored out into deep water, off Grand-Bourg, and cast the net. Two boats were necessary because they trawled the net between them. The students jumped into the water and swam alongside the little buoys which held the net afloat. Gerard steered one boat and Lytho the other. One of the men in Gerard's boat put on a mask and swam ahead, driving the fish back into the long net. The two boats began far apart, then drew closer, closing the circle of the net and pulling it and its contents towards one of the boats. We repeated this five times, and in the east, beyond Capesterre, the sun began to rise. There were long periods of apparent inactivity, but it was pleasant enough to be out on the sea and to watch the day unfold and the dark outline of the island take on character and definition as the sun came up. By the time we were through, it was broad daylight. As we sat in the boat and waited, Lytho talked to me.

He talked about Buddhism, about the Dalai Lama and about mammals. He said that he liked to make 'spiritual' love, that Santois men treat their women like queens, that he adored his girlfriend – a half-French, half-Brazilian white woman – but that, at thirty-nine, she was too old to have children and she had been around; later that day I saw her (she was either lying about her age or had been to hell and back). I asked him whether you could see any whales near Trois Rivières. 'Yes,' he said; there were some calves. I asked how long the whale's gestation period was. He said nine months – just like a woman. I was surprised that it was so short (in fact, it takes between eleven and sixteen months, depending on the species) and asked why, therefore, it could take nearly two years for an elephant to come to term. He said that that was because elephants aren't real mammals – unlike whales. He also volunteered that Raoul was 'un peu lourd' – that he could be 'très gentil' but also, on bad days, 'très méchant'.

From the point of view of fishing, the expedition was a disappointment. Cast after cast yielded an almost empty net. At one point the man in the water saw a huge shoal, but then it swam out of reach. It looked as if Rashid and Fred's trip to Venezuela would have to be postponed. But, with our final throw, we pulled in a small load of silvery *orfie* (ocean gar, or needlefish); they had long pointed beaks and little sharp teeth serrated like a bread knife. Everyone looked relieved.

As we got back to Saint-Louis a schoolbus drew up and disgorged a crowd of small children by the Ecole de Voile. They rushed on to the beach, shrieking like baby birds, and began to don life-jackets, assemble tiny boats and put up sails. Then they jumped into the boats and sailed off into the calm blue, the sound of their shrill voices, drifting back across the water. Gerard sped off in the direction of Basse-Terre to sell the *orfie*.

One day I took the bus across to Capesterre.

Capesterre, on the Atlantic coast, was bathed in brilliant

white light. From a bend in the road on the hillside above it, you could see the town laid out before you, like a series of coloured boxes; beyond it stretched sea, crystalline, turquoise, magnificently transparent, up to the reef, where it suddenly splintered in a spray of white – beyond all was stormy, dark and deep blue. I liked the beach at Saint-Louis, strewn with conch shells, their livid interiors reminiscent of female genitalia – but Capesterre's Ansede la Feuillère was a beach from dreamland.

After lunch – cold red wine and *court-bouillon de dorade* – in a restaurant presided over by a fat man with no teeth – it turned out there were no buses and I stood by the side of the road in the full heat of the afternoon sun for twenty minutes – wondering how I was going to get back to Saint-Louis. Then the postman, in his Post Office yellow Renault 4, pulled up and offered me a lift.

The postman's name was Georges. We made a detour to feed his cow and her calf, and then he took me to see his house and his wife. The house was huge; he had built it on his return from Paris and they let rooms. He showed me photographs of their four children, who were aged between twenty and thirty, and he gave me several glasses of home-made *punch de coco*. His wife's name was Thérèse. She was very black and, initially, seemed rather out of it, but perked up after a couple of drinks; we had a lively conversation about AIDS. While Georges was out of the room, she told me that, on the whole, men didn't like condoms and wouldn't use them. (According to a report, which I later saw reprinted in an Antiguan paper, Caribbean men were all for the female condom: 'It should be less panic and easier on the man's nerves.')

Georges drove me back to Saint-Louis, making restrained advances all the way. I told him that I never slept with married men whose wives I knew. He looked dejected and said he could see that he had made a big mistake in introducing me to Thérèse. He said she wouldn't mind at all and started a long story designed to prove how tolerant and understanding she was. He said that when he had lived in Paris he had become involved with a young white girl. He had thought that she was over twenty-one – which was the age of consent – but actually she was only seventeen. She was mad for him, he said: she wanted to have a child by him. Her parents found out and it got ugly. Thérèse found out too, and had stuck by him, so she was unlikely to mind if he were to sleep with me.

As we drove into Saint-Louis we saw Raoul, who was getting into his car. Georges said:

'Oh, him, he comes from Marseilles. He's involved with drugs.'

That night, after dinner, Raoul came over to the hotel. I was talking on the telephone, to a girlfriend in Washington.

When I had finished, Raoul said that he had something he wanted to show me. 'And what might that be?' I said. 'Ne faîtes-pas la gamine avec moi,' he said, without smiling.

I couldn't decide what to do. Then I made up my mind very quickly and said, 'OK, let's go.'

Johnny's reproachful gaze followed me out to the car. In the car, I thought, 'This is not a nice man. This is a man who doesn't like cats.'

We got to his house. He made me a drink, put on some music and rolled a joint. Then he took off my clothes. I felt remote, detached but perhaps that was the grass. He was a beautiful man, the most beautiful, I think, that I had ever seen, with a body like a coiled spring, but cool, very cool.

Afterwards I couldn't sleep and, around three, I got up and dressed in the pitch-black room. Soon after, Raoul woke and, with perfect good humour, insisted on driving me back to the hotel. I half-expected to find Johnny waiting up for me but all was dark.

The next morning I took the bus to Grand-Bourg. The Swiss came with me. He asked what I done the night before. I said that I had gone out with Raoul. He said that he had thought of warning me against Roul but that he had figured I was old enough to take care of myself. It gave me an odd kind of pleasure, to know I had done something of which he would have disapproved.

One evening Raoul drove me up into the hills. He said, 'I'm going to show you the most beautiful place in the world.'

Away from the coast, in the secret heart of Marie-Galante, life moved at a snail's pace; I felt as if I had taken a giant step back in time. The sugar cane was still brought to the factory in carts pulled by oxen and scattered all over a radiant landscape were idyllic rural scenes which an English painter like Constable would have relished. There were wooden carts, their shafts resting on the ground; stray wheels were propped up against trees; cattle were grazing; the tall walls of sugar cane; a cloud drifted like smoke across the mountain; the light was both dark and golden. Land and sky at this time of day bore no relation to each other: one was dark, nether, hidden the other was luminous and open like a child's face. The sliver of crescent moon rising in the dusk-pink sky belonged to a time of day that was neither day nor night, too pale to survive the dark, detached and pure above the voluptuous blaze of the sunset.

Raoul's friend, Christoph, was half-German and half-Guadeloupean. He looked like an Arab, with shaggy blond hair. He lived in a wooden house that he had built himself at Etang Noire – the black lake – right in the centre of the island; it had a scented garden full of banana, hibiscus, bougainvillaea and other trees and shrubs that I didn't recognise. To the west, catching the rays of the setting sun, stood a traveller's tree, its palms splayed against the light.

Here was where Raoul came to rest, to renew himself after too many late nights, too many joints, too much rum and too many women. He was guided by something he called 'le feeling' which, as far as I could understand, was part-intuition, part-instinct, and he did exactly as he pleased, making no concessions to convention, or to the wishes of others – unless those wishes coincided with his own desires. He had beautiful manners and was sometimes very flirtatious with me – and other women – but he never made small talk, nor made any attempt to put anyone at ease. He did what he wanted and he expected others to do the same. The man in El Moana had described him as 'une force de nature'.

However, even though he followed the dictates of his moods, it didn't follow that this made him happy. As I got to know him better, I realized he had a terrible temper, which, especially when he had had a lot to drink, seemed ungovernable; there was a dark side to his nature that could completely overshadow his charming side. Also he had the constitution of an ox and could emerge, fresh and reinvigorated, after a debauch that would have laid anyone else out for a week. I would tease him, saying that he was like a vampire – the way he came alive after dark. I once asked him why his relationship with the mother of his son had broken up (in French, the word for wife, *femme*, is the same as the word for woman, so you never knew, in the Antilles, whether a man was actually married). He replied that she was very jealous, adding 'Moi, je suis plutôt aventurier.' But Seraphine, a Dominican, who worked for him in the restaurant, said that he used to hit his wife and that was why she had gone back to France, taking the child with her.

He fascinated me. It wasn't just his beauty. He exuded power and force and his apparent total disregard for almost everything was compelling. I wasn't the only one who was mesmerised by him. Everyone in Marie-Galante was. You could tell by the way they talked about him.

Christoph was a vegetarian, almost a teetotaller; he seemed to be a sort of guru, charming and infinitely patient. He made a fairly decent living as a transpersonal astrologer (his card read 'astrologie karmique, astrologie transpersonnelle') but he was also building wooden houses, which he planned to let or sell to vegetarian tourists. I asked him why I always fell in love with Gemini men and why the result was always disastrous; he asked me for the date, time and place of my birth and looked me up on his little Toshiba laptop computer.

'Your sexuality is very important,' he said. 'It is the key to you. Gemini men make love with their intellect which dazzles you but you need something earthier.'

There was nothing in my chart about marriage or children and he said that I would never have any money. I would get by, he said, but I would never be rich. Before we left, Christoph gave me a handful of leaves. When I crushed them in my hand, their perfume rose, sweet and fresh, into the air; it stayed in my bag for days afterwards.

As we drove away, I told Raoul what Christoph had said about Gemini men and he asked whether he had said anything about my relationship with men born under the sign of Libra – which he was. It was, I think, the nearest he came to making a remark which could be interpreted as romantic, unless you count catching me in his arms in a big hug and saying 'Bella,' or the time when he reproved me for saying 'coucher avec' (go to bed with). 'On ne dit pas "coucher avec". On dit "faire l'amour".'

The Antilles is full of superstition of a rather perfunctory and romantic kind. A series of postcards revealed an entire Creole astrology which worked on the same date basis as the one we used but with different symbols. Thus, Sagittarius, which I am, appeared as *ouassou* (a sort of fresh-water crayfish) and Libra as pelican or *grangouzye*.

Every time I walked to the post office in Saint-Louis, in one of those little wooden houses which were being regularly checked for *aedes Aegypti* – mosquitoes which carried yellow fever and dengue fever – dozens of houses carried a little paper notice with the words: *Campagnes de lutte contre l'aedes Aegypti*. I passed a sign which advertised a soothsayer with an African name, whose card I had found at Raoul's, and who was supposed to give you advice about love and money. (In the English islands, that sort of adviser tended to have a more religious bias – Sister Hope would appear on television, offering 'direction' and a telephone number to call.)

After we left Christoph, we drove down through the dark, over rough roads, bordered with sugar cane, to Grand-Bourg where

Raoul had been invited to dinner by a friend, a Swiss called André who owned a little restaurant near the port.

Here the atmosphere was quite different. André was a man in his forties with a big stomach who had lived in Marie-Galante for five years. He cooked like a dream (we ate a *bisque* of *ravé de mer*, then some snail-like things, followed by a *fricassée d'oursins* and finally little pots of chocolate). He made the usual jokes about English cooking – how the only decent meal you could get in England was breakfast, and so on. His philosophy of life was: 'Baiser et bouffer – c'est tout qui'il y a faire dans la vie. C'est la même chose mais quand tu veillisses, tu baises moins et tu bouffes plus.'

He told Raoul that I was 'much better than the last one'. Then he went to the kitchen to fetch yet another delicacy, calling back to me.

'Lucrèce, est-ce que tu aimes les noix?'

I heard 'noirs' and, looking embarrassedly at Raoul, said: 'Bien-sûr, je les aime.'

André reappeared with a dish of walnuts.

Marie-Galante seemed to be full of people like André, sophisticated, *bon vivant métros* who wanted to live well and avoid the rat race. But there was nothing simple about Marie-Galante. It might seem simple, basic even, but André made his *ti punch* with honey or *coulis de framboise*; he had his ingredients flown in from Paris or Geneva and had only superficially adapted to his surroundings. In fact, he had moulded his surroundings to suit him. He told me he hated black people – though I think he was just trying to provoke me; but at least he was honest. I lost count of the number of whites in Marie-Galante who began sentences with the words: 'Je ne suis pas raciste, mais . . .'

Raoul, most of whose friends were white, also had a low opinion of the local people; they drove him mad with their slowness and inefficiency. 'Les gens sont cons,' he would shout, crashing the gears. (He was a very bad driver, extremely short-sighted and often dangerously stoned or drunk. When he was stoned, he would simply drive very slowly, but all over the road. Fortunately there was hardly ever much traffic, but, if I drove, we would squabble – about how fast I was going or about the route.)

The life I was leading was Antillais and rarefied rather than Caribbean; it was quite stifling and I began to long for the vigour of the English-speaking islands. Each island was in a world of its own – or perhaps it was that each island was a world of its own – and on the French ones this was particularly so. I had bought a scrimshaw-carved penknife in Bequia, which Theo had admired, but he had never heard of Bequia. It had been hard to credit.

If it was sometimes tiring to make love in a foreign language, it was even harder to quarrel in one and the relationship between Raoul and myself was becoming increasingly uneasy. He had a strong narcissistic streak and was used to being worshipped. Ostensibly, he could be quite passive sexually (passive-aggressive as Americans say), or maybe he was just lazy, and I suppose my pride or sense of myself rebelled against the degree of abnegation that he seemed to demand. Beneath his sleepy exterior there was a barely-controlled ferocity and it was very easy to cross him. Like a big cat, he could suddenly reach out and give me a lethal swipe with a huge paw. His caresses came to seem like blows. Perhaps it was my imagination, but I was never quite sure how much Raoul liked women – and, as always with black men, I suspected that, mingled with his desire for my whiteness, there was an almost equal loathing of it.

The night before I left Marie-Galante, a journalist from Guadeloupe, an old friend of Raoul's, came to dine in the restaurant. He had been born in Marie-Galante, educated in France, and now ran a weekly magazine in Pointe-à-Pitre. He had come home for a funeral. I quite liked him; he talked about politics, the economy and the independence movement – he thought that Guadeloupe should be independent. Raoul had no help that night, and was busy in the kitchen and so, when Michel invited me to join him, I accepted. While we were waiting to eat, he suggested we might go for a walk.

The sky was a deep midnight blue, simultaneously both dark and light. The moon was hidden behind a cloud. We walked along the beach, then back past the war memorial in the square behind the *hôtel-de-ville*. Suddenly Michel stopped talking about politics and said:

'Sois gentille avec moi. Pourquoi tu n'es pas gentille avec moi?'

I wasn't aware that I was being anything other than *gentille*, but it was immediately obvious that he meant something else. We returned to the restaurant, and throughout dinner he continued to stare pointedly and aggrievedly at me as if I had betrayed him in some way. Suddenly, he jumped up and whispered something to Raoul, looking over his shoulder at me. When he came back and sat down again, nothing was right – neither the food nor the wine and, when he discovered that there was no Grand Marnier, he paid the bill and left in a hurry. Raoul commented on the speed with which he had left. I said that I thought that it might have had something to do with me.

'Yes,' Raoul said, 'he asked me whether you belonged to me. I told him you belonged to yourself.'

That night, very late, after everyone had gone and he had locked the doors and cleared the tables, Raoul and I made love in the bar. We didn't bother to undress. He pushed my skirt up round my waist and pulled my pants down. It was frenzied, extreme, and uncomfortable, more pain than pleasure, more fuel for fantasy than the stuff of easy gratification. The lights were dim and the music was loud. All evening we had been smoking dope and drinking rum and, though I didn't feel at all drunk, I did feel profoundly involved – I remember the sharp edge of the bench digging into my calves, and that I kept shifting slightly to try to get more comfortable, which did not in any way interfere with the intense excitement of the moment. I also felt curiously detached, as if my real self was floating near the ceiling and watching these two figures below; as if there were a single spotlight concentrated on the lovers – as if they/we were caught in the flash of a camera, or strobe, and as if the woman with the long red silk skirt bunched up round her waist was not really me but a stranger.

It was almost three in the morning when we came to; Raoul

cooked a huge steak for himself, then ate it. Fatigue, drink, dope and sex had exhausted me, but Raoul seemed untouched – if anything he was reinvigorated by excess.

I spent the rest of that night in a state of semi-somnolence. I never seemed to properly go to sleep. Raoul had left the radio playing softly and all night songs from my past filtered into my consciousness. I was never sure whether I had really heard them or just dreamt them. It was terribly hot and despite a pine-scented candle that was supposed to deter mosquitoes, there was one buzzing somewhere. I tossed and turned, drifting in and out of sleep. Raoul lay on his back – oblivious, relaxed.

I had to get up at dawn to catch the six o'clock boat to Pointe-à-Pitre. At five I woke Raoul. He opened his big strange eyes, said it was far too early and to wake him again when I was ready to go. Then he went back to sleep, sinking effortlessly into deep slumber. We left half an hour later and I caught the boat, with time to spare. Raoul came on board and breakfasted on black coffee and *tourments d'amour* – little coconut cakes which were a speciality of Les Saintes. I couldn't eat anything. I was not particularly sad to say goodbye to him – rather I was relieved to have survived our encounter; I was looking forward to hours and hours of sleep. Yet of all my lovers in the Caribbean, Raoul was by far the most compelling and the way in which, even now, he enters my dreams – more often than not as a malignant presence – is a testament to the force of his personality and to the havoc he wreaked on my subconscious.

After Marie-Galante, I lost it. I felt Guadeloupe slipping away from me like water draining down a plug-hole.

I took a long bus ride, through rain-sodden villages, to Basse-Terre, Guadeloupe's torpid administrative capital. The bus made many stops. Every time someone wanted to get off, a sort of police siren sounded. In Basse-Terre I carried my ludicrously heavy luggage up a steep hill to a dismal *pension* facing the *préfecture*, where I was shown to a damp underground room, seething with mosquitoes. The bed-linen was clammy to the touch and covered in what I hoped were rust stains. I walked back down the hill into the town – shabby, charmless, frustrating – and called my American lover from a call-box in the main street. The conversation was a failure. There were a couple of dogs barking and howling in a nearby garden. I couldn't hear much of what he said, and what I did hear didn't satisfy me. Our worlds had grown too far apart. I had gone through too many changes in the Caribbean. I might as well have been calling from Mars. The telephone card ran out at a particularly bad moment. I had a beer in a dreary bar and, when I had finished my drink, I went to queue for an hour in the post office to buy another telephone card so that I could ring New York again and try and make matters better. I succeeded only up to a point, but it was all in my head anyhow. He had always been a fantasy figure and now I was simply finding the fantasy more difficult to sustain.

I felt dizzy and sweaty as if I were catching a cold or had a fever. I thought I might be getting my period. I walked back up the hill, stopping in a bookshop. To my surprise there were two copies of Madonna's *SEX* (in a bookshop in Pointe-à-Pitre. I had asked whether they had any books in English. They had one, she thought, said the sales girl, and disappeared towards the back of the shop. She came back, proudly bearing a copy of *Macbeth* with a dual-language text). But the people of the French Antilles showed virtually no interest in learning or speaking English – though Raoul had thought it a great joke to say 'Yes, Mees' to me and correct my French.

Sex, however, was a different matter and the bookshop owner had managed to sell five copies of *SEX* at 300ff each. He said that the people in Basse-Terre, whom he described as *petits-bourgeois*, hated the people in Pointe-à-Pitre. He invited me to come out with him but I felt depressed and returned to the hotel and went to lie down. The cumulative effects of squalor suddenly all seemed too much: the smell of damp, the cold water in the bathroom, the dripping tap, the mosquitoes, the rust-stained sheets. My room seemed unbearably sordid and I went back upstairs to where the *patronne*, Madame Balthus, was eating her dinner and watching television. I joined her and she told me about the 1976 earthquake when Basse-Terre had been evacuated for five months. Her husband had become ill during the earthquake and died. 'Ça m'à laissé une bonne souvenir,' she said gloomily.

I spent a sweaty night, tossing and turning in my damp cave, dreaming all manner of dreams. I dreamt about the man in New York, woke at three, went back to sleep, dreamt about my ex-husband, about a newspaper I used to work for, about lovers in politics and that my cat had died. I woke again and went back to sleep once more. This time, in the bleak hours before dawn, I had a dream about Raoul. I dreamt that I went to see him, that he was being kept naked in a small cage and women paid to have sex with him. When he saw me, he said: 'Parce que c'est toi, tu ne dois pas payer.' I woke up seeping blood.

The next day I went to church with Madame Balthus. The service – French Evangelical – lasted three hours. The preacher, who claimed to have seen the light with a whole group of other people when a big evangelical mission had come to Pointe-à-Pitre, gave a sermon on the benefits of baptism. When communion in the shape of little bits of brown bread was brought round, Madame Balthus prevented me from partaking on the grounds that I wasn't a member of the church. Many people stood up and declaimed about the power of prayer. One woman told a story about praying for a car. It took seven months but eventually God sent her one.

In Matouba, in the hills above Basse-Terre beyond the wealthy suburb of Saint-Claude where the *békés* live, it was pouring with rain. I stood on a wet hillside and telephoned Gina in Trinidad. She said the sun was shining there and asked when I was coming back. Then I called Raoul who said I should have stayed in Marie-Galante and asked if I had prayed for him.

As the bus pulled into Pointe-à-Pitre, there was a dead tabby cat lying in the middle of the road, one eye spilling out of its socket. That evening, in the Normandie, I met a Frenchman who kept buying me drinks. His wife was in La Rochelle in France and he said that he couldn't wait to get back to her. He said that the Antillais were only interested in four things: clothes, jewellery, cars and white women. Behind the musicians, a man opened his flies and peed into a bush. It made me angry. I thought, men always think that because they can pee standing up and with such ease, they have a God-given right to do it anywhere.

The Frenchman was still talking and scribbling illegible *billets-doux* in my notebook. I had more or less stopped listening to him but I sat up when he said: 'J'aimerais t'épouser.'

I said, 'But what about your wife? You've just been telling me how much you miss her.'

He shrugged and said, 'Oui, mais je n'ai jamais recontré une femme comme toi. Tu es ce qu'on appelle en Français une "barracuda".'

I thought, not for the first time, that men will say *anything*.

8

More Than Paradise

I must declare
My heart is there
Though I've been from Maine to Mexico...
(from Jamaica Farewell)

Oh Antigua! If the Caribbean is the Wild West, Antigua is its most distant frontier. I loved Antigua from the beginning.

The Spanish Main, which the guidebook had described as 'an English-style pub', was like no pub I had ever been in. A former residence of either the American consul or the British Ambassador (no one seemed quite sure which), it was a big rambling colonial mansion, opposite the recreation ground on the corner of Independence Avenue and St Mary's Street, with a rabbit-warren of passages and cubbyholes. Though it was shabby, the rooms were large and well-proportioned and the corridors wide. It had neither hot water nor air-conditioning but it was cheap. My room was at the front, on Independence Avenue, and every morning I was woken up as soon as it was light by the noise of the trucks rumbling by, their exhausts backfiring and popping, smoke pouring into the steamy dawn.

Though I was more than ready for the rough-and-tumble of the English-speaking Caribbean, I was not prepared for the almost total immersion in white culture that I got at the Spanish Main. It was true that Denise, the Jamaican lunch-time barmaid, was black. So was Cora, the cleaner, a massive Antiguan woman, and Sylvia, who worked in the customs office during the day, and came to waitress several nights a week. But everyone else was white and English. There was Ruthie who had been knocking around the Caribbean for years. It showed on her face, the years of sun and drink and hopelessness. She was a heavy smoker who would down a schooner of lager for breakfast. There was Beryl, short, stocky, with a bosom the size of a hippopotamus's rump, and a voice which was both booming and genteel, like a grotesque parody of the Queen (whom she would sometimes imitate). Often the first thing I would hear in the morning, over the sound of the trucks, would be Beryl bellowing in the kitchen. Pat, the manageress, came from Hastings in Sussex and, like Ruthie, had been in and around the Caribbean for years. Unlike Ruthie, she wasn't a fallingdown drunk. There was Nicky, the barman, a hairdresser with a pony-tail from Leicester, who was able to explain the technicalities of dealing with black people's hair to me. There was Steph, his niece who also worked behind the bar and who also came from Leicester. There was some kind of link between Antigua and Leicester and many Antiguans who went to England ended up there. Nicky and Steph were so near in age and so similar in appearance that they were more like brother and sister than uncle and niece. Steph's boyfriend, Manuel, was Chilean and didn't speak much English. When Nicky had gone to pick her up at the airport, Manuel had accompanied him and they had been going out together ever since. There was Steph's father, Kevin, married to Nicky's sister who was back in Leicester, and a chubby man called Dave who worked with Kevin in construction. There was Rob who sometimes cooked and ran the place if Pat was away. Rob had been born in Antigua but had managed to remain totally English.

These were the hard-core, who made no apparent concessions to their surroundings. On slow evenings – and there were plenty of these – they played Scrabble in the bar and, if a black face dared show itself, heads would turn and it would be greeted by a steady collective stare.

The only people who appeared oblivious or, at least, impervious to this pronounced lack of interest and unspoken, if not actual, animosity were Denise's admirers who came in at lunchtime and were, anyhow, mainly policemen and a strange young man called Joshua who seemed a bit daft. He took a great and not very welcome liking to me and was always trying to flirt. He had a confident line in chat and would say things like, 'Make me a promise. Think of me.' I ignored him as best as I could but he took to hitting me on the hip or bottom to attract my attention. He seemed awfully young and finally I said: 'How old are you?'

'Twenty-two,' he answered.

'Well, I'm forty so why don't you just fuck off?'

But he didn't pay much attention.

By the time I discovered that the Spanish Main was known locally as 'South Africa' or 'Durban', I was too entrenched to move. Anyhow I didn't know where else to go. Rodney at the Hemingway Café ('This West Indian styled wooden building, built in the early 1800s, is a perfect example of the kind of place frequented by the celebrated author' said the menu) on St Mary's Street said that the Spanish Main 'sucked' and why didn't I stay at a place called Joe Mike's. I walked past it a couple of times, but it looked pretty rough, and I couldn't afford any of the smarter beachside places. I liked being in town and I couldn't help being fascinated by the slice of English life that the Spanish Main embodied. It even provided 'Real English Fish & Chips – Cod & Chips Served Authentically In English Newspaper' and other classics of British cuisine: shepherd's pie; breakfasts of sausage, egg, baked beans and chips; jam roly-poly; spotted dick; trifle. Some nights Rob cooked, experimenting with curries and Thai dishes, and the food was better, but the kitchen always smelt of frying and old grease.

It remained a somewhat embarrassing address and, whenever anyone new asked me where I was staying, I always felt obliged to make excuses.

One evening a week, Barry performed a cabaret. Barry

worked at Newquay in Cornwall in the summer and in Antigua in the winter. His wife, Nicole, was a fortune-teller who said that she had a lot of clients from British Airways, as well as some local people who wanted to know how to keep their boyfriend or girlfriend faithful. And then there was a floating population of hard-drinkers, Americans and English, who were trying to scrape together a living – not very successfully as far as I could see. There was Vince who had been a bartender in Philadelphia for twenty years; he had come to Antigua to start a restaurant which hadn't worked out. He now had a job as a soft-drink salesman, working for Russ who was from Florida and had brought his wife and two daughters with him. The wife had total alopecia. There was a Scot who called himself an artist and spent every penny on drink. I got quite used to seeing people drinking at – or rather for – breakfast. There was a woman who had a mink farm somewhere in North America but claimed to be an artist when she was on the island. They were all perfectly friendly but seemed to have decided to mix only with other ex-pats. It was as if they only felt safe with their own kind.

One evening I came back early. Down the road from the Spanish Main there was a little Chinese restaurant where I liked to go for a bowl of soup in the evening. Barry was in full swing in the bar and it was obvious that I wouldn't get any sleep if I went upstairs to bed, so I thought I might as well take the opportunity to catch his act. He was surprisingly good: best, I thought, when playing hard-driving rock-and-roll on his electric guitar. There was a robust vulgarity to his performance: jokes about black men having big cocks and the difficulties of finding condoms large enough to fit them went down very well with his all-white audience. But there was an edge to everything he said, and he liked to pick on his audience. When a black man wandered into the bar, he played a reggae song, ostensibly in his honour, but his parody of Caribbean English was offensive and the man quickly left. As soon as he had gone, Barry said: 'And let's not forget the Native American' and played 'Running Bear'.

Running Bear loved little White Deer
with a love that was brave and true . . .

That night there were a couple in the bar who, even by
the flotsam-and-jetsam standards of the Spanish Main, were the
absolute dregs of humanity. The woman, a Canadian, was
almost albino with white eyelashes and eyebrows and hair
braided into unbecoming, cornrows. Her lover was Dutch,
good-looking enough, but his face coarsened by alcohol. His
muscular arms were covered in tattoos and he wore a T-shirt
which said: 'Sail Naked – St Martin'. They were both very
drunk and getting drunker by the minute. Suddenly, a fight
erupted between them. She was hanging on to his arm, evidently
pleading with him about something. He pushed her off her bar
stool on to the floor and started to kick her. Nicky and Rob
intervened and picked her up. The man wouldn't speak to her
or even look at her but continued drinking furiously. After a
bit, he went outside, leaving her sitting at the bar. I noticed that
her shoulders were heaving and, in a moment of misplaced
sisterly feeling, went over to try and comfort her. I succeeded
– in that she stopped crying – but everything she told me
revealed a dreary pattern of abuse and alcohol. Soon she had
cheered up enough to weave over to Barry and grab the micro-
phone. It was sad and pathetic and embarrassing all at once.
When the evening finally ended around one, it emerged that
she had no money and that the Dutchman had disappeared.
Rob put her in a taxi and paid for it.

The next day the Dutchman came back and paid their bill.
About a week later, he came in with a black woman (whom
Denise thought was a hooker) whom he introduced as his
fiancée.

The first thing I noticed about Antigua was the number of
tourists (the island which had a population of approximately
sixty-five thousand accommodated over two hundred thousand
tourists a year). They poured off the cruise-ships on Thursdays
and flooded the streets of the capital, St John's. One morning,

The Weather Prophet

a few days after arriving in Antigua, I got up and walked out on to St Mary's Street. Something was different. I couldn't work out what it was at first. Then I realised that I couldn't see the sea. At the bottom of St Mary's Street were the duty-free tourist complexes of Redcliffe and Heritage Quays (old warehouses and slave-holding areas now transformed into restaurants and duty-free boutiques for tourists where everything was charged in US$); their location meant that the first thing the tourists encountered when they disembarked was an opportunity to spend money. You could buy postcards with a photograph of Redcliffe Quay and the consumer motto 'Shop till you drop in Antigua'. Beyond lay the sea and the deep-water harbour. That morning the harbour was completely filled by two massive cruise ships which obliterated the horizon. This, I discovered, happened every Thursday.

Once the tourists had struggled free of the smart shops – the Guccis and Loewes, the Columbian emeralds, the tobacco and liquor stores, the electronic goods and the perfumes – they got to the little souvenir stalls. These were a depressing sight. I saw a T-shirt saying:

> Where the Hell is Antigua?
> Over here in Paradise

In the Body Shop, they sold a postcard which read: 'Messy Mongoose thanks you for contributing to a cleaner, greener Antigua' and showed a cartoon of a sunglasses-wearing mongoose in a hammock throwing a banana skin into a rubbish bin marked 'Don't Mess with Antigua Protect Our Environment'. In fact, the streets of St John's could have done with a good clean-up and every time it rained the air smelled of sewage.

It was a pretty enough town, built on a gentle slope up away from the harbour, dominated by the splendid nineteenth-century cathedral of St John's where, one Sunday, I attended a mass baptism of nine tiny babies. The sermon was as usual all about family values but there was not a father in sight. There were a few fine buildings like the austere grey-stone Ebenezer

Methodist Church on St Mary's Street and the museum, formerly the court house; but the town had suffered two major fires in its history which had taken a predictable toll. The years between 1833 and 1843 were a chapter of disasters: 1833 – a severe earthquake and severe drought; 1835 – an epidemic of yellow fever and a severe hurricane; 1837 – a very severe drought; 1841 – St John's destroyed by fire on 2 April; 1843 – a severe earthquake on 8 February. An advertisement for the New India Assurance Co. (Trinidad & Tobago) was a reminder of the frailty of Caribbean life: '. . . General Insurance Including Fire, Hurricane, Explosion, Riot & Strikes, Earthquake . . .'

There remained, though, dozens of pretty little wooden houses painted in the weather-faded colours of the Caribbean palette. When the sun shone, it was easy to ignore the broken pavements and gaping sewage drains and, at twilight, the town was bathed in a forgiving glow which seemed to conceal the worst ravages of neglect and time. But, wherever the rewards of Antigua's comparative prosperity were going, it was not into the infrastructure of its capital, where it was not unusual to see rats scurrying through the gutters. There were, however, dozens of new cars on the streets, Mazdas, Nissans and Toyotas, which all looked as if they had come straight from the showrooms.

Antigua, the self-styled 'Heart of the Caribbean', seemed to exist on two levels. There was the real Antigua, the Antigua of Liberta, Bethesda, Crosbies, Cedar Grove, remote little villages scattered throughout the countryside, and of St John's, which, despite its shopping precincts and souvenir stalls, retained a certain earthy charm. And then there was the fake Antigua, the tourist Antigua, the Antigua of Sunset Cove ('where love is the setting'); Runaway Bay; Halcyon Cove; Blue Waters; Sandals (a couples-only all-inclusive resort); Harmony Hall, and so on. How people could say these names with a straight face I couldn't imagine. Places like English Harbour, Nelson's Dockyard and Shirley Heights had once been real, but were now reduced to the level of theme parks. If you rented a car, the map that was provided with it was almost exclusively of the fake

Antigua, as if all anybody would ever want to do would be to drive from resort to resort.

Sometimes, a positively surreal 'element would creep into everyday life: such as when Island Provisions 'ideally located in Antigua, the crossroads of the Caribbean', would suggest, via the medium of television, that viewers buy Norwegian smoked salmon and Beluga caviar for their 'discriminating guests'. The radio in turn proclaimed that, 'Once upon a time the fashion-conscious man would travel to Europe or Miami to do his shopping.' Really. Most ordinary West Indians could barely afford the LIAT fare to Dominica. But their worries were over. Handy, local Saint Maarten was now *the* place for shopping.

But it was on the fake Antigua that the country's economy depended. Antigua, more than any other Caribbean island, seemed to gloss over the discrepancy between fact and fiction, between the realities of island life and the visions of the tourist mirage. This extract from a Speedbird brochure captured the essence of the Caribbean dream:

> Close your eyes. Imagine an island they say wears a pearly
>   necklace
> made of 365 white sandy beaches. This is Antigua.
> Imagine a windsurfer with a butterfly sail skidding
> across a turquoise sea on warm trade winds. This is Antigua.
> Imagine a land where buildings seldom rise
> above the tops of the coconut palms. This is Antigua.
> Imagine drifting in a glass-bottomed boat
> over one of the eighty historic shipwrecks. This is Antigua.
> Imagine an island that still remembers
> the glory of harbouring Nelson's fleet in 1790. This is
>   Antigua.
> Now turn that dream
> Into reality.

Antigua did have all those things: the white sand beaches, the warm turquoise waters, the shot-silk sunsets, the balmy climate, and some very beautiful old churches dotted around the country in remote corners where the tourists would never find them. It also had a government notorious for its corruption. Under the leadership of Vere Cornwall Bird, Antigua had, according to *Modern Caribbean Politics*, 'acquired the regrettable image of being the most corrupt society in the Commonwealth Caribbean, hosting a notorious amorality from top to bottom'.

V. C. Bird was born in St John's in 1910. Like Eric Gairy of Grenada and Michael Manley of Jamaica, he had risen to prominence through the trade union movement. By the 1940s Bird was already extremely powerful, though it was not until 1951, when Antigua was still under British rule, that his reputation as the 'Father of the Nation' was created.

According to local legend, one afternoon, under a tamarind tree, out near the remote village of Bethesda in the west of the island, he confronted Alexander Moody-Stuart, the managing director of Antigua Sugar Estates. In a speech which has passed into Antiguan folklore, he told the planter that, until decent wages were paid in the canefields, the workers would go on indefinite strike. 'We will eat cockles and the widdy widdy bush. We will drink pond water,' he is supposed to have said. Moody-Stuart laughed in his face and replied: 'I will crush you into subjection. I will beat your head against a wall.'

How much of this was apocryphal and how much actually happened is by no means clear, but this was the story that Bird told, and it is what many Antiguans believe. There is a tamarind tree on the road to Bethesda – I saw it – and certainly after a bitter strike which lasted six weeks, Moody-Stuart caved in. That year, led by Bird, the Antigua Labour Party (ALP) won all eight seats on the legislative council. From then on, through the various constitutional stages before Independence in 1981 and up to the present day, Bird, 'your Queen's favourite politician', has, apart from five years in opposition, dominated Antiguan politics, either as Chief Minister, Premier or Prime Minister.

V. C.'s two eldest sons, Vere Jr. and Lester, have also played major roles in Antiguan politics since the early 1980s. Both are lawyers, and both have held a variety of cabinet posts (in his time, Lester has been Foreign Minister, Minister of Tourism and Immigration, of External Affairs, Planning and Trade, while Vere Jr. has held, among others, the offices of Minister of Public Utilities, Communication and Aviation, which last earned him the nickname of 'Runway Bird'). Their alleged involvement in many of Antigua's scandals has contributed to the country's reputation for corruption.

Vere Jr.'s most notorious escapade was the 'Guns for Antigua' scandal, in which a large cache of guns and ammunition was discovered in December 1989, during a raid on the farmstead of a Medellin drug baron; the arms were found to have been sold by the Israeli Defence Ministry to the 'Quartermaster General of the Antigua and Barbuda Defence Force', shipped from Haifa to Antigua and thence to Panama. There was no such person as the Quartermaster General in Antigua, and an independent commission of inquiry – requested by the then-Governor-General, acting in accordance with the advice of Cabinet and led by Louis Blom-Cooper Q.C. – discovered that the original plan, masterminded by Maurice Sarfati, an Israeli businessman then resident in Antigua, had been for the establishment of a military training-school on the island, a school which would train mercenaries for the private armies of the Medellin drug cartel. But it became known that Israel was at the same time assisting South Africa in the manufacture of a nuclear bomb. This seems to have made even the normally tolerant Antiguans feel that an arms deal with the Israelis would be unacceptable, and the guns were diverted to Colombia.

Vere Jr., then Minister of Public Works (though he also adopted the title of Minister of National Security for this adventure) was heavily implicated in the affair. As Blom-Cooper put it in his report to the inquiry, '...he [Vere Bird] was a conspirator in the plot'. Although he was stripped of his ministerial position (Blom-Cooper recommended that he 'should not hold any public office again'), he remained a member of parliament and a key player in the colourful world of Antiguan politics, confounding Blom-Cooper's naïve prediction that he would become 'both politically and socially outcast in Antigua'.

Lester, who had called for a full public inquiry into the matter, resigned from the government, ostensibly in protest at Vere Jr.'s involvement. He set up an office of 'government in exile' and temporarily joined forces with Tim Hector, a left-wing activist who had founded the Antigua Caribbean Liberation Movement and was editor of the weekly *Outlet*, Antigua's only opposition paper (on its twenty-fifth anniversary, under the title ran the words 'Twenty-five years of trials, tribulations and undaunted dedication'), and the government's most outspoken critic. This improbable alliance lasted five months before Lester found the distance from the seat of power too hard to bear and returned to the fold.

But, corruption or no corruption, compared to St Vincent or Dominica, Antigua is rich. There is relatively low unemployment and the standard of living is comparably higher. Antigua is a success story, but its successes are based on greed, intrigue, corruption and complicity in all manner of misdemeanours. Almost everyone in Antigua owes their livelihood either to the government or to the tourist industry, and ministerial involvement (in the shape of bribes and kick-backs) is held to be one of the reasons why Antigua has such a developed tourist industry. 'Antigua is the prime example of an economy now highly dependent on the sector [tourism] largely by choice, where other sectors have deliberately been downgraded,' reads a recently-published report on Caribbean tourism.

Antigua has even managed to incorporate tourism into its national flag, designed in 1967 by Mr Reginald Samuel, showing the sun rising or possibly setting, against a black background with a band of blue, then white, narrowing to a 'V' and bordered on both sides by patches of red. The sun symbolises 'the dawn of a new era'; red 'the dynamism of the people'; black 'the soil and African heritage' and gold, blue and white 'together represent Antigua's tourist attractions – Sun, Sea and Sand'. The 'V' 'depicts the symbol of Victory at last'.

Almost all the hotels are foreign-owned and they were among

the fanciest I had ever seen. The roads, however, were among the worst (almost on a par with Cambodia), but that didn't matter, because few tourists ever left their resorts. Though one week the *Outlet* printed a letter from an Anna Garcia in Florida complaining that, 'The roads that one has to travel are a disgrace and a burning shame. The pot-holes are akin to ravines in some areas. Those little old men patching the roads with their shovels make the situation even more laughable. I hate to tell you this, progressive Antigua, but no one repairs roads like that any-more.' (These sorts of repairs were known locally as 'sugar-cake', after a cake made of coconut, sugar and water.)

One of my favourite television advertisements showed a series of Nissan jeeps while a voice-over announced – with no percep-tible trace of irony – 'Hadeed Motors proudly present the surviving heroes of the Antigua roads.' One afternoon I went out to Runaway Bay for a swim. As we bumped along the road to the beach, I said to the taxi-driver: 'The roads are not too good.' 'Not too good!' he answered, 'they're pure shit, that's what they are. Pure shit.' But he was glad that the rain had stopped. Rain was bad for tourism. (It was Thursday, the big cruise ship day, and an opportunity for taxi-drivers to make some money showing tourists the sights.)

'The tourists, they vex, man, if it rain.'

Rain might be bad for tourism but it would have been good for the land. Unlike the volcanic islands further down the Lesser Antilles chain, flat little Antigua suffered badly from drought. It had been ideally suited to the growing of sugar cane, which had made it the most productive of the Leeward Islands, but that had been its only crop. Its bone-dry climate was, however, both one of the main reasons for its popularity with tourists and *the* main reason for its dependency on tourism, and what was good for tourism was good for Antigua. Tourism had undoubtedly played a major part in sharpening black/white relations. St John's was the first place where I was addressed as 'white girl'. One day some black youths downtown suggested I take their photograph. When I declined, one of them said: 'That's right. No black people in your photos,' and they walked off, chanting, 'Racist, racist.' There was a daily radio phone-in called *Talk To Me* and a favourite complaint of callers was about how tourists were monopolising the best beaches and that to reach the beaches, which were public property, local people had to negotiate the often-guarded entrances to resorts, to state their business and so on. So although, theoretically, anyone could go to any beach, it was often too much trouble. One caller complained that 'You got to beat up a security guard to get through.'

The reverse side of that particular coin was that, as a white woman, you were very likely to be bothered by any young black men who had managed to get on to the beach. One afternoon at Runaway, I was approached by one who told me that he had previously enjoyed a very successful relationship with a white woman. I fell back on my old standby and said that I was too old for him.

He looked momentarily discomforted, then rallied and said gallantly:

'But I prefer older women. They are more sensually experienced.'

'That's very kind of you,' I said, 'but I do not prefer younger men.'

Further ironies were available to anyone prepared to look for them. One morning I took a bus from down by the market across the island to English Harbour and Nelson's Dockyard. As we drove out of town into the countryside, we passed a sign saying, 'Speed Traps On This Road Speed Limit.' The road was so full of pot-holes that speed traps were unnecessary – no one, except for the determinedly suicidal or those hell-bent on destroying their vehicles' suspension, would dream of travelling at more than 30 m.p.h. As the bus turned right towards Nelson's Dockyard we passed two more signs. One read: 'Righteousness exalteth a nation but sin is a reproach to any people'; the other, 'Cocaine – just one sniff can make you stiff.' Once again Antigua was hedging its bets.

English Harbour, 'one of the most infernal places on the face of the globe', according to an eighteenth-century account, was set up as a Naval Yard in the eighteenth century to cater locally for the basic needs of warships. Once it was 'the grave of Englishmen', where 'the moral state . . . was deplorably wicked, the Sabbath [was] unknown' and 'when warships anchored, immorality of the worst description was perpetrated'; now it had the unenviable reputation for being 'the heart and soul of the drug world in Antigua', as well as the venue for Antigua Sailing Week and the Wet T-shirt Contest. As a young captain, Horatio Nelson was stationed there in 1784; and the dockyard was named after him.

Nelson's Dockyard, 'the only existing example of a Georgian Naval Dockyard in the world today', was now a National Park and a sophisticated small complex of shops and restaurants. A burly black man with pink polish on his fingernails sold me a ticket. Once through the gate, one first passed a maze of tacky souvenir stalls to emerge, as if from a fetid tunnel, into the dockyard proper with its fine old buildings: former officers' quarters, stores, blacksmith's workshop and so on transformed into craft-shops, galleries and a nice-looking hotel. A magnificent set of stone pillars were all that remained of the boat-house. Inside the museum, the old Admiral's House (where no admiral had ever lived), the usual mish-mash of exhibits prevailed: photographs of Princess Margaret and Lord Snowdon on their honeymoon; an invitation to Nelson's funeral; a replica of the marriage certificate of Nelson and Frances Nisbet; Nelson's tea caddy.

Soon after arriving in Antigua, I went to see if I could find a copy of Jamaica Kincaid's *A Small Place*. Kincaid, now based in Vermont, comes from Antigua, and the book is a scathing indictment of what has happened to the island as a result of colonial rule and the policies of the Bird regime. In the bookshop on St Mary's Street, there were other Kincaid books. I asked for *A Small Place* and was told that it wasn't available on the island. Seconds later an argument broke out about Kincaid. One man said that she shouldn't have written 'that way' about her mother in *Annie John* (her first novel). I said that since the book was a novel it should not be taken literally. The owner of the bookshop joined in and the argument was still going on when I left.

I finally did get hold of a copy of *A Small Place* (sent, via Federal Express, from New York) and took it to read over lunch in Hemingway's. Rodney (who had tried to steer me away from the Spanish Main) saw me reading it and promptly launched into a diatribe against the book and its author, whom, he claimed, wasn't an Antiguan at all. On another occasion, when Kincaid's name came up, the person to whom I was talking told me with unmistakable relish that Kincaid's real name was Eileen Potter, adding that she had 'intelligence and a psyche, two things that are no good to her here'.

A Small Place is a disturbing – and compelling – book; it was particularly disturbing to me because it revealed a loathing and suspicion of white people (perhaps not a loathing of *all* white people but certainly of the former slave-owners and planters, of the past colonial masters and the present tourists) which was exactly what I secretly expected every black person I met to feel. Although I thought that sort of loathing and suspicion would be, broadly speaking, justified, the idea that it might exist made me uncomfortable.

One morning I spent a couple of hours in the museum library where a reading of the archives revealed the following:

1. By 1974, 93% of the population of Antigua was black.
2. The 'salt water' slave, newly taken by force from his African homeland, suffered the hardest adjustment. The 'Creole', born into slavery in the islands, knew no other life.
3. In 1701 Major Samuel Martin was murdered by his slaves at Green Castle when he denied them their Christmas holiday.
4. The planters lived in comfort in the Great Houses attended by their household slaves.
5. The slaves lived in compounds of houses built of wattle and daub or stone with thatched roofs and dirt floors.

One black woman, an Antiguan called Savannah, who had lived much of her adult life in America, told me that, when she returned to live in Antigua, she took a job, in guest relations, in a resort. One day, a tourist approached her, accompanied by another woman. As they got close, Savannah heard the guest saying, 'You know some of them really speak quite good English' and then turning to her, said, 'Say something, dear.' She quit.

I had already noticed that, when white tourists speak to black people, they raise their voices. They would say, almost bellowing, as though, if someone was black, he was somehow also deaf: 'We LOVE your beautiful ISLAND. Everybody is SO FRIENDLY' and so on. And these were the people who meant well.

There was a white woman on the island who had a profitable business publishing magazines for the tourist industry. I had met her in the Spanish Main during Barry's cabaret; then she was so drunk that she could hardly stand, but I arranged to go out to her house so that she could talk to me about Antigua.

She lived out near Fitches Creek, in a lovely big house with an aviary in the garden. What she had to say was, however, not so lovely. According to her, blacks were 'useless – their brains had been atrophied by living too near the Equator'; there were 'no future tenses in African' (she seemed to think that only one African language exists) which accounted for the hopelessness of black people, and 'West Indians have an African mentality'; 'behind almost anything that is functioning, you'll find somebody that's white, or whitish, or Indian'; corruption was endemic and every island, except the French ones, was virtually bankrupt; black people were 'great on rhetoric but that's all'; 'they don't mind if LIAT is run into the ground so long as it is not run by a white man'; and South Africa was 'the last bastion of European civilisation'.

Later I met a white man who seemed more thoughtful than others. I told him about my conversation with this woman.

'She's the most hated woman on the island,' he said.

'Why don't they just burn her house to the ground?' I asked.

'Because black people are the most tolerant people in the world.'

I wondered. It's not surprising, I thought, if they do hate us. And I found their friendliness disconcerting. They know that they need tourism to survive and so they have to conceal their true feelings and put on these smiling faces to conceal their anger at the foreigners who only wanted their sun and sea and sand and sometimes to have sex with their men. I thought that Sartre had got it right when he wrote in *Orphée Noir*:

What then did you expect when you unbound the gag that had muted those black mouths? That they would chant your praises? Did you think that when those heads that our fathers had forcibly bowed down to the ground were raised again, you would find adoration in their eyes?

But among expatriate whites a kind of impatient paternalism was widespread. From the Swiss in Marie-Galante who had complained of the 'insolence' of the local people to the habitués of the Spanish Main, they all expected gratitude. An elderly white woman who ran a gift shop, vilified by Kincaid in *A Small Place*, told me how betrayed she felt, since 'we've done so much for these people'. She also told me confidently that Kincaid was *persona non grata* on the island.

I asked the thoughtful white man if this were true. He laughed and said, 'Nobody's *persona non grata* in Antigua. The devil could show up and he'd be given a ride into town.'

One of the most beautiful parts of the island was over on the wild Atlantic coast and was occupied by a big exclusive development called the Mill Reef Club. This had been started in the late 1940s by some rich (white) Americans who wanted total privacy in a warm Caribbean setting. The Club owned a chunk of land and had leased a further stretch, some thirty or forty acres, on a 99-year Crown lease. The total area covered about a thousand acres (on an island of 108 acres square). It was a state-within-a-state, 'a private club which took care of its members', of which there were some six hundred.

The Mill Reef Club founded the Historical & Archaeological Society of Antigua & Barbuda (HAS) and also established something called the Mill Reef Fund which is contributed to by all the members and pays for all sorts of things: scholarships, parts of hospitals, charities; it is supposed to even up the score. 'It's part of our effort to be good guests' was the official line. 'I don't know how Antigua would manage without us,' people from the Mill Reef Club would say.

The Mill Reefers couldn't understand why their presence might be resented, and the local people couldn't understand why a chunk of the island had been taken over by white people who, in their own words, did 'their best to keep the island out'. The man who said that to me wasn't particularly aware of what he was saying, its implications. But I could see both points of view, as if I were in the middle, and I could also see that neither side would ever be able to accept or understand the other's position.

I had an introduction from Jamaica Kincaid to Tim Hector, the editor of the *Outlet*, which was far livelier than the other Antiguan papers and the papers of the other islands.

Tim lived in Villa, a residential suburb of St John's not far from the capital, in a house with a lavender-coloured garden wall. A large dog wandered around the garden and Tim lay on a red sofa outside in a porch festooned with hanging plants and chain-smoked while he talked. I sat upright in a chair and took notes.

We talked about tourism (it was sometimes difficult to think about anything else in Antigua) and its effects. He said that, in Antigua, unlike in Barbados, there had been a complete transfer from a plantation economy to tourism in 1968. There had been a long history of absentee landlordism but, since the 1960s, the planter class had completely disappeared from the social and commercial life of the island. He described a black BBC producer from England waiting to be served in a hotel dining-room. After he had been ignored for about forty minutes, he made a fuss. Nobody had realised that he was a guest because 'a guest does not come in that colour'. Tourism had altered many aspects of life. For instance, a steel pan band ought to, and used to, consist of fifty or more members; now in hotel foyers you found truncated versions, with ten members playing standards like 'Island In The Sun' and 'Yellow Bird' for tourists. Lobsters used not to be a luxury and in the old days people would catch them, then grill them on the beach. Now they were reserved for the resort hotels, or flown on ice out of the country. The prevalence of Kentucky Fried Chicken outlets meant that the national dish of Antigua (that is, what most people ate most of) was now actually chicken and chips, not fungee and saltfish.

'The country is not really ours,' Tim said. 'It's just here for the tourists.'

He talked about his childhood and the way the Caribbean had changed. He said that there had been a social breakdown on the island, that nobody seemed to care about anything anymore.

'Nothing that I did as a child, my son does. Carnival used to be a simpler, more spontaneous affair. We used to call it the steel pan road festival but the local population no longer connects to it. The responses are not there any more.'

Like old Mrs Creft in Grenada, he painted a picture of an age of innocence, when pleasures were simple: the beach, steel pan, cricket ('when we heard the steel pan, we would drop bat and ball and be off to it'). Steel pan was preceded by something known as an 'iron band', because people would play any old iron.

'And when I was young, every evening at six in Barbuda, the pigeons would return and cast a shadow so you knew it was six o'clock. When I went back recently, the pigeons had been replaced by mosquitoes.'

A woman I met at a meeting of the Environmental Awareness Group told me that tourism was a twenty-four hour activity which left little time for anything else. 'We think that we're free but we're not. We have been colonised by tourism and foreign investors and, when these colonial powers get you, they have total control.' As Tim Hector had pointed out, the West Indies were not so much colonised as created by colonialism.

The traditional Christmas masquerade had been forced to become the summer carnival, because Christmas was high season and everyone was working then.

'People are afraid. Every child you talk to in the schools has a sort of hopelessness. There is no talk of building a society.'

An old woman who had a flowershop near the market said, 'When I was a child, Antigua was clean. Clean. People didn't have any money, their houses weren't painted but they were happy. Now laughter has died. There's no warmth, no friendliness. They feel a deep resentment because they've lost control of their own country. Morally, Antigua has gone to the dogs. Tourism has brought prostitution, drug-addiction and AIDS, and it is making the people lazy. The Prime Minister kept telling the people "Your children have the right to work in banks." Now he has put them back to being servants. Without Tim Hector and the *Outlet*, Antigua would be like Haiti.'

And she quoted the calypsonian who sang,

> Antigua is a democracy
> Everybody do as they please

Not everyone, though, thought that things had deteriorated. The old woman's daughter said that Antigua had 'changed out of all recognition over the last twenty years, but for the better', adding 'I'm not sure what customs they're regretting the loss of. Walking to work?'

It was like looking through the looking-glass. Everything seemed to be a question of interpretation.

A Guyanese taxi-driver who had come to Antigua twenty-five years before told me, 'V. C. Bird he created an atmosphere when everyone could have a house and a car, a vision of a nice and decent and good Antigua.'

Tim attributed the apparent widespread indifference of Antiguans to their leaders' peccadillos to apathy rather than to tolerance. One afternoon I heard a man shouting in the streets of St John's, 'People get the government they deserve.' But slogans like 'THE VERE BIRDS MUST GO', 'DEMON- STRATE AGAINST DRUGS AND GUN RUNNERS' and 'A.L.P. A DE REAL COMMUNIST' (this last was a reference to the ALP's claim that Tim Hector was a communist, he was once described in the *Workers' Voice* as 'a selfish communist destructive wolf parading like a beautiful angel who really loves the people of Antigua') were stencilled on walls all over town.

Nevertheless, the Birds had been returned to power for the past fifteen years. The opposition's performance had been consistently poor with most candidates losing their deposits. Whether the explanation for this was an uneasy combination of fear and patronage, apathy or vote-rigging – there were proven irregularities in the 1989 election, with many registered voters no longer in Antigua, or even in the land of the living – the fact remained that, after the period between 1971 and 1976, when the Progressive Labour Movement (PLM) was in power, and which the business community in Antigua described as the 'five dark years', the opposition had not come within a mile of getting in. Even so, almost no one had a good word for the government. Robert Hall, an elderly white man who had been Minister of Agriculture and Deputy Prime Minister during the PLM years, pronounced V. C. Bird as 'no damn good from the day he was born,' adding 'Every damn one of them is a damn scamp; they're dishonest as hell.'

One young man, a policeman who moonlighted as a taxi- driver, and who was leaving the force because he couldn't 'stand the corruption', told me, 'The Prime Minister sold Antigua to the Antiguans and then he take it back and sell it to the for- eigners.' But I began to suspect that Antiguans take a perverse pleasure in their own tarnished reputation. One man told me, 'Oh, you know, we have the best dirty politics in the Caribbean.'

*

Despite all this or perhaps because of it, I found that I liked Antigua almost more than any of the other islands. It wasn't as beautiful as any of the Windward Islands – it had no rainforest, it had no rain and lacked the lush vegetation which shaped the landscape of the volcanic islands. It was dry and dusty and the countryside had a scrubby desolate look to it. The distinctive, ruined sugar mills, which protruded like thumbs from the ground, only added to the air of desolation, and everywhere the 'cassy', a thorny acacia shrub, had seen off more attractive plants.

Constant claims were, however, made for Antigua's beauty, and the notion that it was paradisal seemed widespread. The government had orchestrated the publication of a book of glossy photographs of the island, entitled *A Little Bit of Paradise*; at a public meeting, Hilroy Humphreys, the Minister for Agriculture, described Antigua as 'more than paradise – a little heaven'; and, when I went to see him, even the Leader of the Opposition, Baldwin Spencer, called it a 'crooked little paradise'.

And the light is wonderful, the sunsets beyond compare, the climate perfect (except for the drought), and those of the island's alleged 365 beaches that I managed to visit were pretty fine. And I had become fascinated by the gossip and scandal which were the daily grist to Antigua's rumour mill. Each Caribbean island was obsessed with itself but, in Antigua, rumour-mongering had assumed the proportions of a national pastime.

And there were so many rumours. X used to pilot Carlos Ledher (Ledher was a leading member of the Medellin drug cartel now serving life without parole, plus 135 years, in Marion County jail). Everybody *knew* this was so because it had been written in the *Outlet* which, in turn, had got its information from a book called *The Cocaine Kings*. When I left Antigua, I looked for this book. It did not exist. I did find a book called *The Kings of Cocaine* but it carried no reference to X.

The young policeman told me that the Birds had a 'hit-man' who was a 'sex freak'. 'He has a supernatural demeanour. He moves as though he believes in witchcraft,' he said, adding that this man was known to break the necks of the Birds' enemies and throw their bodies in the sea, leaving them to be washed up on some distant beach. And, it was said, you could buy Antiguan passports which the government was selling 'like they're going out of style'.

The strangest rumour of all concerned the Deputy Prime Minister, Lester Bird. I was told that when V. C. Bird married, he invited his wife's sister to come and live with them. And he began to sleep with both women. Within months the sister conceived and gave birth to Lester. Soon after the wife produced Vere Jr. Since then there had been terrible rivalry between the two brothers, the one older and cleverer but lacking legitimacy, the other younger, slower, but backed by his mother, the true wife. The only problem with the story was that it wasn't true. Lester was, in fact, the younger of the two brothers by two years, but just as legitimate as Vere Jr.

Antigua was above all a family affair. The tensions between the three prominent members of the Bird family were an open secret. In his report, Blom-Cooper wrote that 'Mr Vere Bird Jr. complained bitterly to the Commission . . . that . . . he was being pilloried by his brother in a campaign to throw the whole blame for the scandal on him', adding 'I have heard a little of the struggle for political power between the Bird brothers . . .' V. C. was believed to favour Vere, but Lester, a brilliant orator and a man of considerable personal charm, was thought to be the more able politician, and therefore ultimately a more suitable successor to his father (Lester succeeded his father as Prime Minister in the 1994 elections).

When I thought of Lester and Vere Jr., I remembered Tennessee Williams' line in *Camino Real*: 'We have to distrust each other. It is our only defence against betrayal.'

The next week the Customs Comptroller, Rolston Samuel, was murdered; this prompted, among other things, a rash of telephone calls from the United States and Britain asking if Antigua was safe for tourists. There were also road-blocks all over the island, as the police searched for weapons and drugs. Antigua was abuzz with gossip and rumour, fuelled, in part at least, by the reports in the *Outlet*:

Murder after Murder

... the murder of the Comptroller of Customs, Mr Rolston Samuel, 45. He had been found murdered in his kitchen, fully clothed. His face bashed in with a stone. His throat cut, probably with his very own, very sharp cutlass. The killer walked from the kitchen to the garage. Cool as ever. Blood was found in Mr Samuel's spanking new, top-of-the-line, Infiniti, one of two on the island, the other owned by the Financial Secretary ... There was a scuffle between Mr Samuel and his killer. Two types of blood were found. Before toppling over in death, collapsing into some cases of soft drinks, one of which came crashing down as his body fell to the floor, Mr Samuel must have drawn blood from his assailant with a valiant counter-attack ...

It seemed that somewhere around 10.00pm ... Mr Samuel let someone into his owner-occupied, more than half-a-million, modestly furnished, solitary home ...

The following week's paper carried this report:

Customs Chief Murdered in Gay Crime of Passion?

... It appears that in the course of an argument with a former homo-sexual partner, the argument became particularly heated.

At some point, unknown to Outlet, Mr Samuel decided that his gun, which was in his spanking new, top-of-the-line, Infiniti was the best form of defence. Apparently, as he made for his gun in the car the suspected killer resorted to force, and the brutal slaying ensued outside the house.

After Mr Samuel was killed he was taken back inside the house. Reliable reports state that not only was Mr Samuel's throat cut, but his skull was fractured in two places as a result of blows to his head, probably delivered with the flat side of Mr Samuel's very own cutlass.

He was also struck with a stone in the face. His body was a gruesome sight.

. . . Startling reports seem to have emerged in the course of the investigation. It is said that some four gay or bisexual men, personal associates of Mr Samuel, were made gifts of cars in the course of their amorous liaisons.

. . . If a bi-sexual gay man is charged with the murder of Mr Rolston Samuel, it will be the first known time that there is a murder in Antigua, arising out of a crime of passion related to a gay life-style.

Stacks of pornographic tapes, with gay content, were found at Mr Samuel's home . . .

And so it continued. The video tapes in particular were a source of endless speculation. Every morning I would go down the road to P.C.'s bookstore and discuss the latest developments. The tapes were rumoured (a) to be homemade and (b) to feature prominent Antiguans (male) in sexually-compromising positions. Of course, no one had seen the tapes.

The report in the *Sentinel*, owned by Vere Jr., ('We Stand Guard, Ensuring Progress, Truth And Justice For All') was more sober in tone:

Homosexuals Targetted (*sic*) As . . . Samuel's Murder Probe
Continues

According to Detective Superintendent, Michael Lawrence of the New Scotland Yard, the police have been questioning members of the homosexual community. Mr Lawrence added that he had no reason to feel that Mr Samuel was heterosexual . . . The weapons used, included a meat cleaver and machete . . . The police dismissed remarks that local persons have been viewed on pornographic video tapes found in the house of the murder . . . in excess of seventy video tapes, were found in the home of the deceased. Most of them were of a pornographic nature . . . local police will be called in to assist in identifying any local resident, if any, who appears on the tapes. Mr Lawrence . . . jocularly said, 'I'm fully aware that for the short time that I've been here that rumour does spread around in Antigua ... we are not keeping blinkers on and going down the path that it was definitely a homosexual murder. From experience, we have had a number of these murders in England and they do tend to be quite brutal ... Having said that, yes, it may well be drug related.'

This was all quite gripping, particularly in view of the general consensus that homosexuality barely existed in the Caribbean. Tim Hector's explanation for the widespread revulsion against homosexuality (men in rum shops would apparently talk freely of ripping homosexuals limb from limb) which was in itself an exaggerated expression of that machismo without which no Caribbean man seemed complete, went back to slavery.

'Because of the nature of slavery, your child was not your own. Your master could sell your children so there was no point in developing a sense of responsibility towards them. These societies of necessity emasculate a man. Promiscuity is the last resort and the only way to define yourself as a man. If you take everything away from a man, all he has left is his machismo.'

I decided that I needed a break from the Spanish Main, and to go to Barbuda for the weekend.

Barbuda, a tiny, completely flat island with a population of just over a thousand, lies some twenty-eight miles north of Antigua. Much to the Barbudans' dissatisfaction, it was packaged with Antigua and the uninhabited island of Redonda when independence was granted in 1981. Barbuda is represented by a single member of parliament, and though Antiguan politicians make a great song and dance of talking about Antigua *and Barbuda*, the relationship between the two islands is clearly an unequal one, and the Barbuda Council spends much of its time suing the government of Antigua.

The island's main claim to fame is its exquisite pink sand beaches. In one of the typically convoluted scams with which Antigua seems so blessed, it transpired that the sand was being mined, causing tremendous damage to the local ecology, then sold to the US Virgin Islands by a company in which Lester and two other government ministers were known to have been involved.

This is how the island is described in *Antigua and the Antiguans* which was published in 1825:

> Barbuda is a small island, about twenty miles broad, and lies twenty-six miles to the north of Antigua. It has belonged to the Codrington family from about the year 1691, when William III granted it to General Codrington, then Governor-General of the Leeward Islands. It raises a great number of horned cattle, ponies, donkeys, etc., and its shores are very prolific in turtle and various kinds of fish; while its beach is strewed with many beautiful shells. Deer, also, range amid its sylvan glades; and their flesh occasionally affords another dish at a West Indian dinner. The chief emoluments arising from this island, however, are the number of wrecks; three or four sometimes occurring in a year. The reason of these frequent maritime disasters is, that the island lies so low, and is generally encompassed with fogs, that vessels are upon the reefs (by which it is almost entirely surrounded) before they are aware ... Barbuda contains about 1500 inhabitants, of which the greater part are employed as huntsmen and fishermen; the former make use of the lazo to catch the wild horses ...

It is also claimed that Christopher Codrington, the sugar planter who ran Antigua in the late seventeenth and early eighteenth century (and turned the Betty Hope Estate, which he named after his daughter and whose ruins are now a major tourist attraction, into the most efficient sugar plantation in Antigua, with over 270 slaves working some 725 acres of sugar cane), used Barbuda for an experimental slave-breeding programme.

Barbudans were certainly big (the mother of Vere Jr. and Lester, both massively 'girthy' – to borrow a local expression –

came from Barbuda) but the Codrington family has always strenuously denied that there was any truth in the slave-breeding story.

Now the island has no less than three luxury resorts. The newest, the 'K' club, owned by an Italian businessman, Aldo Pinto, and his wife, Mariuccia Mandelli, a designer whose clothes sell under the Krizia label, is rumoured to have cost $20 million to build. 'Be the most pampered Robinson Crusoe in the world on the finest beach in the Antilles in a setting which is the jewel of the Caribbean,' trumpeted the brochure:

> Krizia discovered this corner of Paradise some years ago, selected it as her personal Eden for many seasons, then decided she wanted to share her pleasure with others, but only if they were capable of fully appreciating and understanding Barbuda... Every room has a separate dressing-room where you will find your personal kimono, or rather 'yukata', designed by Krizia...

Well, I would be staying at Carter Nedd's guesthouse.

I hadn't been on a boat for a bit and, since the memory of my bruising last experience had faded, I thought it would be fun to go by sea. Pat, who used to live on Barbuda, sent me down to the deep-water harbour to talk to Lindy Burton. Lindy, a handsome man whose father, Eric, had at one point been the island representative, said that he would take me and to be on the dock by ten the following morning. The crossing would last about three hours.

At eleven, cargo was still being loaded. The *Concorde* was a small boat, about the size of the one which had taken me from Carriacou to Union, but without the low hold. It had instead a wheelhouse on deck, backed by a tiny cabin containing two filthy bunks. The long front deck was covered with boxes and building materials. There was a rear deck, about ten foot by five, with a sliding door leading to the cabin. I settled myself on a pile of timber and waited. There were no other passengers, only Lindy and two boys. 'My name is Ken but they call me "Tool",' the one with dreadlocks told me.

We set off soon after eleven and five hours later we were still at sea. For the first half-hour, we were within the protective confines of the harbour but once out in the open sea, all hell broke loose. The waves were easily eighteen feet high; the boat would wash up to the top of one, skid around like a car that had hit a patch of ice and crash down the other side. When a particularly big wave loomed, Lindy would give a warning shout and I would know to cling on even tighter. As soon as we had got going, I had moved round to the little rear deck to avoid getting soaked and I spent most of the journey with my back against the cabin door (until it splintered, then disintegrated, halfway to Barbuda): I clung to the frame of the cabin and braced my legs against the railing. It was like being on a rollercoaster. At one point, I thought, I can get the hang of this, it's like dancing, you just have to follow the rhythm and roll with the boat, but every time I relaxed for a minute, a great mass of salt water would pour over the bows and threaten to wash me over board.

The terror became monotonous in time, but it never really lifted. The boys were predictably insouciant and wandered around the bucking little craft as if they were on dry land. Tool had a huge spliff which dealt with any fear that he might have been experiencing. The other boy, whose name I never found out, was swigging from a bottle of Smirnoff vodka and a bottle of orange throughout the voyage.

'What kind of a boat is this?' I asked.

'A wooden boat,' said Tool.

'I can see that.'

Because Barbuda is so flat, even when we drew near and the water grew calmer, it was still impossible to distinguish land from sea, so there was no way of knowing that we were nearly there. We approached painfully slowly. The island is surrounded by lethal reefs – there are 137 wrecks around Barbuda – and Lindy had to steer carefully with Tool and the other boy leaning over the bows staring into the crystalline water and navigating by sight.

When we finally docked, I stumbled ashore, shaking and soaked, and fell to my knees. The journey had taken five and a half hours, longer even than that from Union to Bequia. A cousin of Lindy's, a man called Sheldon gave me a lift to Codrington, Barbuda's Lilliputian capital.

Codrington was not so much a one-horse as a one-goat town. It was completely flat and gave the impression of having just been plonked down in the middle of nowhere. It had no formal beginning or end and simply trailed away at the edges like a piece of fraying material. You could stand at the crossroads in the centre of town and see for miles.

In the warm light of a rusty sunset, I walked to meet Sheldon at his bar. The Green Door had a billiard table and was full of noisy men. Behind the bar a woman with a resigned expression was serving drinks. She was Sheldon's mother. There was also a camera crew from *Island Magazine*, a weekly television show in Antigua, who were going to film at the frigate-bird sanctuary the following morning. Sheldon thought that I could probably tag along, so we drove over to the house of an American woman who was organising the shoot.

Randi was a blonde New Yorker in her mid-thirties. She had pretty, slim legs and hands and enormous breasts hanging loose under her T-shirt. She also talked non-stop. Yack, yack, yack. The stereo was blasting, the television was on, Randi was chain-smoking. A black man who introduced himself as Elvis appeared.

'They call me the black Elvis of soul,' he said.

They put on a couple of video tapes of programmes which *Island Magazine* had made about Barbuda. I don't remember anything about the first one but the second was full of Barbudans complaining about the way that they were perceived in Antigua and treated by Antiguans.

'They think of us as being inferior.'

'They think of us as being backward.'

'They are delightful people, very open-minded and utterly

receptive to advance,' a spokesperson for the 'K' Club announced to the camera.

Later, back at The Green Door, the clientele seemed rather drunker than earlier. Sheldon had told me that people in Barbuda didn't drink much so perhaps they were making an exception in my honour. I had a beer and fended off some drunken advances from a man who wanted to know if he could be my 'friend'. This was a popular question and easily open to misinterpretation. Of course, I wanted to be friendly, but friendship wasn't quite what was always intended.

The room was filling up and assuming a sort of Hieronymus Bosch-like aspect. When another man approached me and asked if I would 'kindly feel his wood', I decided that I really was too old – and too tired – for all this and left.

Sheldon came the next morning at quarter to nine and we drove down to the wharf where his son was playing on the shore with a little heap of sugar-pink conch-shell fragments. The television crew arrived and it became clear that there wasn't room for me in the boat. I didn't want to spend the day on the beach with Randi and her boom-box, so I walked back into town.

In Codrington's only souvenir shop, I met an American woman from Orange, New York State. She turned out to be Lindy's stepmother, the second wife of the former island representative, Eric Burton. They lived across the road in a house outside which there was a sign which said:

> Man to Man is so unjust
> You don't know who the hell to trust

Some people certainly didn't trust Burton who, it was claimed, 'would say anything for money'.

The house was jammed with every modern convenience and luxury: a huge television set with satellite dish, an elaborate stereo system, a massive refrigerator bursting with imported foods, the latest in coffee percolators and so on. An electricity generator outside provided a continuous and intrusive accompaniment to our conversation. Mrs Burton's parents, tiny old black people, were on a lengthy visit from the United States.

Eric was a big man, almost as girthy as the Birds, who seemed to typify a certain kind of successful Caribbean businessman. He was noticeably richer than anyone else on the island and, if the rumours about him were to be believed, this wealth had not been achieved without some bending of rules. It was clear he liked it where he was – on a tiny island where everybody knew everybody and where he could be, as it were, king of the castle, or cock of the dung-heap.

'I want to help my people,' he told me, 'I have turned my back on wealth in Antigua.' He said that Barbuda had been neglected by the colonial government but that 'if it wasn't for the white people, we would still be cutting sugar cane.'

I spent most of the next day with Mackenzie Frank, nephew of the current member for Barbuda, Hilbourne Frank. Burton, who had lived in Florida during segregation, had said, 'I goes where I am welcome,' but Mackenzie's earliest memory of racism was of being called a 'wog' at the age of ten at a bonfire party on Guy Fawkes night in England.

I went out to the frigate-bird sanctuary with Mackenzie and another man. It was a wonderful place, full of wheeling, calling birds, the males with their inflated red neck-sacs, the females predictably more subdued, biding their time. We glided across the water, into a world where illegal sand-mining, racism and Barbuda's unequal status seemed to fade into unreality.

I liked Barbuda – the light, the peace, the almost-hallucinatory feeling that you are falling off the edge of the world which you sometimes get when you are on a tiny island, as if there is a bright light shining inside your head. I liked the little houses with their sherbet paintwork – lemon, ochre, aqua, raspberry pink – and their well-meaning slogans ('God Is Good Trust Him') and the herds of goats wandering through the rubble that was still left over from the last big bad storm. I liked the juxtaposition of rusting metal and unbridled vegetation that was such a feature of the Caribbean landscape, cars which had stopped in their tracks, and just been abandoned, evidently beyond repair.

At the same time it was the sort of place where it wouldn't be difficult to go mad. It was so small. Mackenzie told me that there hadn't been a murder since 1904 (this was to change – in April 1994, four white people were murdered on board a yacht anchored off Barbuda. Despite wild rumours to the contrary, the motive turned out to have been simple robbery, the perpetrators members of the Green Door gang – named after Sheldon's bar). 'In another year, imported people will outnumber the Barbudans,' an Antiguan woman who worked at Coco Point, another luxury resort, told me.

On the last morning I got up early. Carter Nedd and another man were already downstairs. They had spent the night watching the test match in Australia on television. I walked out on to the runway which backed on to the guesthouse and caught a tiny plane back to Antigua. Throughout the fifteen-minute flight, I couldn't stop looking out of the window at the aquamarine waters below. They looked so calm, so smooth, so very inviting.

Back at the Spanish Main, I met a Barbudan woman who now lived in Canada. She said that she'd rather *swim* to Barbuda than go on Lindy Burton's boat.

9
Black Blood

My mother bore me in the southern wild,
And I am black, but O! my soul is white;
White as an angel is the English child,
But I am black, as if bereav'd of light.
                    (from *Songs of Innocence* by William Blake)

When I got back from Barbuda, I went to the doctor.

I had been feeling strange for some time now: at times fever-ish, dizzy with a sudden roaring in the ears. I would be walking down the street perfectly OK and, with no warning at all, be overcome by weakness. I was perpetually exhausted, waking tired, even after eight or ten hours' sleep, and often going to bed as early as seven or eight o'clock. I no longer felt hungry. I would think that I was and then, when food arrived, I found that I had no appetite. My breasts were tender and then there was the matter of my period. The faint splash in Basse-Terre had not even lasted the day. I had a history of erratic periods and hadn't been bothered at the time, but now this symptom, combined with all the others, as well as a constant sense of weepy vulnerability, made me begin to worry. I was beginning, in fact, to suspect that I might be pregnant and this suspicion filled me with a kind of low-grade anxiety which never com-pletely left me and which, given half a chance, crescendoed to blind terror.

About seven years before, I had become pregnant and, after

three months, I had begun 'spotting', as it is termed, and been taken to hospital in an ambulance. There they did an ultrasound and discovered, to their surprise and my relief, that the foetus appeared to be alive. I was told that when the bleeding stopped, I could go home. I spent a week in hospital resting with my legs up and the bleeding did stop. See you in three weeks at the ante-natal, they said. The day that I was due to leave hospital, they did another scan – at the insistence of the man I was going to marry. This time there was no sign of life. The baby had simply died. The medical term for this is apparently a 'lost abortion'. After the operation to remove the dead foetus, I went home in tears. Within twenty-four hours, I was back in hospital with a high temperature and screaming with pain. Some kind of infection had set in. They put me in a small ward with a heavily pregnant woman. Seven months into her pregnancy, a scan had revealed that her baby had no kidneys and would anyhow die at birth. She had come in to go through labour. This time I stayed in for three days and then was sent home again. I bled off and on (more on than off) for the next two and a half months. No sooner had I begun to recover than I had become pregnant again. This time it was an ectopic pregnancy which, by its very nature, was doomed to failure. Since then nothing.

So if I was right this was, to say the least, unexpected, and a tribute to the unreliability of condoms.

Denise, the lunchtime barmaid, with whom I had become friendly, recommended Doctor Kelsick, a woman doctor at a clinic for women. I called her but she couldn't see me until the following Monday. Once the possibility of pregnancy had entered my mind, I could think of nothing else and immediately fell victim to a host of related anxieties. Some sharp twinges low down on my right side convinced me that not only was I pregnant but that it was another ectopic. I seemed to remember reading somewhere, that women who had experienced one ectopic pregnancy were more likely to have another one. Oh, great, I thought, recollecting the days in hospital, the tidy scar across my lower abdomen just into the pubic hairline, and the three weeks convalescence that had followed. How on earth was I going to manage here? Women could die from ectopic pregnancies. The tube in which the fertilised ovum had lodged couldn't take much pressure and as the embryo grew, so the tube swelled and finally burst and, if you weren't in close proximity to specialist medical care, it could be fatal.

By Thursday morning, my panic had escalated to uncontrollable proportions and I rang the Women's Clinic again. A male doctor with a sympathetic voice answered and I explained my problem. 'Come this morning,' he said. 'Dr Kelsick will fit you in.'

Dr Kelsick, a light-skinned, almost white, woman of my age, was reassuringly competent. I would have trusted her with my life. She examined me, confirmed that I was indeed pregnant, and told me to get dressed and then we would talk about it.

I dressed in the cubicle and went to sit down opposite her.

'How do you feel about this?' she asked.

I said, 'I don't know how I feel but I know that I don't want to have an abortion.'

'Well, I can tell you one thing. You are forty years old and with your history, if you don't have this child, you won't have one.'

I nodded. 'I know.'

She said that it was too early to tell if it was an ectopic but that normal pregnancies brought all sorts of strange little pains with them. She took some blood, to confirm the pregnancy, to test hormone levels (which would apparently assist in determining whether the pregnancy was ectopic or not) and I asked her to do an AIDS test. She looked surprised.

I said, 'Don't you think it's sensible? I thought all pregnant women were supposed to be tested.'

'Of course it's wise but I don't usually suggest them because people take offence.'

I arranged to see her again in a couple of weeks and left the surgery.

Outside everything was just the same. The same brilliant sunshine, the same effortlessly blue sky, the same dusty streets.

Everything looked the same yet everything was different. In a matter of hours, no, half-hours, my life had changed. I walked to the cathedral. I didn't know where else to go. I needed somewhere quiet. Once inside the vast calm and cool, I collapsed in a pew and burst into tears.

The next day I went to Montserrat. I had been planning to go anyway but now the need to be somewhere quiet, anonymous, away from the Spanish Main, was overwhelming.

Montserrat is one of Britain's remaining Caribbean colonies (now known as 'dependent territories'), the only Irish Caribbean island, the self-styled 'Emerald Isle of the West'. Just a stone's throw from Antigua, a hop across an azure sea in one of those tiny LIAT planes, it was, if the tourist literature was to be believed, 'The Way The Caribbean Used To Be'. The tourist board also makes much of the Irish connection, distributing leaflets which reveal that Montserrat is three thousand miles west of Ireland, that it became a sanctuary for victims of religious persecution in the seventeenth century, attracting Irish settlers from Ireland, Barbados and Virginia, and lists some seventy-three Irish surnames to be found on the island: Fagan, Farrell, Galloway, Maloney, O'Brien, O'Donoghue, Reilly and Ryan were among the more obvious. Catholicism is the main religion. 'Present-day natives of Montserrat have retained many Irish customs and beliefs,' continues the shamrock-festooned pamphlet, 'A popular folk dance the "Heel and toe" has been attributed to Irish customs as well as the national dish, "Goatwater" which is believed to be a popular Irish stew.' I already knew about 'goatwater' from my guidebook which had recommended Annie Morgan's restaurant ('A must . . . for goatwater'). 17 March, St Patrick's Day was a public holiday because the Montserratian slaves had chosen it to stage a rebellion, and, as you came through immigration, your passport was stamped with a shamrock.

'Welcome home. Welcome to paradise,' said the huge taxi-driver and then asked if I minded if his cousin caught a lift with us.

'No,' I said, 'it's your cab [minibus actually], give anyone you want a ride.'

So we picked up various characters along the way as we weaved across the hills and valleys of Montserrat. The island was indeed splendidly emerald and scattered with cottages like Irish cottages, though made of a dark volcanic stone. Even so, it was oddly disconcerting to drive through Kinsale, Cork and Galway.

Montserrat had been badly hit by Hurricane Hugo in September 1989 which had destroyed many of the buildings and rendered over two and a half thousand people homeless. No part of the island had been untouched by the storm. In Plymouth, the toy-town capital, much of the damage was still evident in the battered houses and wrecked harbour; the 180ft quay which had completely disappeared in the hurricane, making it difficult to land relief supplies. The semi-submerged hull of a boat which had been torn in half by the storm still wallowed in the harbour, its jagged edge breaking through the water like shark jaws rising to attack. Three years later the roof of the Philatelic Society had still not been replaced. In the preface to a verse account of the disaster – which I had picked up in the airport gift shop – Lowell Lewis, the island's Director of Health had written: 'Sustained winds of 130 mph were experienced for eight (8) hours with damage to 95% of buildings 20% destroyed. The main hospital lost its roof and most health centres were severely affected.'

The poem itself gave a vivid impression of what the night of 17 September must have been like.

> It was Mayhem
> 300lb solar panels
> With trailing tails of Copper piping
> Leaped off the roof
> Floating down
> to the courtyard below
> Smashing into reinforced concrete . . .
> Those which did not move
> Suffered likewise
> From holes torn open

Black Blood

By passing sheets of galvanise
Now propelled by absent engines . . .
At 100 miles per hour or more . . .

But no one could spend long in the real Caribbean without being aware of the terrible destructive potential of nature and also learning to love the jumble of vegetation and debris which formed such an integral part of the landscape. This was one of the reasons why I hated the resorts, with their manicured perfection. In their efforts to shut out reality, they became totally artificial.

In Plymouth I attempted to check into a gloomy hotel into where I was supposed to have booked. Despite my having telephoned from St John's and made a reservation, it turned out to be full. I was relocated to a depressing apartment building over the road and given a suite of grimy rooms. I pulled a folding chair outside and sat in the late afternoon sun, watching a big lizard with a turquoise head make its way across the grass, and thinking about what had happened to me.

I couldn't really begin to absorb the enormity of the change which lay ahead. I had always thought that I would have children. I had grown up believing that that was what at some point in my life would happen and one of the traumas of reaching forty was having to accept that children, even one child, looked increasingly, acceleratingly, unlikely. I had been trying to come to terms with this lack, with this, as it seemed to me, failure. And now suddenly, a whole new set of adjustments were required. It was too much. I lay back in the chair and thought about the baby.

Once the initial shock had diminished, I found that I was thrilled. I felt not just physically different but suddenly emotionally, spiritually, intellectually different. I was a pregnant woman, a precious object. I had life within me and this knowledge gave a rosy tinge to my vision of the world. As I looked out at Plymouth's ravaged face, I felt benign, tender and infinitely fragile, like the crumpled petals of a flower opening in the sun. And the baby was the focus of all this soft, welling emotion.

*

219

The Weather Prophet

The next morning I made a dutiful attempt to explore the island. On arrival I had tried to obtain a local driving-licence without which it was impossible to hire a car. But, despite alleged enthusiasm on the part of the Montserrat tourist authorities for tourists and their money, the police station department which issued driving-licences was closed and destined to remain so for the duration of my stay. This was a Caribbean characteristic which I had observed again and again: despite unimaginable laxity, no end of bending-of-rules and corruption, there was nothing more obdurate and inflexible than Caribbean official-dom when it so chose. Everyone knew that anything was possible but, unless you knew exactly which buttons to press and which palm to grease, you might as well have been in the middle of a law-ridden country like Sweden or Belgium.

However, my altered physical state hadn't yet completely sapped my will. The barman/chef at the hotel restaurant ('Make the Critics Choice for BREAKFAST, SNACKS, LUNCH, DRINKS, DINNER' BB's Restaurant & Bar) said that he had a friend who had a car which I could hire for a couple of days. We went to find the car, a beat-up blue automatic of indeterminate vintage and provenance. And we had just concluded a mutually satisfactory agreement, and I was just getting into the car, when the owner's dog, which had been barking hysterically at the end of a chain throughout the transaction, bit me on the calf. I insisted on going to hospital (I could imagine the headlines in the *Montserrat Reporter* 'PREGNANT WOMAN IN RABIES ALERT') where a fat nurse glanced casually at my now-bruised and swollen leg and said that there was nothing they could do for me, that they never did *anything* about dog bites, but not to worry, there was no rabies on Montserrat.

My new friend, Leroy Fitzpatrick ('Call me "Leftie" '), said that there was no need for me to bother to drive all the way to the airport, where there was a faint chance that I might be able to pick up a driving-licence and offered to accompany me on a tour of the island. Though I would really have preferred to be alone, I didn't see how I could refuse, so we set off.

Montserrat was all velvety hills and valleys scattered with ruined houses of dark volcanic stone. The old car strained up tiny curving roads at the summit of which would be one of those heart-stopping Caribbean vistas, that intense conjunction of sea and sky, a watery savannah of graded blues, starting with the soft turquoise of the shallow waters, darkening, darkening as the water deepened until it reached the darkest indigo depths.

Leftie took me to a workshop where they made glass. I bought an ashtray with a frilly emerald green rim and a handful of black volcanic sand trapped between two layers of glass. I asked if there was one without the sand and, for that matter, one that didn't say 'Montserrat' but the salesgirl looked offended and said that was the whole point. Then we trekked on to the Galways Soufrière – a desolate moonscape burping sulphur. One whiff of the sulphur was enough for me and I declined to climb up for a proper look. I could see that I was going to use my pregnancy, acknowledged or not, as an excuse not to do anything I didn't want to do.

Comparisons between Montserrat and Antigua make no more sense than comparisons between any of the islands but Antigua's proximity invited them. Montserrat was calm where Antigua was turbulent. Montserrat was clean and Antigua dirty. Montserrat was orderly but Antigua was chaotic. The roads in Montserrat were not riddled with pot-holes, presumably because of a continuing subsidy from a reluctant British government. A sign advertised a Best-Kept Village Competition. Perhaps I was wrong to think that this would have been unimaginable in Antigua. And perhaps Montserrat's torpid façade was deceptive.

A black American woman told me that it was 'a middle-class island full of sullen racist blacks'. She and her husband, an Englishman with the classic good looks of Stewart Granger, ran a little restaurant outside Plymouth where I had lunch. He used to be in the movie business in Los Angeles, he said, and they had come down here in search of a comfortable retirement – but hadn't found it. She was full of anger – at the way the blacks treated her, them, animals. She said that their dogs would bark at Montserratians but not at white people, or at black people, from Europe or America. She said that the local blacks were inferior to black Americans. It wasn't a rewarding conversation. I drove back into town and parked the car. On the pavement near the hotel, I found a tiny ginger kitten, not more than three or four weeks old. It seemed to be dying with glazed eyes and blood seeping from its baby nostrils though, when I picked it up to shelter it in some laurel bushes, it began purring at my touch. I didn't know what else to do, so I left it there.

That evening, in the feather-pink light of dusk, I fell into conversation with an elderly man who was practising golf strokes on the grass outside my apartment. He came from Calgary but had had a house in Montserrat where he had usually spent six months of the year. When Hugo hit, he had lost everything and because he had been under-insured, couldn't afford to replace it. Now he rented an apartment in Lime Court. It was a poor substitute for his house but, he said, he needed the sun.

Sunday in Montserrat was just like Sunday everywhere else in the Caribbean. Slow. The only excitement was provided by a couple of street preachers bawling into microphones about Judgement Day. One of them seemed to have completely flipped out and was yelling, 'Listen to me, somebody. Anybody.' Nobody did. A boy sidled up to me and asked, 'Do you have a friend here?'

'No, but I have one in England.'

'Is he black?'

The following morning, before leaving for the airport, I went to take a photograph of the decapitated Philatelic Society. As I aimed my camera, a man waving a machete lurched towards me shouting and screaming. I tried to explain that I was photographing the building, not him, but he couldn't or wouldn't hear. He came very close, so close that I could feel his spittle on my face and brandished the machete under my nose. Two schoolgirls walking by came to my rescue.

'Leave de white woman alone, man,' they said and he went away. I looked over the edge of the little stone bridge on which

222

this encounter had taken place, then up at the blue hills, then burst into tears.

On the plane back to Antigua, I sat behind two Americans in shorts and sneakers. One of them, a woman in her fifties, was leaning across the aisle and addressing a stout middle-aged black woman in a piercing voice,

'OH WE JUST LOVE YOUR ISLAND. EVERYONE IS SO FRIENDLY THERE. AND IT'S SO BEE-YU-TI-FUL.'

After Montserrat I took one more short trip, this time to St Kitts and Nevis, with Savannah, the pretty Antiguan woman whom I had met one Sunday at a picnic at Darkwood Bay, which Vince, the utterly hopeless ex-barman from Philadelphia who haunted the Spanish Main had taken me to. (This picnic had a mildly irritating sequel: Vince, apparently miffed by my reluctance to fall into his arms, though he hadn't actually solicited any such thing, told Hawkeye, Savannah's part-Sioux Indian boyfriend, and some other men with whom he regularly played pool, that I was a lesbian. Needless to say, the Antigua gossip-machine, functioning as always better than anything else on the island, ensured that this rumour came to my ears.)

Savannah had been born in Antigua but had spent her early life in Trinidad and most of her adult life in California where she had been married twice, both times to white men. But she claimed always to have planned to return to Antigua where her mother, a pillar of the Moravian Church and a fount of useful information, lived. Now she had a business making souvenirs – bookmarks, key-rings, fridge magnets – incorporating all the pretty stamps of the region, and she often had to travel to other islands, collecting money and delivering orders. I had told her that I was pregnant – I had to tell someone – and when it became clear to me that the days for serious solo research were over, she suggested that I accompany her on one of her lightning tours.

We arrived late in St Kitts ('The Secret Caribbean'), thanks to a five-hour delay at Saint Maarten airport. The little guest-house was shuttered and there was no answer however hard we banged. But we found another, ate a fish dinner, down on the windy quay, and tumbled into bed.

St Kitts was supposed to be Columbus' favourite island and was also the first to be colonised by the British, hence its appellation as the 'mother of the Caribbean'. It was also one of the few remaining Anglophone islands where sugar cane was still grown, and at dusk the waving canefields looked like armies of the dead, phantasmagoria risen from the shadowlands of the past. The taxidriver gave us a little running commentary as he drove.

'This here is Bloody Point where two thousand Caribs were killed when the English and French were fighting. Lots of Rastamen live near here. They so dirty. One of them had a terrible headache and he went to the doctor but it still wouldn't go away so the doctor told him to cut off his hair and when he cut it, there was a centipede living in there feeding off his brain.'

In Nevis, birthplace of Alexander Hamilton, holiday destination of the Princess of Wales, I went to look at St John's Fig Tree Anglican Church where the original marriage certificate of Nelson and Frances Nisbet, a copy of which I had seen in English Harbour, was on display. The actual ceremony had taken place on 11 March 1787 at Montpelier, the house of Fanny's uncle, John Herbert, the President of Nevis; Montpelier is now a 'great house' hotel. Nevis then was, according to one of Nelson's biographers, Tom Pocock, 'unlike the other British islands in being richer, more fashionable and its merchants and planters more arrogant' and Herbert was 'very rich and proud'. Fanny Nisbet, his niece who acted as his hostess since the death of his wife, was a twenty-seven-year-old widow with a small son. She had spent almost all her life on Nevis, her late father having been a senior judge there: her first husband had been the doctor who had attended him at his death.

Like most Caribbean churches, the church at Fig Tree was lovely with grey-blue shutters, but of greater curiosity was the Nelson museum which had been put together by a demented American Nelson enthusiast. In 1987, celebrations were held in Nevis to commemorate the two hundredth anniversary of the Nelson-Nisbet wedding with participants dressing in eighteenth-century dress. The museum contained, among other Nelson memorabilia, the dress 'created' by the late Mrs Louis Bjorstad (Marjorie) for the event. The 'Horatio' costume of her partner had been made by a tailor in Charlestown, the capital of Nevis. There was also a photograph of the pair in full kit. They were, needless to say, both white.

The subsequent disintegration of the marriage and the role Nelson's life of Emma, Lady Hamilton, for whom he had abandoned the unfortunate Fanny in the most callous and public fashion, had evidently been ignored in the interests of pageantry – as well as, perhaps, the desire of a certain section of Nevis society to be part of some great historical tradition.

Back at the Spanish Main, everything appeared unchanged. The only development was that Steph had suddenly started to wear loose smocks and make long lists of improbable names for babies (Halston, Hemingway, Cabochon, Martinique, Kylie, Saturn, Andromeda and so on). She was four months pregnant by Manuel, her Chilean boyfriend. Nicky's little marmalade cat, Chorley (named after what sounded like a typical Spanish Main character, a former guest from Chorley in Lancashire known as 'Chorley Pam'), was also expecting. And, of course, so was I. But I decided to keep the good news to myself – partly out of superstition, partly because, at forty and unmarried, I wasn't sure how dignified pregnancy was.

Life settled into a pleasant enough routine. I felt tired all the time and found it difficult to bestir myself; the odd, almost familial, atmosphere of the Spanish Main drew me in. It was tempting just to lie on my bed and read trashy novels, of which there was a plentiful supply at P.C.'s bookshop down the road; and I spent a fair amount of time doing just that, the little orange cat purring and kneading my stomach.

In the mornings, I would come downstairs to find Denise behind the bar clearing up from the night before. 'Saltfish', an old calypso of Sparrow's from the early Seventies, had just been reissued and was playing on the radio all the time (saltfish had some claim to being the national dish of much of the Caribbean but the song was not really about saltfish at all; it was about the joys of pussy – a popular theme in calypso). We both loved it and it came to encapsulate that time for me. When I hear 'Saltfish' now, I can see Denise dancing and I am back in Antigua.

There was a sudden rash of powercuts at night and the hardcore would play Scrabble by candlelight in the bar. One morning the lamp-post outside the Spanish Main caught fire. Pat went to England for a couple of weeks and left Rob in charge. The food improved but I still didn't feel hungry. Two men were arrested and charged with the murder of the Customs Comptroller who, it turned out, had indeed been killed with his own cutlass. The motive was simple theft, and the rumours about homosexual orgies died away. I made sporadic efforts to increase my knowledge of Antigua and, in doing so, met a man I liked a lot who took me to visit a couple of fine old churches. We went to the octagonal church at Old Parham, a building as beautiful as it was anomalous, and then on to St George's out at Fitches Creek. The graveyard faced out to sea and standing there, amid the shattered tombstones, these lines from 'Saltfish' ran through my head:

> I will die a happy man
> If I close my eye with some saltfish in me hand
> Bury me in de cemetery
> Any money
> Put a saltfish picture on me tombstone
> Saying Saltfish
> Sparrow was its greatest lover . . .

Increasingly my inner world took precedence.

I thought all the time about the baby, alternating between bovine contentment and desperate anxiety. These were my main anxieties: would the baby be OK; how would I support the baby; how would I look after the baby and still manage to write my book; where would the baby sleep (I solved that one quickly enough – it would start off with me in my room and, when it was old enough, move to the spare room); what colour would the baby be (I knew that Theo was the father – that last careless morning in Saint-Pierre, and spent hours trying to calculate the child's probable colour, I worried (a) that if the child was very dark, it would have a more difficult time with a white mother, and (b) that I might feel less able to love something – I couldn't think of it as a person yet, more a sort of superior kitten – so different from me; by the same token, I hoped desperately for a little girl); and finally, how would my mother react to the news.

One day I went to have lunch with a group of lawyers and businessmen in a Chinese restaurant downtown. Before ordering, I went to the bathroom and discovered that I was bleeding very slightly. I felt no pain, but so much fear that I couldn't eat.

From that moment on, everything seemed to move very fast. The bleeding stopped almost the same day but left me permanently anxious about the progress of the pregnancy, despite all Dr Kelsick's attempts at reassurance (she told me that sixty per cent of women experienced some bleeding during pregnancy). I fell in love again – or thought I did – with the man who had introduced me to the glories of Antiguan architecture. I was already bewitched by the Caribbean and all thoughts of New York had been banished utterly by the discovery that I was pregnant.

Pregnancy rendered me uncertain and emotionally fragile and the additional vulnerability left me wide open. Falling in love is so much a question of timing, of receptivity. It rarely has anything to do with the actual qualities, let alone the suitability or even availability, of the beloved object. In my frail, tremulous state, I was an easy target.

This man was an old acquaintance of a friend in England, and it was by the purest chance that we met at all. I had called my English friend to wish her 'happy birthday' and she had suggested that I look him up. There was an intense instant rapport between us – I don't think I imagined it. He reminded me of a great earlier love, from a time when I still believed that life was full of promise, that I had a future, and though, for any number of practical and other reasons, there was no future here either, I fell utterly under his spell. Like the man in New York, he was a fantasy figure, but this time the rush of emotion that I felt for him was rooted in a far more specific fantasy. It is possible that subconsciously I was looking for a father for my baby and, despite the brevity and unconsummated nature of our association – we never even kissed or barely, which almost certainly only served to intensify the hopeless dreamy romanticism of the whole thing, I fastened on him. Everything came together – all these different elements: my pregnancy and the cornucopia of sensations that it evoked; the knowledge that I would soon be leaving; even the impossibility of it all – all combined in a heady romantic brew. In the space of two, maybe three meetings, he assumed a colossal importance in my life.

That condensing of time and emotion was, I had noticed, characteristic of the Caribbean. You could live a lifetime in a matter of days, sometimes hours, and then, when you moved on, it was as if it had never happened. Something new took its place. But now it was different, perhaps because of the pregnancy which fixed my feelings for him like the butterflies trapped forever in Perspex, which they sold as paperweights in souvenir shops. I didn't tell him that I was pregnant – I didn't dare – and, to add to my existing anxieties, I now worried what he would think when he found out.

I still couldn't figure how I was going to manage in England and eventually hit on the perfect solution. I would come to the Caribbean and live in a little house on an island with my baby, and this man with whom I had fallen in love would come and visit us. I felt obscurely guilty about my new attachment. I didn't think pregnant women should feel desire but I couldn't help it.

The taxi-driver who drove me to the airport to catch the flight to Trinidad had the last word.

'People your colour better than people my colour. People my colour want everything too quick. Write something nice about Antigua.'

*

10

Stop That Train

Stop that train
I wanna get on
My baby, she is leaving me now . . .
(from *Draw Your Brakes* from *The Harder They Come*)

If you can walk you can dance
If you can talk you can sing
(Zimbabwean saying)

In Trinidad, Gina was pregnant. So was her friend, Diane. So was Caroline who cooked in Gina's bar.

But it was Carnival, when nothing waits for no one, when all normal considerations are put on hold till the madness, the bacchanal, is over. Port of Spain was throbbing with anticipation. Every night was 'fête', huge parties going on till the early hours, a mayhem of music and dancing and 'wining' and fucking. As one of the calypsos went,

If there's no 'wine',
Carnival never come.

I wasn't up to any of it.

Since I had left Antigua, I had felt as if I were unravelling, like a piece of old knitting. I was winding down – very fast. I didn't exactly want to go home but, since I had to, I wanted to get on with it. Trinidad had unintentionally become a postscript. I needed to prepare for my re-entry into the real world and Port of Spain at Carnival-time was not the best place.

Savannah had come with me as far as St Lucia where we had spent a couple of expensive nights in a chic little hotel near Les Pitons. The drive from the capital, Castries – incongruously twinned with Taipei – along to the west coast of the island took nearly three hours on roads which were, if anything, worse than they had been four years before. They were remaking the surfaces – if that was any kind of excuse. I wondered how, with these roads, tourism could be such a major industry but I supposed that, as in Antigua, once the tourists had safely snuggled into their resort, they just stayed there till it was time to catch the plane home. The scenery was spectacular – banana plantations, rain forest, jungle, dizzying panoramas down to the sea – all in the warm rosy light of dusk and finally, as we rounded the corner on a stretch of road that looked as if it had been dynamited, Les Pitons hove into view, magnificent in a red glow.

But, when we finally reached The Humming Bird Inn, the security guard assumed that Savannah was a taxi-driver (wrong colour for a guest) and the receptionist, in curlers and a scanty sarong, was taking a nap at the desk. It wasn't an auspicious start and the room prices, which had somehow doubled since Savannah had booked the room the previous evening, didn't help. I was too exhausted to object, or go somewhere else – and it was now dark. This all, however, cast a predictable pall over the whole enterprise, and the sight the next morning in Soufrière of a fat black woman with a face like a boot sporting a T-shirt that said,

> Too Hell With Work
> Let's Have Fun in Antigua

did nothing for the depression that had crept up on me. I felt sick and sick at heart. Dr Kelsick had given me some pills that were supposed to help the morning sickness but they weren't working and there was nothing I could take for the other pain.

Over the next two days, Savannah and I squabbled in that way people do when they have totally different objectives and preoccupations and I think we were both relieved when the time came to say goodbye.

Trinidad was the final lap, the last straw.

Gina had to get up every morning before dawn to get to town to open the bar at 6.30. I would doze on until about nine, then make breakfast – fruit, boiled eggs, fresh milk, healthy stuff – and loll around the house listening to the radio, until about eleven, when I would catch a maxi into town to see her and have a bowl of cow-heel soup and a glass of juice at the bar. Then we all would review our pregnancies.

One morning, Loridel came by with Mark, her Chinese brother-in-law, her husband's brother, with whom she was desperate to find somewhere to fuck. He was smaller than her, a slender little man with a droopy black moustache. They said rapid hellos and disappeared into Rupert's room. I immediately put on headphones and turned the walkman up loud to be sure that I wouldn't hear anything I shouldn't. I thought of the old calypso 'The Big Bamboo' which has a verse that goes:

> Well, I know a Chinaman called Ling Pan Lo
> Married and he went to Mexico
> His wife divorced him very quick
> She want bamboo and not chopsticks
> She want de big big bamboo . . .

In St Vincent, you could buy a brand of cigarette papers called Big Bambù. The lovers emerged after an hour or so, looking incredibly pleased with themselves – evidently Mark's bamboo was up to scratch or perhaps it was the way he used it – and sauntered off their separate ways. According to Gina, this had all started because Loridel's husband had encouraged her to sleep with his brother because he wanted to know who was the better lover.

As Ash Wednesday and the start of Carnival got closer, you could almost feel the city heating up. (Carnival took place on the two days preceding Ash Wednesday, one final fling before the doom and gloom of Lent during which, until very recently, it had been forbidden to play calypso.) The *Trinidad Guardian* reported that church leaders were calling for a postponement of Carnival on the grounds that it was 'a flaunting of the flesh and enhancing debauchery'. Pastor Nelson of the Woodbrook Pentecostal Church denounced it as 'nothing more than demon worship' and a reader's letter complained that: '. . . people in Trinidad and Tobago are obsessed with sex and fête. Sex has become a drug . . .' One of the Carnival hits of the year was a song called 'Watch' by the Watchman. There was no mistaking the message:

> I wish I could take you home and sweat,
> I wish I could wine down you in big fête . . .

A more sober note was struck by the radio announcement which counselled, 'Remember on Ash Wednesday, you'll have to get on with the rest of your life. Leave no room for regret.'

Every time I heard this, it sent a chill through me. By Ash Wednesday, I would be back in New York and getting on with the rest of my life – and I was not looking forward to it.

I had decided not to 'play *mas*' and was busy negotiating for the return of the deposit I had left on my snake costume (there were apparently always eleventh-hour requests from people who, at the last minute, couldn't bear not to join in the fun and they were confident that they could sell it to someone else). But Gina, for whom Carnival was the high point of the year, was mad keen on every aspect of the whole noisy business and would go out till all hours of the night – to fêtes and to listen to music ('Masqueraders, bump and wail up/The music they pumping too hot/Everybody jumping non stop/The soca beat generating a heat . . .'). She said that, even when she was pregnant with Rupert, she had played *mas*. Merle Hodge, a writer and a lecturer at the University of the West Indies whom I went to see at the Trinidad campus one afternoon, told me, 'Women feel powerful in Carnival-time. Carnival is a woman's thing.'

One evening we went to a Calypso Spektakula – five hours of calypso in one of the big calypso tents compèred by a comedian called Tommy Joseph. A lot of the jokes were too local for me to get, almost as if they were in code, and I couldn't always understand exactly what he or the calypsonians were saying but the gist was usually clear enough. Sex and politics were the main themes. The older calypsonians, Chalkdust 'Chalky', Black Stalin and others tended to have a more worthy message while a lot of the younger ones were just plain filthy and the audience loved it.

In my notebook, I wrote:

What should a calypso do?
1. Tell a story.
2. Make a point.
3. Instruct.
4. Politicise – rather than moralise or preach.
5. Be witty.
6. Challenge.

When the Watchman, who was also a policeman, sang about Scotland Yard detectives coming to Trinidad to investigate police corruption at the invitation of the government, everyone knew what he was on about. The local police, offended by this high-handedness and worried that it might set a precedent, had organised a protest march round the Red House (the Trinidadian seat of government). Watchman took himself pretty seriously, and at the end of his act, made a little speech saying that this was the last year he would be singing calypso unless the judges put him in the finals for the Calypso Monarch. He claimed that they discriminated against him because his songs were too political.

'I'm not in this business for money. My songs are songs of conscience. They can make a difference.'

Not all of them. 'Watch' was just to get the crowd roaring.

But the calypsonians who were most likely to be the victims of discrimination were the Indian ones. 'They never let an Indian song win,' said Gina. 'They prefer, though this would be anathema too, to let a band from the south win. The Indians taking all the power, all the money, they kill their own families for money. The Indians prefer to bribe people rather than do anything straightforward.'

Earlier Merle Hodge had told me that there was a 'silent pact to keep the Indians out of political power. That's the only reason that the PNM [the governing People's National Movement] can stay in power.'

'Every now and then you get the call of blood,' she said.

The Watchman was followed by Colin Lucas with an incredibly salacious calypso about eating chicken in a box, presumably the ubiquitous Kentucky Fried Chicken; it was full of lines about a 'box-eating experience', 'eat your box with pride' and 'bring your box and come'. I thought of Tim Hector telling me that chicken and chips had replaced saltfish as the national dish. In the Seventies, Sparrow had recorded 'Saltfish', making th dish a metaphor for pussy. Now chicken had taken its place even in that context. Tommy Joseph said: 'I'm a man who's eating no box. I'm eating cun . . . tainers.'

Another night we heard a calypsonian called Brown Boy sing a song called 'Cat Race in the Savanah'. 'Cat', of course, was the West Indian word for pussy. Brown Boy sang that he wouldn't be riding any foreign pussy, only Trini cat. But even then, in among the lewd lyrics, was a word of warning: 'Cat jockey is ma first love/So Ah travelling with me gloves', a reference to condoms.

Thanks to Rupert, with whom I had had dinner the previous evening in an Indian restaurant while Gina snatched a quick – and, according to her, *very* necessary – hour in bed with her lover, I got it. Rupert had been wearing a T-shirt with the same message which I thought was something to do with boxing. Not at all.

This evening, the M.C. was a man called Sprangalang, who featured in a terrific David Rudder song called 'Dus' In Deh Face' – which you could hear bending the ten-foot speakers stationed on every street corner (it was extraordinary, the speakers actually bulged every time a bass note was struck). Sprangalang introduced Brown Boy, who came on stage in jodhpurs and carrying a whip, saying, 'All you come out this evening, wake up this evening, bathe, put on clothes and all your minds stay dirty. Never see that. Clean, clean clothes and dirty dirty minds.'

The whole of Trinidad seemed to be in the grip of a collective madness. There was a 'road march' song (road marches were designed to get the crowd going) called 'Whoa Donkey' – the Donkey was a dance of unparalleled vulgarity if the newspapers were to believed – and every time you climbed into a maxi, which would have added an extra twenty or so speakers, equalisers, boom-boxes and brain-busters in honour of Carnival, the whole bus would be full of swaying, shaking passengers, all tossing their heads as if in the throes of an epileptic fit and howling 'Whoa Donkey'.

The Saturday before Carnival, I went out to the country with a friend of Gina's, Sue, and her husband. Gina, a quintessentially urban character, declined to come, though we took Rupert along. I think that she planned to spend the day – or as much of it as possible – in bed with her married lover, whose wife appeared to be either very easy-going or very trusting, or, possibly, relieved to see the back of him.

Sue, an Indian woman married to an African man, was an exception to the rule of hostility between the two races. She agreed with Gina about Indians. 'Indians are a very racial people. They stick together.'

We drove out to the wild Manzanilla coast. All along the coconut-strewn beach, known as the Cocal, were abandoned villas. 'People can't afford two houses any more,' said Sue, 'so they just have to leave their beach house.' There were miles of coconut palms battered by the Atlantic winds and mounds of greyish coconuts; Sue told me that a ship carrying a cargo of coconuts had been wrecked off the coast to add to the volume. A crane flapped its wings languidly over the ashen waves. A flamboyant tree lent a splash of colour. We drove through bamboo groves and banana and coconut plantations, on to Pitch Lake. In the back, Sue's sister-in-law, Betty, sang along to the radio: 'Whoa Donkey', then another song the refrain of which was 'Wine on a bumsee' – which was an incitement to grind your crotch into someone's ass. Another road march song had the refrain 'Bacchanal time, bacchanal time' again and again till the singer – and presumably the audience – reached a pitch of frenzy; yet another repeated 'Whip the donkey, whip the donkey' over and over. More head-shaking material.

Sir Walter Raleigh claimed to have discovered La Brea, the Pitch Lake, in 1595 during his search for El Dorado, though it seems more likely that it was his advance guard, Robert Dudley, who first happened on it. Hard enough to walk on in parts, it laid yet another claim to be the Eighth Wonder of the World and consisted of ninety-five acres of solid pitch which, according to Sue's husband, supplied the roads of the world. 'That's why our roads are so bad because we are sending all the pitch away.' Rupert had never been there before. Actually he had almost never been to the country before.

We trailed back into town in a crocodile of returning traffic. The car in front had a bumper sticker which read 'Pure Hate'. It was hotter than hell and the air was soupy with the fumes from hundreds of cars with faulty exhausts and overstretched carburettors.

Sunday, *Dimanche Gras*, the eve of Carnival. Caroline's two children, a boy and a girl with big solemn eyes, were spending the day in the bar. I took them to check out the children's parade (tiny infants staggering about under the weight of spectacularly elaborate costumes – one child was got up as a spider, trapped in the centre of a huge web) and bought them ice-creams.

In the centre of Port of Spain shopkeepers were boarding up their windows in preparation for the night ahead. Carnival was to begin at four in the morning with *jour ouvert* (shortened to *'j'ouvert'* and pronounced 'jouvay'). In the late afternoon it began to pour with rain – torrential rain which smeared the streets and caused the gutters to stream with dusty water.

Jouvay morning. The official start of Carnival. Gina hadn't been to bed all night but went straight out to work. The bar was to be open from two on Monday morning. I dragged myself out of bed as a damp dawn was breaking. I had had a dream about the baby. I dreamt that my mother wouldn't believe that she was a girl until I opened her little legs and pointed out her tiny vagina.

I caught a maxi into town. Though it was barely light, the music was blasting and the streets were thronged with bedraggled revellers – it had rained throughout the night. I sat in a booth for a couple of hours while drunken carousers fell in and out of the bar. There was no shortage of people who had smeared themselves with mud and paint and fashioned costumes out of rags, all looking like extras from a futuristic film in which humans had been forced to take to the sewers while androids ruled the world. That kind of costume was called a 'nasty' *mas*. Gina said that white people liked to play 'nasty' or 'dirty' *mas* in the morning and then 'pretty' *mas* – sequins and feathers – in the evening. She herself could never play 'nasty' *mas*. An older man came in and said that when he was young, you could get 'a copper breastplate and everything for $30. Now you just get a g-string for $500. It's getting like Rio – all vulgarity.'

Around eleven we left the bar for Gina to go home to change into her *mas* costume – a skimpy pink leotard and head-dress which had cost a small fortune. By then maxis were few and far between and we had to walk to find one that would take us back to Petit Valley. The streets were strewn with streamers and tinsel and discarded bottles and beer cans and some very drunk stragglers. The smell of urine caused a wave of nausea to wash over me.

At the house I found that I had started bleeding again. I was so scared that I almost couldn't move. With Carnival absorbing the hearts and minds of Trinidad, I could have been dying in the street before a doctor could be found and even then he or she would probably be prancing behind a float loaded with steel pan – or else on cholera alert (every day the newspaper carried warnings about drinking the water and watching out for symptoms of the disease). I had never really felt much enthusiasm for Carnival and now the whole thing turned to ashes in my mouth. I hated the noise, the seeming mindlessness of it all, epitomised by the inane braying of 'Whoa Donkey'. Lying on Gina's bed, I forgot everything that I had grown to love about the Caribbean. The last few days had been too much for me. I wasn't at all sure that the Caribbean as a whole hadn't been too much for me. I seemed to have lived a thousand lives and now time and reality had kicked in. I spent the rest of the day in bed, crying and worrying, and finally sleeping. The only thing that sustained me was the knowledge that I was leaving the following day and could get to a doctor in New York. Like a mantra, a line from an old song ran through my head, 'This time tomorrow reckon where I'll be . . .'

That night – my last – I stayed over at Sue's who lived five minutes from the airport. Sue never played *mas* and had a lowish opinion of Carnival. 'Ash Wednesday every man jack too tired to go to work,' she said contemptuously.

As the American Airlines flight rose into the sky over Port of Spain, I settled back into my seat, exhaling hugely. There was an hour's stop-over in San Juan. At the airport bar, I ordered a Bloody Mary.

The taste of freedom had never been so sweet.

Postscript

Things do not explode,
they fail, they fade,
(from *Endings* by Derek Walcott)

New York was crisp and cold and bright, and the light had all
the intensity and none of the subtleties of the Caribbean. The
woman in whose apartment I was supposed to be staying
appeared to have forgotten that I was coming, but, nonetheless,
I persuaded the doorman to let me in. I was to have dinner
with the man with whom I had fallen in love all those years
ago – or so it seemed – in another life. He came through the
door all kisses and smiles. I told him that I was pregnant.

'You'll have to get your mother to help you,' he said, sound-
ing not entirely thrilled by my news.

'Maybe,' I said.

The next morning I went to a bookshop and bought a book
called *Your Pregnancy Week-by-Week*.

When I went back to the apartment, I was bleeding again. I
called a succession of New York gynaecologists.

'We only deal in unwanted pregnancies,' said the first.

The second couldn't see me for days.

Third time lucky. How was I going to pay, was the first
question I was asked.

I lay on my back in a consulting-room on Manhattan's Upper Eastside, my feet in stirrups. The doctor interrupted the examination to have a lengthy discussion with his broker.

Everything *seemed* to be all right, but he thought that I should have an ultrasound to be on the safe side. I thanked him and handed over $150.

I left him and went to have lunch with a couple of magazine editors. I said that one of the things that I had learnt in the Caribbean was that there are no advantages to being black.

'I can think of one,' said one of the women.

'Really, what?'

'Black people don't show their age.'

The ultrasound revealed that the baby had stopped growing some weeks before and that there was no foetal heartbeat. It was either dead or about to be, another 'lost abortion'. The doctor was sympathetic but positive. I thanked him and handed over $225.

Later that afternoon I went to the country. As we drove through a clear cold dusk, the radio announced that, in the city, a bomb planted by Middle Eastern terrorists had exploded at the World Trade Centre. There was a new moon. I was going to spend the weekend with a girlfriend in her clapboard house in the wooded hills above the Hudson River. The ground was covered with snow, the river was frozen and there were icicles a foot long hanging from the bushes and the eaves of the roof.

'Perhaps it's for the best,' she ventured.

After dinner, a photographer friend telephoned. He had spent the afternoon photographing a psychic. I had seen him the previous evening and given him a handkerchief of mine to show her.

'Your friend is English and very blonde,' the psychic had said. 'She's also pregnant. She really wants this baby but her body isn't going to let her.'

Worn-out, I cried myself to sleep. I woke once in the night, far too hot and thinking about my small tragedy.

As soon as I arrived in England, I went to the local hospital where they did what was necessary and after that nothing was left of my pregnancy. There remained only the mark on my wrist where my watch had kept out the sun, a thin white line that I had briefly crossed, to tell me that it hadn't all been a dream. When I had been back for about three weeks, I received a letter from Gina saying that she had miscarried about ten days after I had left. And one evening, as I was sitting in front of the fire, listening to Mozart's *Don Giovanni*, the telephone rang. It was the man in Antigua – I had sent him a copy of my first book. We talked for a bit and, as the conversation was winding down ('Me gone' he said – as they say in the Caribbean), I thanked him for calling. 'I had to,' he said, 'I needed to.'

But nothing was ever to come of it and, for months afterwards, driving through the rain-sodden Oxfordshire countryside, I would punch Sparrow's 'Saltfish' into the tapedeck and, as his rich, warm voice filled the car, I would remember walking on a brilliant Antiguan January day through the beautiful graveyard of St George's church overlooking Fitches Creek Bay, full of hope and excitement, and begin to weep and wish that I could have my life over again.

Afterword

Sometimes I think that the Caribbean was the last great love affair of my adult life. During the initial trip that I made for this book, I was as happy as I have ever been anywhere in the world and at any time in my life. I fell in love with the Caribbean, and with everything about it, almost as soon as I arrived. It bewitched and enchanted me, and a large part of the enchantment was the incredible sense of freedom that I felt there. I didn't stop to analyse what I thought that freedom meant. I just knew that in the Caribbean I felt free (whatever that was) and infinitely at ease. I loved the landscape, perhaps even more than the sea (though I loved that too), the mountains and the valleys, the rain forests and the rivers, the cane-fields and the oxen bringing in the cane in wooden carts; the goats on the hillsides and the horses wandering loose on the roads of Antigua; the banana plantations and the long coral beaches festooned with driftwood and conch shells; the black sand beaches which glinted like metal in the sun and got so hot that the soles of your feet burnt when you tried to walk on them. I loved the light and the way the sun set like a curtain ringing down – there was no dusk, no gradual drawing in of the night as we know it, but just a sudden, velvety blackness which covered the land, stealing over it like dye seeping into fabric. I loved the weather, the damp warmth that opened your pores and relaxed your limbs so you felt well, better than you ever had before, better than you had imagined was possible. I loved the music and the way that music was everywhere so that even when you weren't aware of hearing it, it would be there somewhere, like a subtext to everyday life, a drumbeat like a heartbeat. I loved the language, which was like another kind of music: the divine gurgling of Creole (not a word of which could I understand); the rude wit of the English islands (which I grew to understand); the constant banter that went on morning, noon and night; the way any excuse for an argument was good enough. I loved the markets, which were like a vision of fecundity: mounds of fruit and vegetables and the buckets of exotic flowers. I loved the smell of the Caribbean: a strange, ineffable blend of cinnamon, vanilla, coconut, rum, frangipani, jasmine, fish and sweat, all mixed in with the mustiness of rotting vegetation and the tang of the sea. I loved the cheerful chaos of the islands; the near-anarchy that bubbled just below the surface; the *laisser-faire* tolerance of the place.

And I loved the people; I loved the way they had an opinion about everything; I loved their friendliness, their humour, their courage, or insouciance, or sheer 'fuck you'-edness or whatever it was that made them swagger through life, and the poetic streak that ran deep through them. I loved the way nothing seemed to matter. It wasn't that people weren't capable of being serious, but that they seemed able to take everything in their stride. Serious things were taken seriously, but, to paraphrase the ad, they didn't make a drama out of a crisis. They seemed to have a knack for assessing whether a situation was really desperate or not, and if it wasn't, they didn't make a big production out of it. Death, bereavement and family were serious, but love or sex and money were not and consequently they were treated light-heartedly.

In the men, I loved the way a kind of earthy sexuality combined with an old-fashioned romanticism and the way they swore fit to beat the band. In the women, I loved their feistiness, their independence, and their sassiness, and the way that they wouldn't take any shit from the men, but, nonetheless, took so much of it all the time. I loved the contradictions of the place and the way that those contradictions co-existed, apparently, with such ease.

I hadn't been prepared for any of this. Not consciously, though now, looking back at the person I was then, I think that

I can detect a vulnerability, an openness, a receptivity, which might account for the rapidity with which I succumbed to the place. I was ready for this; I was ripe. When I think back over my life, I divide it into pre- and post-Caribbean. The Caribbean changed me, made me the person I am today. God knows what I would be like if I had never had that experience.

*

The longer I spent in the Caribbean, the more I loved it. So it happened that I grew to love Antigua most (because I had spent more time there), though it wasn't as beautiful as either Grenada or St Lucia. But I knew it best and it knew me best. So, for years, I loved Antigua best. I loved its politics, its dirty politics (once, in a spat with an Antiguan man, I said, 'Oh, I knew I should have gone to Guadeloupe'; quick as a flash, he came back, 'But, darling, you know we have the best dirty politics in the Caribbean'), the way they dominated life there. I loved the gossip, the way everybody knew everybody's business.

Actually I love the size, the smallness that is, of the islands of the Lesser Antilles. You can get round them in a day or less. They are contained, manageable. It's possible to know an island, or to think that you do, which is a wonderful feeling. Yet another wonderful feeling is the way you will go on making discoveries about a place, little discoveries: a plant, a view, a corner of a beach, a bar, a dish, a quiet place to swim where the water is so clear that, even out deep, you see down to the bed of the ocean. You never really know a place, but the Caribbean's gift is to allow you a considerable degree of familiarity. Now I think that, in some ways, I love Marie-Galante best, even more than Antigua, though Antigua will always have a special place in my heart. But Marie-Galante is so beautiful and so small. It's secret, private, undeveloped, slow, tranquil. A place for lovers or hermits, an Antiguan friend commented dryly.

Like the song says, the Caribbean is 'in my blood like holy wine … so bitter and so sweet.' Since that first trip, getting on for a decade ago, I have been back to the Caribbean many times. In *What the Twilight Says,* Derek Walcott writes, 'The traveller cannot love, since love is stasis and travel is motion. If he returns to what he loved in a landscape and stays there, he is no longer a traveller but in stasis and concentration, the lover of that particular part of earth, a native. So many people say they "love the Caribbean", meaning that someday they plan to return for a visit but could never live there, the usual benign insult of the traveller, the tourist.'

In my case, Walcott has got it wrong. I really do 'love the Caribbean,' and all its faults. The more I get to know it, the more I see, not just its problems (many of which are not of its own making), but also its faults, and I still love it. And I have tried, over the years, to think of a way in which I could, if not actually live there full-time (do I want to live anywhere full-time?), spend much more time there. But I can't think of a way that I could do it. There are practical reasons: I doubt, for instance, that I could make a living there. But, even supposing all the practical stuff could be worked out, I have come to the sad conclusion that the Caribbean, ultimately, is no place for a single white woman. Once the heady sensation of the kind of sexual freedom people dreamt about in the Sixties wears off, you are left with the problems created by that kind of freedom and the behavior that goes with it. The last few times I have been to Antigua, Antiguan friends have said, 'Why, you, you an Antiguan.' They mean it in a friendly way, as a compliment; they mean that I can fit in, that I know the ways of the island, that I know my way around. I take the remark in the spirit in which it was intended, though I know now that actually nothing could be further from the truth. Of course, I am not an Antiguan. I have only just begun to scrape the surface of the place. As a white, foreign woman, I am a fish out of water in the Caribbean, a stranger in a strange land. White people who go to live in the Caribbean can never really belong there, and, indeed, why should they?

*

Being an outsider is part of its charm for me; on the whole, I like not belonging. Anyhow I'm not sure that I can belong anywhere, not sure that I even want to. I like moving through different worlds. But the Caribbean calls to me. Something in me recognises some special quality there; all its beauties and all its woes have combined to produce something wonderful and evocative which tugs at my heartstrings. I know it's not perfect; I know it's flawed – how could it fail to be, given the way its present society was created – but, for me, it has quasi-magical properties. And I worry about it; I feel protective towards it; I hate it when people dismiss it as crude or lacking in culture. They're just ignorant. What do they know? I worry about how it will develop. That seeming carelessness can't last forever. The Caribbean, despite appearances to the contrary, is not a Garden of Eden, except insofar as it is rife with serpents. There is the serpent of tourism on which the region is utterly dependent; the serpent of drug dealing by which the Caribbean is caught, vulnerable, between Latin America and the United States; both of these lead to the kind of corruption for which the Caribbean is noto-rious and which so few Caribbean politicians seem able to withstand. But it needs tourism – it has nothing else. Sugar is long gone, bananas soon will be – Latin America can produce them so much more cheaply.

*

For all its easygoing charm, the Caribbean is a troubled place. It suffers from marginalization; it is peripheral to the affairs of the rest of the world. Only when a hurricane hits or a white tourist is murdered does the Caribbean make the front page. Tourism and trouble – these are the only means through which the Caribbean can command the interest of the wider world. Is it any wonder that the impetus to build a dynamic, productive society is lacking? Yet many, if not most, people in the Caribbean are decent, hard working, God-fearing and intelligent. They want the best for their children, but, in their hearts, they know that the likely outcome for those children is at best a job in tourism, waiting on rich white tourists (because the Caribbean is not cheap). Can it be coincidence that most Caribbean writers (and it has produced some wonderful writers) live in exile? And, if they are not in full-time exile, then they are gone for much of the year, seduced by wealthy, politically-correct American universities and the opportunity to be recognised on an international stage, returning home only sporadically to recharge tired batteries before going back to prove to the world that people from the Caribbean do actually have something to say. A 1978 *New Yorker* cartoon showed a middle-aged couple talking over drinks; it bore the caption: 'Let's go to the Caribbean or someplace and give our brains a rest.' The French islands are generally deemed to be more 'interesting' because of the French culture which pervades.

I remember a man in Antigua telling me that Jamaica Kincaid was always going to have to leave the island because she had 'an intellect and a psyche and they are no use to her here.' Yet all Kincaid's writing stems from her Caribbean roots and every time she visits Antigua, it is reported in the local paper. I remember another man, the editor of a newspaper, telling me that he used to take the *New York Review of Books*, but, after his wife was murdered, he cancelled his subscription because there was no one left on the island with whom he could discuss the articles in it. Sometimes the sun and the sand and the sea and the heat and the light are just not enough.

Last time I went to the Caribbean, I called a friend there to ask if there was anything I could bring. 'Is there anything you want?' I asked. 'Nothing you can buy. What I want,' said my friend, 'is another dimension.'

The Caribbean is my other dimension and I feel lucky to have it.

LUCRETIA STEWART
London
May 2001

Index

Index

Index

Select Bibliography

Blackburn, Robin: *The Overthrow of Colonial Slavery*, Verso, 1988
Blom-Cooper, Louis: *Guns for Antigua*, Duckworth, 1990
Césaire, Aimé: *Cahier d'un retour au pays natal*, Présence Africaine, 1983
Cleaver, Eldridge: *Soul on Ice*, 1968; Panther, 1971
Coram, Robert: *Caribbean Time Bomb*, Morrow, 1993
Fanon, Frantz: *Black Skin White Masks*, 1952; Pluto Press, 1986
Ferguson, James: *Far From Paradise*, Latin America Bureau, 1990
Gonsalves, Ralph: *History and the Future: A Caribbean Perspective*, Kingstown, 1994
Green Gold, Latin America Bureau, 1987
James, C. L R.: *Beyond a Boundary*, 1963; Random Century, 1990
James, Winston, and Harris, Clive (eds.): *Inside Babylon*, Verso, 1993
Kincaid, Jamaica: *Lucy*, Farrar, Straus and Giroux, 1990
———: *Annie John*, Farrar, Straus and Giroux, 1983
———: *A Small Place*, Farrar, Straus and Giroux, 1988
Knight, Franklin W.: *The Caribbean*, Oxford University Press, 1990
Kurlansky, Mark: *A Continent of Islands*, Addison Wesley, 1992
Lamming, George: *In the Castle of My Skin*, 1970; Schocken Books, 1983
Leigh Fermor, Patrick: *The Traveller's Tree*, 1950; Penguin, 1984
———: *The Violins of Saint-Jacques*, 1953; Oxford University Press, 1985
MacPherson, John: *Caribbean Lands*, Longman Caribbean, 1990
Naipaul, V. S.: *A House for Mr Biswas*, 1961; Penguin, 1969
———: *The Middle Passage*, 1962; Penguin, 1969
———: *The Overcrowded Barracoon*, Vintage, 1984
Phillips, Caryl: *A State of Independence*, Faber, 1986
———: *The Final Passage*, Faber, 1985
Rhys, Jean: *Voyage in the Dark*, 1934; Penguin 1969
———: *Wide Sargasso Sea*, 1966; Penguin, 1968
Rohlehr, Gordon: *Calypso and Society in Pre-Independence Trinidad*, Gordon Rohlehr, 1990
Said, Edward W.: *Culture and Imperialism*, Chatto and Windus, 1993
Selvon, Sam: *The Lonely Londoners*, 1956; Longman Caribbean, 1985
Shand Allfrey, Phyllis: *The Orchid House*, 1953; Virago 1991
Smith and Smith: *To Shoot Hard Labour*, Edan's Publishers, 1986
Thomas, G. C. H.: *Ruler in Hiroona*, 1972; Macmillan Caribbean, 1989
Walcott, Derek: *Collected Poems 1948–1984*, Faber, 1986
Walvin, James: *Black Ivory*, HarperCollins, 1992
Williams, Eric: *From Columbus to Castro*, 1970; Vintage, 1984
Wouk, Hermann: *Don't Stop the Carnival*, Fontana, 1966
Wyndham, Francis, and Melly, Diana (eds.): *Jean Rhys: Letters 1931–1966*, Penguin, 1985

Song Credits

COMMON READER EDITIONS

As booksellers since 1986, we have been stocking the pages of our monthly catalogue, A COMMON READER, with "Books for Readers with Imagination." Now as publishers, the same motto guides our work. Simply put, the titles we issue as COMMON READER EDITIONS are volumes of uncommon merit which we have enjoyed, and which we think other imaginative readers will enjoy as well. While our selections are as personal as the act of reading itself, what's common to our enterprise is the sense of shared experience a good book brings to solitary readers. We invite you to sample the wide range of COMMON READER EDITIONS, and welcome your comments.

www.commonreader.com